P9-DNF-874

Ten Sewing Tenets

tear here

1. Always straighten the grainline before laying out and cutting fabric. Block so that the lengthwise and crosswise grains are at right angles.

2. Always pretreat fabric before cutting by putting it through its usual wash cycle: Launder and dry hand- and machine-washables; steam and/or dry-clean fabrics that are dry-clean only.

3. Never use sewing shears on anything but fabric; especially avoid paper, a shear pet peeve.

4. Always stop machine-stitching with the needle down when you plan on pivoting and stitching on.

5. Always press a seam before crossing it with another seam. Heat sets the stitches, imprinting the seam in place.

6. Always reduce seam allowance bulk. Grade when there are multiple layers. Pay particular attention to points.

7. Staystitching and basting are a necessity rather than a nuisance in the following cases: Always staystitch any seam cut on the bias or a circular area, such as a neckline; always baste set-in sleeves, first when easing and second before stitching permanently in place.

8. Always buy a pattern size according to the body measurement rather than the overall size—pattern sizing doesn't correspond to store sizing!

9. Always position the bust buttonhole first, spacing the others accordingly. The bust is the center of the buttonhole universe!

10. Always try on and then try again—first as you sew, making alterations, nips, tucks, and hemlines that work for you.

alpha
books

Yardage Conversion Chart

Fabric Width:	32"	35-36"	39"	41"	44-45"	50"	52-54"	58-60"
Yardage	1 7/8	1 3/4	1 1/2	1 1/2	1 3/8	1 1/4	1 1/8	1
	2 1/4	2	1 3/4	1 3/4	1 5/8	1 1/2	1 3/8	1 1/4
	2 1/2	2 1/4	2	2	1 3/4	1 5/8	1 1/2	1 3/8
	3 3/4	2 1/2	2 1/4	2 1/4	2 1/8	1 3/4	1 3/4	1 5/8
	3 1/8	2 7/8	2 1/2	2 1/2	2 1/4	2	1 7/8	1 3/4
	3 3/8	3 1/8	2 3/4	2 3/4	2 1/2	2 1/4	2	1 7/8
	3 3/4	3 3/8	3	2 7/8	2 3/4	2 3/8	2 1/4	2
	4	3 3/4	3 1/4	3 1/8	2 7/8	2 5/8	2 3/8	2 1/4
	4 3/8	4 1/4	3 1/2	3 3/8	3 1/8	2 5/8	2 5/8	2 3/8
	4 5/8	4 1/2	3 3/4	3 5/8	3 3/8	2 3/4	2 3/4	2 5/8
	5	4 3/4	4	3 7/8	3 5/8	3	2 7/8	2 3/4
	5 1/4	5	4 1/4	4 1/8	3 7/8	3 1/4	3 1/8	2 7/8

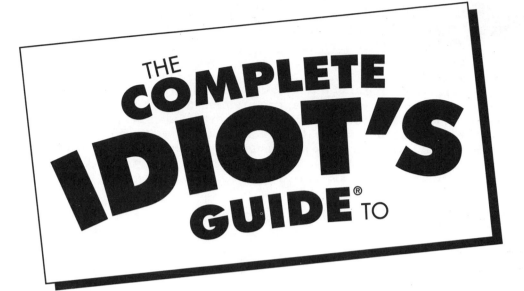

THE

COMPLETE IDIOT'S GUIDE® TO

Sewing

by Lydia Wills

alpha books

Macmillan USA, Inc.
201 West 103rd Street
Indianapolis, IN 46290

A Pearson Education Company

To Lydia Cavallo and Natalie Cavallo Wills; I am but one recipient of their constant generosity and curiosity.

Copyright © 2000 by Lydia Wills

All rights reserved. No part of this book shall be reproduced, stored in a retrieval system, or transmitted by any means, electronic, mechanical, photocopying, recording, or otherwise, without written permission from the publisher. No patent liability is assumed with respect to the use of the information contained herein. Although every precaution has been taken in the preparation of this book, the publisher and author assume no responsibility for errors or omissions. Neither is any liability assumed for damages resulting from the use of information contained herein. For information, address Alpha Books, 201 West 103rd Street, Indianapolis, IN 46290.

THE COMPLETE IDIOT'S GUIDE TO and Design are registered trademarks of Macmillan USA, Inc.

International Standard Book Number: 0-02-863891-3
Library of Congress Catalog Card Number: Available upon request.

02 01 00   8 7 6 5 4 3 2 1

Interpretation of the printing code: The rightmost number of the first series of numbers is the year of the book's printing; the rightmost number of the second series of numbers is the number of the book's printing. For example, a printing code of 00-1 shows that the first printing occurred in 2000.

Printed in the United States of America

Note: This publication contains the opinions and ideas of its author. It is intended to provide helpful and informative material on the subject matter covered. It is sold with the understanding that the author and publisher are not engaged in rendering professional services in the book. If the reader requires personal assistance or advice, a competent professional should be consulted.

The author and publisher specifically disclaim any responsibility for any liability, loss, or risk, personal or otherwise, which is incurred as a consequence, directly or indirectly, of the use and application of any of the contents of this book.

Publisher
Marie Butler-Knight

Product Manager
Phil Kitchel

Managing Editor
Cari Luna

Acquisitions Editor
Amy Zavatto

Development Editor
Amy Gordon

Production Editor
JoAnna Kremer

Illustrator
Brian Moyer

Cover Designers
Mike Freeland
Kevin Spear

Book Designers
Scott Cook and Amy Adams of DesignLab

Indexer
Tonya Heard

Layout/Proofreading
Angela Calvert
Svetlana Dominguez
Bob LaRoche

Contents at a Glance

Contents

Appendixes

Foreword

You probably already know that sewing is a valuable life skill—that's why you're reading this, right? What you probably don't know yet is that it's so much more than that. More than a life skill, it's a life tool. Sewing is a creative expression. If you just need to clothe yourself, you can purchase clothing, but if the inner designer/creator in your soul is just screaming to come out, you are ready to learn to sew.

For me, it began more than 40 years ago when I wanted my Little Miss Revlon doll (who I was living vicariously through at the time) to be as well dressed as my favorite movie stars. At that point in life, I had no hang-ups about whether I was doing things the right way, and my creativity soared. Through the years I've honed my sewing skills and have experienced great personal satisfaction in creating special garments for my family and friends as well as for myself. From christening gowns to wedding gowns, Halloween costumes to boat covers, a sewer's life is full of cherished memories involving sewing projects.

When sewing my granddaughter's first red velvet Christmas dress, I felt connected to my own mother who had sewn my daughter's (almost identical) first red velvet Christmas dress 20 years earlier. Connected not only by the skill to sew but even more, by the love that goes into every stitch. Sewing connects us to preceding generations of women who found magic in the side benefits. It's saying "I love you" with our hands.

Sewing is empowering—it gives you limitless choices and puts you in charge. If you can envision it, you can create it. You want that collar, those sleeves, and a waist length 2 inches longer, in your favorite shade of lime green? No problem!

Whether you're fantasizing about your very first project or returning to sewing after some time away, you'll be amazed and inspired by the new techniques, fabrics, notions, and machines available today. The education, support, and camaraderie available to today's sewing enthusiast are beyond what our mothers could have imagined. The home sewing industry supports us through classes and workshops in retail stores across the country; the Internet is full of enthusiastic sewers ready to share knowledge and encouragement at sewing-related Web sites at the touch of a keyboard. The American Sewing Guild (with chapters all across the country) exists to serve the sewing enthusiast by providing the broadest range of sewing information, education, assistance, and support. It's a great place to meet sewing friends and add joy to the journey!

The Complete Idiot's Guide to Sewing will give you the information and guidance you need to develop your sewing skills and set you on the path to sewing success. Whether a novice or seasoned seamstress, you will return here over and over again for the answers to your sewing questions. The creativity that you bring to the experience will make it a rewarding adventure and result in garments of which you'll be proud.

Margo Martin

Chairman, Board of Directors

American Sewing Guild

For information about the American Sewing Guild, call 1-877-I-CAN-SEW toll free or visit their Web site at http://www.asg.org.

Introduction

So you've decided to learn how to sew ... or maybe just brush up on your sewing tools so you can whip that wardrobe into shape. Either way, you're on the brink of a great creative adventure. Taking a piece of flat fabric and fashioning it into something you, your home, or your friends can wear is so satisfying.

It took practice, a few professional classes, and many ripped seams, but I learned to sew fast and sew clean with a host of simple and time-saving techniques that I'm going to share with you. And these nifty tricks, little nips and tucks, can't be found in any other book.

Even though I grew up in a family of sewers (my grandmother made bridal gowns at her Smart Shop and handcrafted all her own clothes), I never learned to sew at home. After I moved to New York and started a business, I thought my life was far too hectic to fit something as skill-based and time-consuming as sewing into my schedule. But necessity took over, and I realized that easy techniques and sure-fire shortcuts can make sewing not only simple and quick but pleasurable as well. I relish the time that I get to sit at my machine and concentrate on pillows or a set of drapes that are not only fun to make but also beautify my home. And the real joy of sewing is that you get to have just what you want—the exact fabric, the exact fit, the exact financial investment—which frees you up in so many ways.

And this freedom is exactly what sewing is all about.

How to Use This Book

Any sewer worth his silk knows that time spent at the machine is a minuscule part of the whole project. The real time investment comes before—setting up the work station and machine, organizing notions, choosing, preparing, laying out, and cutting the fabric, measuring, the list goes on and on. **Part 1, "Tools of the Trade,"** and **Part 2, "No More Hemming and Hawing: Getting Set to Sew,"** will walk you through these crucial early steps, from gathering your notions together to setting up a sewing space that really works.

Once you've made it to the machine stage, **Part 3, "A Stitch in Time Saves Nine: Basic Techniques,"** will provide you with all the techniques needed for the most basic repairs, from hems to zippers to buttons. When you've got these under your (home-made) belt, **Part 4, "Fashion in a Flash,"** will show you how to bring these skills together into a whole garment, from understanding patterns to creating the perfect fit. In **Part 5, "Home Sewn: Home Accents and Gifts,"** you can make sure your home is as well accessorized as your wardrobe, adorned with curtains and pillows that reflect your flair.

By the end of the book, I know your home and closet will be stocked with the fruits of your home-sewn labor, a real reward for the time and effort you've invested. But the best reward is when you're able to respond to that wonderful compliment of your new dress or vintage duvet cover: "I made it myself."

Tips Along the Way

Throughout the book, I'll give you all sorts of hints and details, the kind that make the difference between something that looks handmade and something handmade that looks designer.

Noteworthy Notions

Interesting facts and helpful hints to add flair and zip to any sewing project.

Sew Far, Sew Good

Tips to make your sewing experience "seam" much more pleasant.

Sew You Were Saying ...

Definitions of those key sewing terms to make it all "sew" simple.

Stitch in Your Side

Warnings to steer you clear of needle and thread catastrophes.

Acknowledgments

First and foremost, I'd like to thank Mercedes Quijije, a superbly talented professional, generous and patient teacher, and inspiration. I also owe much to my colleagues at Artists Agency, especially Sita White, for their help. And I can't forget Hilary and the rest of the gracious staff of The Hotel Twin Dolphin, for their enormously long extension cord so that I could write and watch whales at the same time.

Trademarks

All terms mentioned in this book that are known to be or are suspected of being trademarks or service marks have been appropriately capitalized. Alpha Books and Macmillan USA, Inc., cannot attest to the accuracy of this information. Use of a term in this book should not be regarded as affecting the validity of any trademark or service mark.

Part 1

Tools of the Trade

Think that getting set to sew means setting up your machine? Think again! Before you even set foot on the sewing machine accelerator, you need to get a grip on all the accessories that make sewing so much faster and easier. I'll help you stock up on the necessary notions to get any sewing job done. You need a sewing toolkit that includes measuring, marking, and cutting tools, as well as all the extras such as zippers, elastic, interfacing, pins, and needles. The problem is that all these different tools use different terminology—this part helps you decipher thread codes, needle numbers, and interfacing facts.

After you've pooled your spools and filled your sewing toolkit, you can turn to your big-ticket items—your machine and ironing equipment. We'll assess your sewing machine needs, matching the man to the sewing machine. And never neglect pressing tools—your iron and pressing surfaces make a world of difference.

Finally, we get to fabric. Instead of being cowed by the dazzling array of fabric types, blends, finishes, and facts, this part will have you bolting through fabric like a pro.

Chapter 1

Shear Essentials

In This Chapter

➤ Get a clear notion about notions

➤ Sharpen your knowledge of scissors and shears that are a cut above

➤ Measure your marking and measuring tools

➤ Build your sewing toolbox

➤ Face down interfacing

Whenever anyone thinks about sewing, the image of a sewing machine immediately pops up—but before you get to the machine, you've got to have a clear idea about what supplies are involved in any project. In other words, you need to have a clear notion about notions—the essentials of any sewing project.

Notion is a loose term that applies to all the parts of a sewing project except for the fabric—from thread to pins and needles to interfacing. Notions are found in a variety of stores, from five-and-dimes like K-Mart to specialized outlets like my favorite one in New York, Greenberg and Hammer, which sells only sewing notions.

This chapter outlines the "shear" essentials—the notions you should shop for once or twice a year to fill your sewing basket (my "basket" is actually a filing cabinet, but we'll get to that later). This way, as long as you have your fabric, you can start any project, any time. Planning ahead will save you countless hours and keep your energy where it belongs—on the project—instead of running around looking for thread!

Cutting Up: Any Sharp Sewer's Necessities

Any sewer is only as good as her dullest shears or most run-down needles. It really pays to have sharp, well-cared-for tools. After all, would you want a carpenter with an old rusty saw working on your new addition? Well, I feel the same way about my beautiful woolens and silk pajamas—they deserve the best tools (which also happen to be the most time-effective)!

You don't need to run out and buy every sewing tool on the market, but there are a few simple items that you should definitely have on hand. If you start out with the right tools for the job, you'll find that you've cut your project time in half before you've picked up a single piece of fabric.

Sew You Were Saying ...

Notions are all the extras involved in sewing—excluding the fabric—that make it possible to cut, mark, measure, and create your finished project. Without shears, pins, tape measures, zippers, and interfacing, for example, we'd all be back in the sewing stone age.

Noteworthy Notions

Since you are forking over some cash for them, you want to make sure you take good care of your shears. Here are some guidelines to keep your shears sharp:

➤ Don't use them to cut anything besides fabric, especially paper or your pet Pekinese's fur!

➤ Don't lift the shears from the table as you cut. Make sure the bottom blade is always touching the table and that the fabric is always stationary, never moving around.

➤ Don't forget to sharpen and clean the blades and oil the screw on a regular basis. You can do this at home with a Gingher sharpening stone, or you can take your shears to be professionally serviced, my preferred way of maintaining top-notch tools.

Shears

Here's where you need to invest in the best you can afford, because a great pair of sewing *shears* can make one of the more labor-intensive parts of sewing—cutting fabric—almost effortless. High-quality shears can last a lifetime. In fact, they can even improve with age if properly cared for. My sewing teacher has had the same pair of shears for the last 20 years and is meticulous about sharpening and maintaining them. She spent 20 dollars on them back then, which adds up to a whopping dollar a year! So, don't skimp. Crummy shears can ruin your fabric as well as your sewing experience.

Rotary Cutter and Cutting Mat

Don't be fooled by the rotary cutter's appearance; while it may look like a harmless pizza wheel, it's actually a sewer's secret weapon. A rotary cutter is really a circular X-Acto knife that cuts the fabric as it rolls over the fabric surface. The truly great thing about it is that you never have to lift the blade from the surface of the fabric—it always stays in contact with the cutting surface, eliminating a lot of cutting errors that occur when fabric is moved and shifted. It's particularly useful when working with slippery, silky fabrics or when you need to cut two layers at once (such as interfacing and fabric pieces).

Just like an X-Acto knife, rotary cutters need a "self-healing" cutting mat that won't be damaged by the blade. These mats come in various sizes and are gridded, which makes cutting and measuring much easier. It's smart to buy the biggest that you can afford—just make sure you have room for it—so that you can cut large pieces of fabric without having to move them around.

Stitch in Your Side

Fabric and notions aren't often sold in the same place, so if your notions pantry isn't already stocked, plan on making a few trips when you decide to whip up a wrap to go along with that fantastic red evening dress.

Sew You Were Saying ...

Shears are longer than 6 inches (the length of your average scissors) and have a larger bottom loop to more easily fit your fingers (there are models for both righties and lefties, so make sure to ask for the correct ones!). Given my druthers, 8-inch Gingher shears are my choice every time.

Must-Have Mainstays

Sure, you could probably get through a project without the items in this section, but why try? The point here is to make your project as easy as possible.

Sew Far, Sew Good

Next time you're shopping for notions, buy an extra seam ripper. I know, I know, I sound like a negative nudge, but you will make mistakes as you sew, and it's worth having two—or even three—on hand so they are always easy to find when you need them the most!

➤ *Scissors.* These are for cutting patterns, stray threads, tape, and so on—but never for fabric.

➤ *Pinking shears.* Despite their rather froufrou name, these are useful shears with a serrated edge. Use them to cut a seam so it won't unravel, for decorative cutting, or for cutting interfacing so the edges won't show through to the fabric.

➤ *Seam ripper.* My favorite and least-favorite tool all in one! It's useful because, if you're careful, you can remove thread from a seam without damaging the fabric—which is great—but it also means you've made a big sewing mistake. A seam ripper is basically a 2- to 4-inch handled tool with two prongs: One is a crescent-shaped blade, and the other is short and bulbed to protect the fabric.

Measuring Up: It Pays to Be Accurate

After cutting, your most important tools are for measuring. I used to hate measuring hems or other sewing jobs for a few reasons: I didn't understand how to do it properly (why won't that fabric sit still?), and I didn't have the proper equipment. You only need a few things, but boy, are they important!

➤ *Clear, 18-inch-long-by-2-inch-wide ruler.* It's crucial that this tool is see-through so you can do just that—see how much fabric you're measuring under the ruler. It's a great straight edge as well.

➤ *Tape measure.* I always saw my grandmother, the seamstress, with a tape measure around her neck, whether she was sewing or not! You don't have to keep yours there, but it does have to be handy.

➤ *Six-inch metal sewing gauge with sliding marker.* This invaluable tool is a metal ruler with a sliding plastic marker. Perfect for making alterations, marking hems, turning fabric—the list goes on and on. Pick one up, use it, and you'll wonder how you ever lived without it.

Marking Up: Points Well Taken

A few marks here and there will guide you during your sewing. Here are some tools to help you get good marks.

➤ *Tailor's chalk.* Chalk, the standard fabric marking tool, is available in a few different forms. Triangle chalk or chalk squares are solid and come in a few different colors—white, red, and blue—for use with different-colored fabrics. Try to get old-fashioned tailor's chalk, which is made of chalk rather than a chalk/wax blend. Run your nail along the chalk to determine its make-up; a waxy brand is harder to remove and "sets" into your fabric with heat.

A chalk wheel is packed with loose chalk that marks the fabric as the wheel rolls. A chalk pencil is used just like a normal pencil.

➤ *Fabric marking pencil.* This is a thin lead pencil made specifically for marking up fabric. It works better than your average Number 2, contains less graphite, and washes well. And you can use it on paper in a pinch.

➤ *Water- and air-soluble markers.* The former makes marks that wipe away with water; the latter makes marks that disappear within 12 to 24 hours.

Staying Up: Holding It All Together

From pins to the finishing touches of buttons and clasps, you'll need these items to keep everything together—both while you're sewing and when the project is complete:

➤ *Zippers.* It's smart to stock up on the basic colors—black, white, and gray—as well as your personal favorites. There are three basic kinds of zippers: traditional, invisible, and separating. See Chapter 10, "Win One for the Zipper," for some zipper guidance.

➤ *Snaps.* I recommend a few different sizes and colors such as metal, black, and white.

➤ *Hooks and eyes.* A great name for a useful notion. These are the closures that are on the back of bras, as well as other areas that need some hooking up, such as the side of your slacks. Again, stock up on an assortment so you have various sizes and colors on hand.

➤ *Elastic.* There are many different kinds of elastic to choose from for all kinds of applications. The best all-around elastic to have on hand is nonroll, which is made to do just that—retain its shape and not bunch up in the casings for elastic waists, wrists, and so on. While there are many types and widths of elastic available, it's smart to keep several yards of one inch nonroll on hand.

Stitch in Your Side

Before you start a project, test all markers on your fabric just to make sure the marks disappear. You won't be very happy if you end up with a garment with permanent writing all over it! And take these precautions: Mark on the wrong side of the fabric and avoid pressing before the marks are gone—heat often "cooks" the marks into place.

Noteworthy Notions

Buy zippers longer than you need instead of the specific length for each application. (Remember ... you can always shorten, but you can't lengthen.) Better yet, check out bulk rolls of zippers with color-coordinated pulls. The zipper is sold off of a roll by length—just cut to the desired length and bar tack (we'll get to that later) across the bottom, and you'll be zipping through without a hassle!

➤ *Buttons.* Needless to say, viva variety! It really pays to have the standards around all the time, from clear to black, and brown to pearly white. Buy them in a few sizes and styles—$1/2$-inch to $1^1/4$-inch four-hole buttons, as well as buttons that have a toggle on the back. Buy the quantity of buttons according to their size:

1. Four to eight medium-size buttons

2. Four large, or coat-size, buttons

3. One specialty button—such as a unique button that will grace the top of a coat or jacket

➤ *Seam sealant.* This is a clear resin that prevents seams from unraveling, especially on buttonholes. Try a brand like Fray Check.

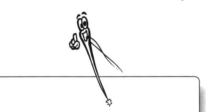

Sew Far, Sew Good

Whenever you spot them, pick up specialty buttons at flea markets, garage sales, or even vintage boutiques. A unique Bakelite or carved button can turn a simple handmade handbag or garment into a one-of-a-kind creation.

➤ *Straight pins.* Pins are the number one notion need. You should always have them around, easy to grab, easy to store. They're categorized by length, which is measured in $1/16$-inch gradations, and by the shape of the head. They also come in different widths, with the average pin .5 mm thick. Here are some guidelines for picking pins:

Number 17 dressmaker's pins. These are the standard-size pins for use with most fabrics. They're $1^1/16$ inches long and have a flat head.

Ballpoint pins. Ballpoint pins are just that—they have a bulbous tip instead of a sharp point. Use them with knitted fabrics—instead of slicing away at the threads, causing snags, the bulb separates the knitted fibers.

Glasshead pins. Glasshead pins are topped with a colored ball made of either glass, or more likely, plastic. This makes them easy to spot when pinning, especially with thick, piled fabric. Be careful not to leave them in when sewing or pressing—the bulb can damage your machine, break the needle, or melt if ironed.

T-pins. These are longer pins with a T-shaped top. They work well when you need to do some heavy-duty pinning on upholstery and other crafts.

➤ *Weights.* Rather than laboriously pinning fabric and pattern pieces together when laying out and cutting, I almost always use weights. You just position them intermittently on the edges of the pattern and fabric, and you're ready to cut. Look, ma ... no fabric slippage!

➤ *Transparent tape.* Scotch Magic brand has a place in your sewing toolkit.

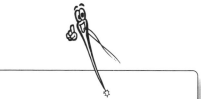

Sew Far, Sew Good

Even though you can use anything to weight your fabric—cans, rulers, staplers—you'll be much happier with the average curtain weight. These square weights are sewn into the bottom of curtains so that they hang properly, but they're also perfect for weighting fabric while cutting. Plus, they're cheap, small, and easy to store.

Noteworthy Notions

In a pinch, clear nail polish works as a seam sealant. Think about it—it certainly does the job on hosiery runs.

➤ *Glue.* A good craft and fabric glue (Sobo or Magna-Tac are top-notch brands) holds things together before you get to the final sewing stage. Always test to make sure it disappears when it dries.

➤ *Basting tape.* This is a thin double-sided tape that serves the same purpose as basting; it keeps fabric layers, zippers, and more in place before and during sewing. I find the thinnest width—$^1/_8$ inch—the most useful.

➤ *Spray starch.* Besides using for basic ironing, spray starch is good for adding some firmness to fabric as well. Although starch does come in various strengths, I like to use the heavy-duty dosage.

Keeping Interfacing Easy

One of the great things about new fabrics, threads, and interfacing is that they've made life a lot easier for the sewer. *Interfacing*, which is a layer of fabric that adds shape, stability, durability, and control to garments, has been totally transformed in the past few decades and become much more user-friendly.

Interfacing is a fantastic way of "edging" a garment, giving some structure and stability to armholes, necklines, and the front edges of jackets and blouses. It adds some stiffness and crispness to details like collars, cuffs, and pockets so they won't wilt. It reinforces fabric that needs some extra anchoring, such as the buttonhole area or a shoulder seam.

Interfacing isn't just used in clothing; it's also great for stiffening the edges of a European pillow sham or adding strength and stability to the tops of curtains so that they hang rather than droop. New technology and the creation of foolproof fusible—that is to say "iron-on"—interfacing has made it a snap to create contouring without all that old-fashioned hand sewing.

Sew You Were Saying ...

Interfacing is a woven or non-woven fabric that provides stability and shape to a garment. It's traditionally used on the edges of a garment or project—jacket fronts, collars, cuffs, necklines, and armholes—adding strength, extra oomph, and durability. Fusible interfacing is backed with a heat-reactive layer that bonds to fabric; stitchable interfacing must be sewn on.

Noteworthy Notions

Fabric and interfacing are almost always cut from the same pattern pieces, so why not cut your fabric and interfacing together? Simply position the interfacing and fabric together with the pattern piece on top and cut away! Better yet—use your rotary cutter to cut down on layout and cutting errors.

Choosing Without Blowing a Fuse: Fusibles vs. Stitchables

There are two main kinds of interfacing: fusible, which is coated on one side with a heat-activated resin that sticks to fabric for good when pressed; and stitchable, which has to be sewn on. This is probably obvious, but I almost always use the fusible variety! It's much easier to simply iron on than it is to go to the trouble of more sewing. There are a few fabrics that call for a stitchable, though:

➤ Fabrics with a pile or nap, like velvet, corduroy, or the like, the raised surface of which will be damaged by the chemicals or fusing process.

➤ Fabrics like silk that react badly to moisture.

➤ Fabrics that are treated with a stain- or water-repellant finish. These chemicals not only repel stains and water—they repel fusible interfacing, so no bond is created.

In addition to the categories of stitchable and fusible, there are many varieties of "base" fabrics that are used to create interfacing. The base fabric, which is treated with resin if it's a fusible, can be made out of woven or nonwoven fabric (usually nylon or polyester or a blend), knit tricot, or what's called weft-insertion fabric. Instead of focusing on the technical aspects of the interfacing make-up, try touching, stretching, playing with, and draping the interfacing. See how it moves with your fabric.

Face to Face with Interface

Interfacing is sold off of bolts, just like fabric, so you can't return your purchase if you discover you bought the wrong kind. I found this out the hard way when I was shopping in the garment district in New York City and bought some bargain-basement interfacing. I used it on a jacket—I think you know where I'm going with this—and promptly ruined the entire garment because the bargain was a bust and I didn't test it first. Big mistake, but at least you can learn from my error!

So, use my interfacing table from this chapter to start off on the right foot; remember, interfacing involves a number of variables—the interfacing itself, the fabric, heat, moisture, and pressure—all of which have to combine in the right way to be successful. The only assurance you have is through testing with small swatches. For more detailed information on testing interfacing, check out Chapter 12, "Pressing Matters: Ironing Out the Wrinkles."

Stitch in Your Side

So you don't have to go back to the store—or worse!—start the whole project over, avoid making these interfacing mistakes:

➤ Using an interfacing that is too heavy for your fabric— no one wants to wear a cardboard coat!

➤ Using a dark interfacing on a sheer or light-colored fabric.

➤ Forgetting to check whether the interfacing is fusible, only to realize that you have to sew it on.

Fusible Interfacing Guide

Weight/Fabric	Fusible Interfacing	Fabric Content/Colors/Details
Sheer or soft shaping for light- to midweight fabrics such as silks, gauzes, organza, faille, charmeuse, lightweight shirting and cottons, lightweight synthetics, crepe	Touch O' Gold	All rayon/b/w/nude/has a tendency to come off after repeated use, so it's often called a hybrid or "fusible sew-in"
	Soft'n'Silky	100% poly/b/w/ivory/gray
	SofBrush	100% poly/b/w/ivory/gray
	SofTouch	100% nylon/b/w
	SoSheer	100% poly tricot/b/w/crosswise stretch
	SofBrush	100% poly/b/w/g/ivory
	Pellon 906F Sheer-Light	100% poly/only white
	Pellon 911F Feather	100% poly/w/gray
Soft shaping for midweight fabrics: cotton, broadcloth, linen, shirting	Shape Flex	100% cotton/b/w/natural
	Whisper Weft	64% poly/36% rayon/b/w/gray
	Weft	60% poly/36% rayon/b/w/gray (good all-purpose shaping)
	Form Flex	100% cotton/b/w/great all-purpose interfacing
Crisp shaping for cuffs, shirting, pockets, etc.	Fuse Shirtmaker	Only white
	Pellon Craft-Bond 808	100% poly/only white
	Wigan	Only gray (very stiff)
	Pellon ShirTailor 950F	100% poly
	Fusible Formite	100% cotton/b/w

Weight/Fabric	Fusible Interfacing	Fabric Content/Colors/Details
Mid- to heavyweight fabrics: denim, wool, gabardine, heavy linen	Fusible Acro	5% goat/52% rayon/43% poly/ natural color
	Pellon 931 TD	100% poly/only white
	Fusible Formite Canvas	100% poly/b/w
Knits: jersey, sweater knits, double knits, terry	SofKnit	100% nylon/w/nude (for lightweight knits)
	Pellon SofShape 880F	80% nylon/20% poly
	Knit Fuze	100% nylon
	Fusi Knit	100% nylon tricot/b/w
Bulky material and craftwork	Fuse Fleece	100% poly/deep-piled fleece that's great for padding and quilting (white only)
	Heat and Bond Laminate	Perfect for waterproof placemats, tablecloths, bags, etc.
	Pellon Décor Bond 808	60% rayon/20% poly/20% nylon (only white, very crisp)

13

The Weighting Game

As you can see from the table, there's a huge variety of interfacing available and the array of names, types, and construction techniques can be downright dismaying. Just take to heart the most important things the sewer should know: Make sure that the interfacing weight matches that of the fabric and that it fuses properly.

To match weight, hold the interfacing and fabric together in your hand, moving them around and draping them over your arm. Be observant: Does the interfacing give with the fabric but still add some shape? Be aware that fusible interfacing stiffens slightly after pressing when the resin hardens, so always use an interfacing that's slightly lighter than the fabric. And test, test, test—this is the golden rule of interfacing!

I recommend buying 4 or 5 yards of three different weights of interfacing to have on hand at all times. They're sold primarily in white, black, and gray, and while I use white much more than black, you should buy a few yards and types of black as well.

With these minimum materials, you can whip up almost any project at any time. All you need to do is select the proper needles, thread, and fabric, and you're good to go. The next chapter narrows in on the two details that relate specifically to your project—needles and thread, focusing on needle know-how and a quick thread education.

The Least You Need to Know

➤ Always keep your sewing shears in tip-top condition, sharpening and oiling them on a regular basis.

➤ No matter how talented a tailor you are, you're going to make mistakes. Have your seam ripper handy at all times; better to redo a seam right away instead of redoing a whole outfit.

➤ Remember that fabric and thread alone do not a sewing project make: You always need pins, a tape measure or ruler, markers or chalk, and closures (zippers, buttons, snaps, etc.).

➤ Even the easiest projects require some shaping and crisping: Keep fusible interfacing on hand for drape, not droop, in all your fashions.

➤ Don't get caught with a bubbly blouse: test fusible interfacing on a fabric swatch and you'll save yourself wear and tear.

Chapter 2

The Eyes Have It: Needles and Thread

In This Chapter

➤ Needle through hand-stitching needles

➤ Get to the point of machine needles

➤ Pull it all together with the right thread type

➤ Don't snap under the pressure of matching thread to fabric

Once you've decided to toss your hotel sewing kits in favor of some serious needles and thread, you're in for quite a ride! There's a vast array of needles for every imaginable use—for both hand and machine stitching—all of which play a big part in how your finished product will look. Rather than blindly grabbing what looks like a generic needle, it pays to acquaint yourself with the types and sizes of needles.

Ditto for thread—besides the obvious conundrum of matching the fabric and thread color, how do you choose from the many different thread makes and weights? I used to be so worried about all these variables that I was almost paralyzed by thread dread. Don't succumb! This chapter gives you a basic thread education, deciphering needle and thread sizing, converting the numerology into plain old English, and simple instructions. Soon, needle and thread knowledge will be second nature (and if not, just use the handy charts!).

Finding the Right Needle Among the Haystacks

Hand and machine needles are completely different—they have different shapes, sizes, and construction, and for obvious reasons. Hand needles have a long shaft with an eye at one end for threading and the point at the other end, whereas machine needles have a shank that's made to fit snugly into your machine and a threading eye near the tip.

While it's easy to spot this difference, it gets a bit harder when you get into the minute size gradations of each needle and needle shape. When you need a needle, this is the drill: First, you have to decide on the needle type. Once you made that call, it's time to choose the size. Just to make things more difficult, both hand and machine needles use different sizing systems. Not to worry—first I'll take you by the hand so that you can choose hand needles of all sizes and types. Then we'll move on to machine needles—you'll be a needle pro in no time!

Hand-Sewing Needles

The all-purpose hand-sewing needle is called a sharp (which, I suppose, differentiates it from a dull!). A sharp is a medium-length needle for everything from hand hemming to a quick tack for a stray cuff. The size is scaled from 1 to 10, the number of which is inversely proportionate to the size. This means the smaller the number, the larger (that is, longer and thicker) the needle. A size 10 is used for fine, thin fabrics that need a delicate touch—silk, chiffon, lace, organza, and so on—whereas a 1 works on heavy denim and canvas. The sizes that are used for most of your sewing needs are 7 through 10.

Noteworthy Notions

When hand sewing with the standard sharp, follow this simple rule: Choose the smallest needle (the one that has the biggest number) that you can easily use.

If you have other hand-sewing needle needs, use this quick guide:

➤ *Betweens:* These are shorter than sharps, for more detailed hand sewing and quilting.

➤ *Embroidery:* These are medium-length needles with a slightly longer and rounder eye for buttonhole twist or embroidery thread.

➤ *Curved, or upholstery:* This is a nice, thick, curved (naturally!) needle for hand stitching upholstery, mattresses, and so on. It's used in hard-to-reach areas, such as a sofa cushion, where a long straight needle just won't do the trick.

➤ *Sailmaker's:* The name says it all—these are long, thick, heavy-duty needles with a sharp, tapered point for heavy-duty fabrics such as canvas sails, work denim, and so on.

➤ *Beading:* These are very long, thin, sharp needles with a small eye for detailed handwork on delicate fabrics.

Machine Needles

I wish I could tell you that picking a machine needle is simple—by color, by size, or by type of fabric. Unfortunately, it's not that easy. The industry still hasn't standardized sewing machine needles, and different brands from Europe and America use different numbering and grading methods, which means you have to know your stuff to make the right choice.

There are several different types of needles, and within these categories, there are different sizes. All these variations actually *do* make a difference—the needle shape, size, and eye correspond to different fabrics. The wrong needle can literally shred your new dressing gown, so don't rush in pellmell without some know-how.

Sew Far, Sew Good

Still noodling about for the right needle size, and confused about numbers? Remember that testing on a swatch takes the guesswork out of all your sewing tasks. Try several size sharps and make sure they slide with nary a snag. If there's the slightest hitch in your stitch, try for a larger number, meaning a smaller and thinner needle.

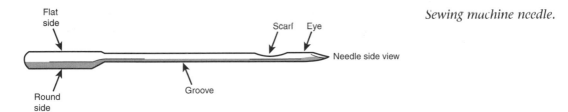

Sewing machine needle.

To the Point

The shape of the point of a needle varies with the intended use. In plain English, this means that needles are classified according to their tip and eye shape, which corresponds to certain types of fabric and stitching. For example, a leather needle, which has a sharp beveled point, must be used for piercing skins. Needles are further broken down into size, a numerical indication of how thick and large the needle is. It's smart to choose the type of needle that will suit your fabric and use first, and then move on to the size. Here are the most commonly used needle types:

Noteworthy Notions

Still confused about which brand to use? While Singer is the most common needle manu-facturer, and easiest to find and use, I much prefer Schmetz, a top-notch needle maker. Their superior quality shines through on all your sewing projects.

➤ *Universal point:* This is the standard, all-purpose needle that you should have stocked at all times. Great for many types of fabric, I keep a Universal in one of my machines for quick fix-me-ups. The Singer brand codes these with a red band. (The European designation is 130/705H.)

➤ *Ballpoint or stretch:* These needles are used with stretch or knit fabrics. You can spot them by their slightly bulbed tip. The bulbous bottom prevents skipped stitches or snags in the stretchy fabric. Singer codes them with a yellow band. (The European designation is 130/705HS.)

➤ *Denim:* This is a sharper-than-average needle for piercing heavy fabrics such as denim, duck, upholstery fabric, canvas, and so on. (The European designation is 130/705HJ.)

➤ *Leather:* Made specifically for suede, plastics, skins, leather, or heavily-piled material, these needles have a telltale long, flattened point and beveled tip for slicing through the thick stuff.

➤ *Microtex:* These needles are very thin and sharp for cutting through microfibers like Ulstrasuede. (The European designation is 130/705 HM.)

➤ *Topstitching:* These long, sharp needles have an extra-wide eye for "fat" thread when you're doing embroidery and decorative topstitching, or when you need heavier thread for upholstery.

➤ *Double needles:* This neat invention sews two completely even stitching lines; the needle itself has two parallel needles that merge into one prong. To use a double needle, your machine must be able to perform a zigzag stitch.

The sizing of this needle is unique to the double needle, and ranges from 1.6 mm to 8.0 mm. This measurement indicates the space between the needles, which in turn becomes the spacing between the two parallel stitching lines. Use the closest size (1.6 mm) for pin tucking on very fine, delicate fabrics; move up to the largest (8.0 mm) for topstitching on heavyweight fabrics. Sometimes there are two numbers on the double needle size, for example, 4.0/90. The first number is the needle spacing, and the second number is the size of the needle.

➤ *Triple needles:* These are just like double needles, except with three parallel needles that make three stitching lines.

Size Does Matter: Needle Numbers

Unlike with hand-sewing needles, the size of machine needles goes up as the needle gets larger. (This is just to confuse us, so don't think you're nuts.) Larger-sized needles are usually used on thicker fabrics; smaller on more fine and sheer fabrics. To make matters even more complicated, there are European numbers and American numbers, and they're often listed together, with the European gradation first. For example, a standard medium to heavyweight needle size is 90/14 (the European number is 90, the American 14). The numbers usually start at 60/7 and go up to 110/18. Following is a quick reference chart to match your needle size to your fabric.

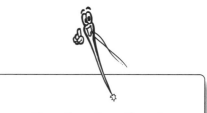

Sew Far, Sew Good

When you have a spare moment on your hands, change your sewing machine needle. The next time you sit down at your machine, you'll have a fresh needle and will be ready to roll.

Sewing Machine Needle Size Chart

European/American	Fabric Use
60/7 or 8	*Delicate*—silk, very sheer cotton, voile, georgette, gauze organza, tulle
65/9	*Lightweight*—lightweight blends, mediumweight silks, crepe de Chine, faille
70/9 or 10	*Light-* to *mediumweight*— shirting, crepe, polyester
75/11	*Mediumweight*—stretch knits, cotton, tricot
80/12	*Medium-* to *heavyweight*—wool, velvet, broadcloth, cotton and cotton blends, rayon, light linen, jersey
90/14	*Heavyweight*—tightly woven, heavy cotton, corduroy, worsted, velour, poplin, heavy linen, gabardine
100/16	*Heavyweight*—canvas, duck, flannel, fleece, denim, leather, and suede
110/18	*Very heavyweight*—upholstery fabrics, very heavy canvas, and duck

Noteworthy Notions

I can never get my needles back into their little packets, which leaves me at a loss when I need to know the size and type of a stray needle. I solved this problem by buying a small tackle box, labeling the compartments, and just dropping the right size into the right needle bin. No more fishing around ....

Pulling It All Together: Thread

I used to be completely stymied whenever I went to pick out thread. Besides the obvious pickle of matching color and weight to fabric, how do you pick what *kind* of thread to use when there's such a variety of brands, makes, and materials? I would find myself staring blankly at rows and rows of spools, unable to make a decision—any decision—that I thought made sense, only to grab the wrong one in the end. This section will provide you with some quick pointers to take away the guesswork in choosing thread.

The first thing to remember when using thread is that old, worn, and frayed thread is the sewer's enemy. What I call "dead thread" will waste a great deal of time in breakage and rethreading, not to mention the problems it causes in your garment. So, don't skimp on thread by using your Aunt Tillie's cache of spools that you found in the attic. Not only are they likely to be worn, making them prone to fraying and breakage, they haven't benefited from recent thread technology—thread has really come a long way in the last decade.

No Spooling Around: Thread Varieties

Following is a rundown of the most commonly available thread varieties and how and when to use them, without getting all wound up.

➤ *All cotton:* All thread used to be all cotton. And for good reason: Cotton is a beautiful fabric, and when spun into thread, it produces a shiny, sleek, and very strong thread that works well with many fabrics. Good cotton thread is put through a mercerization process that gives it its unique sheen. It usually comes in two- or three-ply, meaning that two or three strands are intertwined to create a durable thread. Get out your magnifying glass if you want to check out your cotton thread construction—you can actually see the intertwined strands.

You got to love all cotton, but it does have its pitfalls. It has a tendency to dry and shrink over time; it rots and mildews with exposure to water (so don't use it on your deck chairs or sailing cushions), and doesn't "give," so avoid using it on stretch fabrics. And finally, never use it with leather or suede. The chemicals used in tanning eat away at all cotton thread.

➤ *All-purpose polyester:* I myself am a synthetic material girl. While I can marvel at nature's wonders, I'm also dazzled by the versatility of synthetic fibers. This is definitely the case with polyester thread. It's strong and stretchy, and resistant to wear and tear from repeated use and exposure to heat, water, and chemicals.

➤ *Long-staple polyester:* Long-staple polyester is the best all-around thread, in my opinion. It differs from all-purpose because of the way it's made; instead of using short (about $1^1/_2$ inch) fibers in the spinning process, long-staple uses longer (5–$6^1/_2$ inch) fibers, making it sleeker, stronger, and shinier.

Stitch in Your Side

It may seem obvious, but you should never neglect to catch the end of your thread in the special notch in the spool, specifically designed for this purpose. It keeps your sewing kit from looking like a teased bouffant hairdo and makes finding the end of the spool that much easier.

If you notice such things (and you will), use long-staple poly on finer quality sewing—silks, lingerie, organza, evening wear, satin pillows, and so on. Not only will it look better, it will also wear better, adding sparkle to your seams and top-stitching. My favorite brand is Gutermann, a German maker that's been around since the turn of the century (the last one!) and is widely available. Some other good brands are Metrosene and Molnlycke.

➤ *Cotton-wrapped polyester:* This is polyester thread that's encased in fine cotton. Since cotton looks great but doesn't wear well, cotton-wrapped polyester is de-signed to give strength and good looks. It is indeed stronger and stretchier than 100-percent cotton, but it also has some of its drawbacks. For example, it rots with water exposure and doesn't work well with certain chemicals.

➤ *Buttonhole twist:* This thread, which can be made of silk, polyester, or cotton-wrapped polyester, is thick thread. It's used for buttonholes (imagine that!) or for decorative topstitching that calls for a heavier and thicker thread.

➤ *Silk:* All silk thread is stunning to look at: It practically glows from the lustrous shine of silk. It's much, much stronger than cotton or polyester thread. Its strength can actually slice through fine or sheer fabrics, so reserve silk for top-stitching or decorative stitching. And remember—it's pretty pricey, so buy for each use instead of stocking up ahead of time.

21

➤ *Silk buttonhole twist:* This fancy thread combines the beauty of silk and the thickness of the buttonhole twist.

➤ *Invisible:* Made out of 100-percent nylon filament, this is an almost completely invisible (hence the name) type of thread. While it's not recommended for everyday sewing, it does have its uses. The transparent quality makes it a good choice for bobbin thread when you need a quick fix, for finishing when you don't want any stitching to show (like appliques and pockets), and for working on sequins and lace, for example. Besides clear, it's also available in a smoke color.

➤ *Fusible thread:* This is polyester thread that's wrapped in a nylon fusing agent, a resin that becomes sticky and gluelike when activated by the heat from an iron. It's sometimes used to bond seams and for basting.

➤ *Serger cone thread:* This is polyester or cotton-wrapped thread to be used only with a serger. It is wound on cones in a distinctive cross-weave way that makes it easier to unwind at top serger speeds. Serger thread is two-, rather than three-ply, making it less durable than sewing machine thread. Sergers use so much thread that is looped together, making it possible to use cheaper and less strong thread. Serger thread is also available in special decorative finishes such as Glamour, which is a metallic sparkly thread. If you use a serger a lot, check out the great thread products that are out there.

Noteworthy Notions

Gale Grigg Hazen, a stellar sewing expert, teacher, and author, suggests that if you do have some cotton thread that has started drying out, try putting it in the vegetable crisper of your fridge along with the cabbage instead of throwing it out. It will absorb some of the moisture and may bounce back into shape. If it doesn't, get rid of it!

Threadbare: Don't Be Caught Without Your Threads

The greatest do-ahead timesaver is pooling your spools; go shopping once or twice a year for your favorite threads in your favorite colors. Buy the standards—black, white, and gray—in larger economy sizes. Also, look around your home and your closet, and go with your instincts. If you favor muted colors, stock up on those. If you've got a closetful of brights, clean up on colors. It's taken me some time, and certainly some trial-and-error, but I now have thread for almost every occasion, from day-to-day needs to fancy duds.

Matchmaking: Well-Suited Threads

In a perfect world, we would always have fabric and thread that match … but you don't need to be obsessed with an exact match. There's one rule that will really help when you are trying to match: Buy a spool that is a shade or two darker than your fabric—as the thread unwinds, it'll look lighter than when it's on the spool. Also, thread blends better with fabric when it's a bit lighter (as opposed to darker thread, which stands out a bit too much).

Weighty Thread Matters

Have you ever grabbed a spool of thread, only to discover that you picked the wrong weight? Too thick and heavy or too fine … it's so hard to know which end is up and what all those numbers mean. As with needles, where an advanced degree in needle-ology seems necessary, thread has its own number scale that has a mind of its own. Usually you only need two weights—the regular kind and the heavy kind, to put it simply. But what if you want a better understanding of your options?

Your best guides are the numbers printed at the bottom of the thread spool. There are usually two numbers, for example, 50/3. The first number is the thickness of the thread; the second is the number of plies that are twisted together to form the thread.

Noteworthy Notions

If you can't find a perfect thread color match for your fabric and don't want to travel to another state to find it, why not try a complete contrast color? This is why I love white and have it in all its varieties and weights.

The thickness of the thread is measured inversely—the thinner the thread, the higher the number. A 30/3 number indicates a heavy-duty thread, used for denim, upholstery, and other maximum wear-and-tear projects; a 50/3 or 60/3 can be used for average, mediumweight projects; and an 80/3 is only used for very fine and sheer fabrics.

Buttonhole twist is usually 40/3; fusible thread is 85/3; serger thread is 40/2; and invisible thread is not sized according to the same scale.

Whew! You've made it through the maze of numbers, sizes, and types of needles and threads with hardly a snag. Now it's time to move from the needle in the haystack to more pressing matters—your machine and ironing systems.

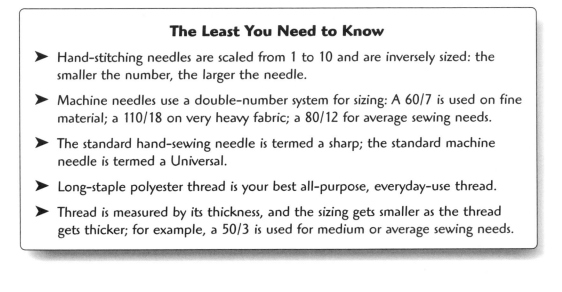

The Least You Need to Know

➤ Hand-stitching needles are scaled from 1 to 10 and are inversely sized: the smaller the number, the larger the needle.

➤ Machine needles use a double-number system for sizing: A 60/7 is used on fine material; a 110/18 on very heavy fabric; a 80/12 for average sewing needs.

➤ The standard hand-sewing needle is termed a sharp; the standard machine needle is termed a Universal.

➤ Long-staple polyester thread is your best all-purpose, everyday-use thread.

➤ Thread is measured by its thickness, and the sizing gets smaller as the thread gets thicker; for example, a 50/3 is used for medium or average sewing needs.

Chapter 3

Power Stitching and Steam Heat

In This Chapter

➤ Choosing between mechanical, electronic, and computerized sewing machines

➤ Giving in to the urge to serge

➤ Knowing when a shot-of-steam iron will suffice or going for gusto with an ironing press

➤ Understanding what's the perfect pressing paraphernalia

Now that you've pooled your spools and gotten together your notions, it's time to turn your attention to your two big-ticket items—your sewing machine and your pressing equipment. Buying a machine can be a big investment, so you need to figure out exactly what your sewing needs are and what kind of machine will address them properly.

For many years I did all my sewing on an old, all-metal Singer from the 1940s and was perfectly happy with it. Now, I've graduated to a more complex mechanical model with a variety of stitches and other gizmos that I can't live without. Even so, I still don't have a fancy computerized model that other sewers swear by. The point is to figure out which sewing machine works for you. With a few guidelines, you'll be able to choose with greater confidence and ease. All you need to know is which questions to ask and what answers to expect.

The most important thing to remember when buying a sewing machine is to use a reputable dealer and buy a recognized make. Pick a dealer whom you trust—someone who responds to your questions and concerns, who'll be around long after you buy your machine, and who'll even supply lessons if you need them. Your machine should last a good long while and your dealer should be there to help you service it.

If you become a serious sewer, you may want to look into purchasing a serger. This is a machine that performs a number of sewing tasks at top speed: It sews a seam, cuts the excess fabric, and finishes the seam all in one fell swoop. A serger is a fantastic complement to your sewing machine, requiring special skills and knowledge. I'll help you decide if you need to go for the serging gusto later in the chapter.

The other big investment, though not nearly as costly, is an iron, ironing board, and other pressing supplies. It wasn't until I started using a professional iron and steamer that I realized just how crucial pressing is to make anything—from curtains to a tailored suit—look snappy and crisp.

The Ultimate Driving Machine

There's a huge variety of sewing machines out there at all price points—from plastic "beginner" models that just perform the basics to 5,000-dollar computerized whizzes. If you're going to go out and drop a bundle on a new top-of-the-line model, you should be very sure that you will actually get 5,000 dollars' worth of use out of it. This means that you'll need to know how to use all of the options and consider them essential to your sewing needs!

There are basically three types of sewing machines on the market: mechanical, electronic, and computerized. One motor that connects to gears—or what's known as cams—which operate different stitches, operates both the mechanical and electronic machines. The main difference between the two is that most of the features of the mechanical machine are operated by the sewer; for example, stitch length, speed, tension, and needle position. An electronic machine still has one motor but it takes many of these features to a new level and calibrates them electronically, taking away some of the guesswork on the part of the sewer.

Noteworthy Notions

Before shopping for a machine, prepare a bunch of fabric swatches so you can test the machine while you're at the store. Cut out some strips of about 2 × 10-inch pieces of fabric in different weights like silk, cotton, and canvas. Use them as you test and you'll get a good idea of the feel of the machine and how it reacts to different fabric.

The computerized machine has a whole different setup: There are often several different motors for different, specialized movements and a main circuit board for the electronic impulses. Rather than using dials to indicate settings, computerized machines usually have push buttons. Virtually everything is calibrated by the circuitry, resulting in up to 500 stitches and a complex memory for storing stitches, buttonhole lengths, and so on. This computerized technology is being perfected every day. According to *Threads* magazine, computerized machines have about the same rate of repair as mechanical machines, and—as with computers—newer and improved models are appearing all the time.

I don't mean to turn my nose up at this new technology, which really is dazzling, but I still find that I really don't need all those bells and whistles to get the job done. I simply don't have the time to commit to learning the operation of a complicated machine, and have no need for the extra frills those machines provide. It's amazing how quickly and easily I can accomplish a pretty fancy tailored jacket with my mechanical machine. However, in the interests of making your own choice easier, I've divided the different features into three categories—essentials, nice extras, and unnecessary extras—to help you decide on a machine.

Just like any other piece of equipment, each machine has its own personality, so it's crucial that you take it for a test run to get the feel of it and see if man and machine are in sync. Tell your dealer what your price range is, and ask her to show you several machines and demonstrate their features. Then, give the machine a good workout, testing each of the different stitches, buttonholes, and bobbins.

Sew Far, Sew Good

If you already own a machine, make a quick list of what you like about it—presser foot, speed, and so on—and what you don't like about it, or even what you don't need. If you don't own a machine, make a list of what you plan on sewing and what you want to accomplish. Show the list to your dealer—don't be shy!—and she can help you match your wish list to your purchase.

Essentials

These features are not just important, you really can't sew efficiently without them! Keep these in mind when you go machine-shopping:

➤ *Good, fast-moving motor.* Make sure you test out the speed in the store. You can only sew as fast as your machine will let you, and some mechanical home models are painfully slow. The top-of-the-line machines have a speed regulator, a feature that's especially useful if you're going to be working with younger sewers or beginners.

➤ *Sturdy body.* Most machines today are made out of plastic parts (with the exception of the motor). Sometimes this results in an extremely flimsy body that is prone to breaking. Pick up your machine. Does it feel like it will withstand your wear and tear? You should also ask your dealer what kind of plastic is used on the machine. The better choices use Lexan, a heavy-duty nylon that's also used on space shuttles. Believe me, there is a difference in plastics!

➤ *Easy bobbin feature.* You'll be winding a lot of bobbins, so test this as well in the store. Is it simple to use? Can you wind the bobbin with speed? Does the bobbin slip in and out of the bobbin case with ease?

➤ *Removable presser feet.* The presser foot holds the fabric in place while you're sewing. There are many different kinds of presser feet, the most important of which are the regular (or zigzag) foot and the zipper foot. Mine just pop on and off—a great feature!—as opposed to older machines in which they are attached with a screw.

➤ *Buttonhole feature.* Without a buttonhole feature, you just can't make machine buttonholes, and if you've ever tried hand-sewing a buttonhole, you know what a complete pain in the fingertip it is. I use my buttonhole feature all the time, and even the lower-priced models have them these days.

➤ *Zigzag stitch.* This is basically a zigzag stitch that is great for finishing seams so they don't unravel, an essential tool if you don't own a serger. The zigzag stitch is also important for making buttonholes, double-needle stitching, and other options.

Noteworthy Notions

If you have an older machine without a buttonhole feature, don't despair! You can finish everything but the buttonholes, mark their placement on the garment or pillows (I like to add buttons to the back of my pillows to keep their shape), and give them to your local tailor. There's even a store in New York that just does buttonholes for you! (Check out Appendix B, "When the Sewing Gets Tough—Finding Help and Resources," for buttonhole resources.)

Nice Extras

Sure, you could probably do without these and never really notice—until you get a chance to try them! Although this is definitely not a "must-have" list, it sure helps to incorporate these features into your new sewing lifestyle:

➤ *Free arm.* This is a removable arm that snaps off, leaving you room to sew small circular areas like sleeves and cuffs. My machine has a great feature: a removable arm with an accessory compartment in it. It's there that I stow my extra bobbins, seam ripper, and a screwdriver. I'm always slipping the arm off and on for sewing ease!

➤ *Automatic tension.* This is a feature on many newer machines that takes the guesswork out of creating the right tension. To sew properly, the tension between your bobbin thread and top thread has to be properly calibrated. If it's out of whack, your stitches won't be even and the seams may unravel. Calibrating the tension takes an understanding of how it works, but mostly, it's trial and error on the older machines. An electronic machine can do this simple but important job for you.

➤ *Needle stops up or down.* This is a feature that allows you to set whether your needle will stop down (anchoring the fabric in place) or up (freeing you to move it around). My sewing teacher repeated over and over that you must stop with the needle down, in the fabric, before moving, shifting, or pivoting, or you'll skip stitches. So, rather than hearing my teacher's mantra, this feature will do it for you!

➤ *Sewing speed selection.* Pick your speed—slow for beginners, faster as you get up to speedy sewing.

➤ *Low bobbin warning.* Electronic machines have a sensor or an eye which turns on a warning light detecting when the bobbin has started to get low.

Stitch in Your Side

No matter how fancy your machine, you should test the stitching for correct tension on a swatch of the fabric you'll be using. There's no need to ruin a fine silk scarf because the tension isn't calibrated properly!

Stitch in Your Side

Whenever your machine is idle, make sure you lower the needle into a swatch of fabric so that it stays put, rather than leaving the needle up. Otherwise, dust can get into the feed dogs and needle hole, and the needle and its mechanisms might shift, causing damage.

Unnecessary Extras

These items can be nice, but really aren't worth the extra investment or time spent learning how to use the feature, particularly for new sewers. But in either case, at least you'll know what they do if you decide that you're worth it!

➤ *Computerized buttonholes.* Yes, it is great to have perfect buttonholes that are programmed into your computerized sewing machine. This is a standard feature on the more expensive models, and it does indeed make your life easier—but only if you're planning to sew a lot of buttonholes! These machines will also make a wide variety of buttonholes, such as the keyhole shape.

➤ *Designer stitches.* The pricier the machine, the more stitch options you get, until you get to the top-of-the-line machine that allows you to design and program your own stitches. These stitches have an enormous variety of widths and lengths, and you can change the stitch pattern with the press of a button. Once you get over the thrill of monogramming and playing around with all the embroidery stitches, however, it comes down to one basic truth: All these toys are fun, but not necessarily functional, and they definitely don't fall into the "daily use" category.

A midpriced machine satisfies the needs of your average home sewer. But if you find yourself sewing a lot faster than your machine, maybe you need to step up your production and move on to a serger. For the extremely productive sewer who's interested in turning out professionally serged seams, read on …

Stitch in Your Side

A serger sews at a much faster rate than an ordinary machine, so it's like going from 0 to 100 in no time. It really is like buying a new Porsche when you've been driving a Chevy; you need a wide expanse of open road, some practice time, and a touch of daring to get all you can out of the experience. But if you're willing to weather the learning curve, it's worth it.

The Urge to Serge

I used to see sergers in the window of sewing machine stores and think they were from another planet. What kind of machine uses up to five spools of thread and a million different knobs and buttons? There obviously was some secret sewing going on somewhere—Mars, maybe—where they possessed super sewing skills, ones that I'd never be able to master.

It took me a while to figure out that this was no ordinary sewing machine, and it did, indeed, have super sewing powers. This is the serger, a machine that sews a seam, finishes it, and then cuts off the extra fabric all at top speed (see the following figure). Most store-bought clothes have serged seams. You can spot by the telltale looping that keeps the seams from unraveling, finishing sewn pieces without bulk or bother.

A serger is usually a complement to a sewing machine, not a substitute for it. How do you decide if you need a serger? If you do enough sewing to be concerned about saving time when sewing seams, you could probably use a serger. But the buyer needs to beware: A good serger (and you should get a good one) is a real investment, often costing more than a regular machine. But the real investment comes when you're learning your serging Ps and Qs. All those buttons and knobs really do make a difference, calibrating between two and five spools of thread and tension at one time. To get your money's worth, you need to be a serging student.

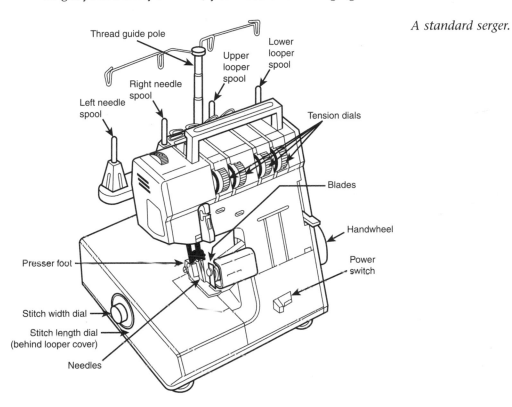

A standard serger.

Thread guide pole

Upper looper spool

Lower looper spool

Right needle spool

Left needle spool

Tension dials

Blades

Handwheel

Presser foot

Power switch

Stitch width dial

Stitch length dial (behind looper cover)

Needles

Here's a quick run-down of pros and cons of the serger vs. the standard machine:

➤ *Faster than a speeding bullet.* The serger is much faster than a traditional machine. If it turns out you need to make Santa suits for the whole class, then serging is the way to go.

➤ *Seam finishing without flair.* Serging finishes the raw edges of the seam allowances with encased loops. If you're making a garment that needs to be as beautiful on the inside as it is outside, then go the traditional route with finely finished seams. For speed and utility, serging rules. For quality rather than quantity, like a fancy French seam, use your standard sewing machine.

31

➤ *Doesn't hug corners.* Sergers are notoriously inaccurate around tight corners and edges. If you have some sticky maneuvering, better stick to your standard.

➤ *No room for error.* If you're not sure how the finished outfit is going to fit, be careful about serging. A serger cuts off the extra fabric, leaving no wiggle room for alterations.

➤ *Thread-thirsty.* Sergers use special thread that has a distinctive diamond cross-weave look on large cones rather than spools. The cones pack a real wallop, and come in quantities of 2,000 to 10,000 yards. Sergers are thread gobblers, which makes sense if you look at the loop-the-loops that finish the seams. Because it takes two to five threads to form the stitches, sergers can use a finer, two-ply (rather than three-ply) thread to create a smooth sheen and finished seam. If you're watching your pennies, beware of the surge in thread use with a serger.

➤ *Buttons without a hole.* Sergers can't sew buttonholes, a good reason to hang on to your sewing machine.

When finishing seams starts to drag you down, you know it's time to invest in a serger. Let your productivity guide you; if your machine is slowing you down, upgrade.

Steam Heat

I used to wait until my sewing project was well underway before getting to the iron. It wasn't until I took a class with a professional steamer and sewer (my teacher) that I learned just how important pressing before, during, and after is to the quality of anything sewn.

From the very start, when you should press your fabric and tissue pattern pieces, to the very end, when you want a crisp, professional look, pressing will determine whether you will end up with a limp, lifeless garment, or one that's got a swingy swagger. After all, that's the goal here—not only to have fun and be able to relax while sewing, but also to make something that looks swell!

Pressing paves the way to a great-looking project, and can also mask any small mistakes and slubs as you go. I once made a complicated welt pocket five times, only to have it fall into place when properly pressed!

Clearly, the most important tool in pressing, in addition to an iron, is a good ironing board. There are a few features that your iron should have, which I'll outline for you, but you also need some other tools. Like your sewing machine, these items should be of high quality and built to last. This is not the place to skimp, whether on the money you spend or on the time you spend pressing. Remember, pressing, as well as practice, makes perfect.

Essential Elements of the Perfect Iron

First of all, make sure that you buy a good brand of iron with a warranty. I got mine at a big department store when they were having a holiday sale (always a good time to go!) and I saved a bundle. Keep an eye out for sales rather than buying an inferior brand. When shopping around, look for these features for stress-free pressing:

➤ *Shot-of-steam feature.* With a press of a button, you can get a quick blast of steam heat, essential for hard-to-press fabrics and fusing interfacing. This also allows you to steam garments as they hang vertically, which gives that "just back from the dry cleaner" look to your clothes. Buy an iron with a lot of steam holes on the iron plate—it works better, especially on fusing.

➤ *Large water container.* The biggest pain while sewing is refilling the water container of your iron. You're going to go through a small container faster than you can say "s-s-s-steam heat," so look for the largest container you can find.

➤ *Nonstick surface.* This isn't essential, but I love it! This means that you don't have to clean the iron nearly as often, and sticky stuff like starch won't build up on the iron as much.

➤ *Self-cleaning feature.* Okay, so it's not crucial, but what sewer wouldn't want this feature?

Sew Far, Sew Good

Always keep your iron clean so it's ready at a moment's notice. You can buy special cleaners made for irons, such as Rowenta's Soleplate Cleaning Kit, or Clean and Glide. Don't use household cleaners; most of them will damage the plate (except for WD-40, which can fill in for an iron cleaner in a pinch).

Noteworthy Notions

Even if your iron has a spray nozzle for misting your fabric while ironing, it's much easier to keep a spray bottle on hand right next to your ironing station. This way, you won't go through the water container of your iron as quickly—a definite plus because refilling is a drag, and reheating a time-waster!

➤ *No automatic shutoff.* An automatic shutoff feature will shut off your iron, usually after it hasn't been used for about eight minutes. This of course means that your iron will constantly shut itself off, so you may need to reheat it over and over. Of course if you have children or pets around you may want to consider the safety issues of having an iron on all the time, so think before you choose.

➤ *Long cord.* This should be self-explanatory, but just think about it—how well can you iron if you're attached to the wall outlet by an 18-inch tether?

Pressing Matters

Besides your iron, there are a few more things you should invest in. Here's a list of pressing essentials:

➤ *Ironing board.* I know, it's obvious, but make sure you buy one that is sturdy and has a thick cover. You can mail-order specialty ironing boards that have a larger surface area and a metal holder for your iron. Or, better yet, get a Shirtmaker ironing board, which is 21 inches wide. The biggest enemy to the sewer is an old, rickety ironing board that's covered with a flimsy or stained cover. These stains, no matter how old, will seep through to your fabric during steaming, ruining both your fabric and your desire to sew.

Sew Far, Sew Good

You can buy a premade press cloth from your notion store, or you can use a common cotton or linen kitchen cloth that you already have. It's also practical to use a sheer cloth so that you can check placement as you're pressing—it's no fun to press a whole garment and then realize that there's a cockeyed crease running all the way down the middle of it!

Noteworthy Notions

Tired of tiny ironing boards that make you waste time by constantly shifting fabric around and re-ironing? Make your own large-scale pressing surface out of a plywood board that's been cut to order, and covered with laundered, heat-absorbent wool that's been stapled to the underside of the board. Tack a piece of muslin to the top of that, and you're ready to roll!

➤ *Tailor's ham.* We're not talking honey baked here! This is a thick, heavy, ham-shaped cushion that's used for pressing open seams—especially in curved areas like darts, sleeve caps, collars, and waistbands.

A tailor's ham.

➤ *Press cloth.* A press cloth is used in between your iron and the material, protecting the material from overpressing and that ugly, telltale "iron shine" that can make even the best fabric look old and worn.

Nice Extras

You can do without these, but they only make the job that much easier:

➤ *Pressing mitt.* Simply slip this padded, double-sided mitt over your hand for pressing those hard-to-reach areas like sleeves, or use it to protect your hands when pressing down on heated areas.

Noteworthy Notions

If you don't own a pressing mitt, try an oven mitt. They're both heat-resistant and perfectly shaped for your hand to slip into some fabric. Just make sure there's no leftover pot roast on the mitt!

➤ *Sleeve roll.* This is a sausage-shaped (what is it about meats and pressing?) cushion that's perfect for pressing sleeves. It can be frustrating to get to all parts of the sleeve, especially the seams, but this simple sausage just slips inside the sleeve so that there are no unsightly creases and the pressing lines don't appear on the other side.

A sleeve roll.

➤ *Point presser and clapper.* This wooden contraption has two purposes: One side has a pointed surface for pressing points open—especially on collars and cuffs— and the other is a flat, wooden block that's great for serious creases. You use the flat side for things like opening seams and turning facings and collars. After pressing with an iron, simply place the clapper on the fabric, and press down with both hands until the material cools. It works on the simple principle that the hard wood of the clapper draws the heat out of the fabric, allowing it to cool quickly and set the crease.

A point presser and clapper.

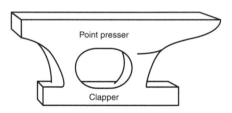

Point presser

Clapper

➤ *Sleeve board.* This is a mini-ironing board that is double-sided for sleeves and small details.

➤ *Table-top ironing board.* Bigger than a sleeve board but smaller than an ironing board, this gives you more ease and variety for pressing. It fits neatly on top of just about any table you could think of!

Not-So-Pressing Features

You don't need these tools, but if you have the space and the money, they can sure make sewing faster and easier:

➤ *Ironing press.* This is also known by the brand name Elnapress, and while expensive ($200 and up), it's a great tool if you plan on doing a lot of interfacing. You've probably seen an ironing press in your local tailoring shop—it looks almost like a copy-machine cover with a handle! Just place the material on the pressing surface, pull down the upper plate, and you'll get about 100 pounds of pressure with almost no effort on your part. This makes fusing and pressing large surface areas just about effortless, and would be a great upgrade for the sewer who wants to save time and prevent getting Popeye arms from doing too much pressing!

➤ *Professional steam iron with upright water container.* This has a gravity-flow steam system that hangs on your wall, or, in any event, higher than your iron, providing a large supply of constantly heated water and serious steam.

The equipment that I've described here is really an investment in your sewing future. If taking care of your own hems, learning how to fix a broken zipper, and making throw pillows are what's in store for you, that's fine, but buy accordingly. If you think you're into something more, splurge on a new machine and a top-of-the-line iron. It'll be worth the money if it makes your sewing experiences more pleasant!

The Least You Need to Know

➤ A good sewing machine should have the following features: fast motor, sturdy body, zigzag stitch, buttonhole feature, easy bobbin use, and simple presser foot removal.

➤ If you're moving faster than your sewing machine and stitching up a storm, you should probably invest in a serger.

➤ Invest in the best iron you can—a small amount of money makes a big difference, and always make sure it has a shot-of-steam feature.

➤ Keep your pressing essentials—ironing board, press cloth, tailor's ham, and water mister—within an arm's reach when working on any sewing project.

Chapter 4

Going with the Grain: Fabric Facts

In This Chapter

➤ Nature's way: natural fabrics

➤ Fantastic fakes: synthetic fabrics

➤ Shopping savvy: how to pick a fabric

➤ Which width: wising up on width and yardage

Every chef knows that he's only as good as the ingredients he uses; you can't make a great omelet with rotten eggs. This applies just as much to sewing. Your creation will only be as good as your basic ingredient—your fabric. The infinite variety of fabrics, in a rainbow of colors, weights, patterns, and grades, is truly dazzling, giving the home sewer the raw materials for an embarrassment of riches. I'm like a kid in a candy shop whenever I go into a great fabric store. The fabric is a real inspiration, and I can easily walk out with enough fabric to keep me busy until the next millennium.

How do you decide, when there's such an intimidating array of fabrics, what is appropriate for those work pants and what's better for black tie? Whether a crisp cotton is ideally suited to your summer suit, or if you should opt for a man-made cotton/rayon blend? Don't be daunted by the strange terminology (what exactly is gabardine? how about crepe?) or the endless varieties of fabric at your fingertips. I'll take you on a quick course that'll have you bolting through fabric like a pro.

Fabric Facts

Just like cooking, which involves a hands-on knowledge of your ingredients and how they react with other foods during the cooking process, sewing is intimately involved with the tactile sensation of working with fabric, of creating something three-dimensional out of a flat piece of cloth. What a rush! Fabric has a life of its own, and it helps if you think of it as a living, breathing being (if you've ever worn fabric that doesn't breathe, like really bad polyester, you know what I'm talking about).

A lot of books and courses will give you all sorts of technical mumbo jumbo about fabric content and fiber construction; but all those facts can still leave you clueless when faced with hundreds of fabric bolts at your local store. You have to jump in, play with the fabric, and see how it plays with you. In other words, you have to touch the fabric, feel its weight, drape, and workability, understand whether it works for your project, and find out how to care for it before you plunk down some cash.

Noteworthy Notions

If you own a piece of clothing that you love and wear constantly, clip a swatch of the fabric from the seam allowance, or, if it's not too bulky, stick it into your bag when you go fabric shopping. Ask for some help finding a similar fabric, and you're set to copy your favorite dress.

Most fabric stores display the fabric rolled up in bolts with small swatches attached to the end. Do not be intimidated by this presentation. You must pull out the bolt, unfurl it, caress it, and dig in. Lay it across your arm, imagine it as a swingy coat, drop it to the floor in front of a mirror to see if it would work as a full-length skirt. If all this sounds scandalous, it's not. A good fabric salesperson is all too happy to roll out her goods and have you handle them. "Feel this—you'll love it" is my favorite phrase from a fabric person. And you should both feel and love it before buying.

Any experienced sewer knows that the drape of the fabric means the difference between a stiff, lifeless garment and one that dips with your hip and glides with your stride. So don't feel guilty if the salesperson is furling and unfurling fabric for you while you're making your choice: It's an investment to buy even a few yards of quality fabric, and you should be sure it's what you want. And, please, please, don't be afraid to ask questions; you're not born knowing this, and any savvy salesperson will be more than happy to share her knowledge.

Nature vs. Nurture: Natural and Man-Made Fabrics

You don't need an advanced degree in fiber fabrication to work well with fabric, but you should know a few basics about natural and synthetic fibers and how they react to you and your needle. All fabrics are made of fibers. Fibers are the building blocks of the fabric, and contain everything you need to know about the fabric—how it feels, drapes, moves, wears, and holds color—just like your own genetic make-up tells you an enormous amount about what makes you, well, you. Whether they're natural or man-made, fibers are either woven or knitted together to form sheets of fabric that reflect their unique make-up.

There was a time (and it was a long time) when all fibers came from nature, created entirely from either animals or plants. Although we've refined the techniques for producing natural fabrics, they're still made from the same sources. The broad categories of natural fibers include wool, cotton, linen, and silk. Within these broad strokes are an infinite variety of permutations. Following is a rundown of these main categories with a sampling of some of the most common types of fabric and a few pointers on special care, needle know-how, and use. In no way is this an exhaustive list; for a more complete course, check out Sandra Betzina's *Fabric Savvy*, a great resource for anyone who's on a fabric fact-finding mission.

Cotton

Cotton is spun from cellulose-based cotton plants into long, lustrous fibers. Although cottons come in a huge variety of weaves and makes, there are a few tried-and-true cotton rules. Always preshrink cotton repeatedly. Most cottons require serious steaming and pressing. I love cotton, and think it's got a zillion uses—it's strong, has a fantastic look and sheen, and is woven and finished in a myriad of ways. But don't overlook some of its drawbacks—cotton fabric, much like cotton thread, can fade and deteriorate with exposure to sun and water, causing mildew. But what fabric lasts forever?

> ➤ *Canvas:* Tightly woven heavy-duty cotton. Used for crafts, home decorating (curtains and cushions), and outdoor gear. Use a serious machine needle (110/18).

> ➤ *Cotton batiste:* A finely woven lightweight cotton that can be used to make elegant garments (blouses, baby clothes, etc.) and as an underlining. Use a straightstitch/jeans presser foot and a 60/8 or 70/10 machine needle.

Sew You Were Saying ...

You say **satin,** I say **sateen.** Is there a difference or is it all in a name? Well, the difference is in the material. **Satin** is made of silk or synthetics, such as polyester and rayon. **Sateen** is cotton. Know your fabric names and you'll know what's in store for your stitching experience.

➤ *Broadcloth:* A fantastic closely woven cotton that has a slight rib.

➤ *Cotton chintz:* This 100-percent cotton has a special fabric treatment that leaves it shiny and smooth, making it terrific for home decorating—curtains, cushions, and so on.

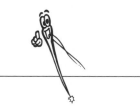

➤ *Cotton pique:* Mediumweight cotton fabric that has a raised nubby surface. Easy to care for (sew, launder, press).

➤ *Cotton shirting:* Lightweight 100-percent cotton that makes fantastic menswear shirts, pajamas, and boxers. Simple to care for, but always use lots of steam to press perfectly.

➤ *Cotton voile:* Crisp lightweight cotton that's used for garments that won't get a workout.

➤ *Denim:* One of the most heavy-duty cottons. Great for work clothes, jeans, jackets— everything that Mr. Levi Straus showed us over the years, and then some. Denim is in fashion these days, making it available in several different weights. Use a 90/14 to 110/18 needle, depending on the weight. Always preshrink repeatedly and watch for color "bleed."

Sew Far, Sew Good

If ever there was a fabric that needs to be preshrunk, it's cotton. You'll need to subject some cottons to three (yup, count 'em), three washings so that you don't end up shrink-wrapped in your shorts. It's worth the extra effort.

Noteworthy Notions

I always used to get confused about organza and organdy—what's the difference and why the almost-the-same name? It's simple—organdy is cotton and organza is silk. Use, sew, and treat them the same: presteam, dry clean, sew with a straightstitch/jeans foot, and use a 60/8 or 65/9 needle. French seams are *de rigeur*. I love organza/organdy for evening wraps that stand at (and call for) attention.

➤ *Seersucker:* This falls into the category of cotton crinkles, which have surface texture. These fabrics need special care: Always preshrink, steam lightly (never

press with high heat; it removes the crinkles),
avoid interfacing that flattens the surface texture, and use a small zigzag stitch.

➤ *Terry cloth:* This thick, absorbent cotton is
used for robes, towels, beachwear, and home
decorating. Use a Teflon presser foot.

➤ *Velveteen:* Either a 100-percent cotton or cotton blend, velveteen has a duller and slightly
stiffer look than velvet.

Linen

While it's very similar to cotton, linen has a life of
it's own. It's made out of flax plants rather than
cotton, giving it more stiffness and less drape.
Linen comes in all different weights, from stand-up
stiff stuff to lightweight linen. Pretreat the fabric
just as you will the finished garment. If you plan
on hand or machine-washing linen, it will definitely shrink, lose color, and change the crisp look
(which you may want). Dry-clean any linens that
you want to retain their stiffness and look.

Linen takes some heat for being tough to take
care of—and for good reason. Linen needs a lot of
steam heat and pressing time to reduce wrinkling.
Take this into account when choosing linen for
any project.

Silk

Silk has a richly deserved reputation for being
pricey, luxurious, and elegant. Made from the filaments spun from the silkworm's cocoon, these
strands are the strongest fiber that nature produces,
reaching up to 2,000 feet long. But don't think of it
as a snooty, standoffish fabric; silk has many uses,
whether its Hugh Hefner-ish satin sheets, silk blouses, or dupioni curtains. Cleaning and caring for
silks depends on the type: Some are dry-clean only,
some can be carefully hand washed and air dried.
In doubt? You know the answer—test on a swatch.
Wash in Woolite and see how it hangs when dry.

Sew Far, Sew Good

Terry cloth and velour are the
fabrics that just keep giving—not
only with their looks and durability, but also in their shrinkage.
That's right—these fabrics continue to shrink even after the first
few washings. Take this into account when buying this type of
fabric—pick up at least an extra
$1/4$ to $1/2$ yard and throw the fabric into the washer and dryer
with your towels and the fabric
linens. You'll end up with clean
towels and ready-to-sew terry.

Stitch in Your Side

Although Jerry Seinfeld says that
clothes can't get more dry than
dry, that's not true. You can actually overdry clothes, especially
cotton. To care for cotton, set
your dryer on the regular dry
cycle, and remove quickly to
prevent shrinkage, damage, and
overwrinkling. Don't dry the life
out of your clothes!

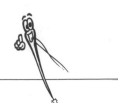

Sew Far, Sew Good

You need to treat your linens with care, but you also need to buy them carefully. I received a set of beautiful linen sheets as a gift, only to have them sit on the shelf of my linen closet. The care—washing and laboriously pressing them—takes hours, hours I'd rather while away on my sewing machine, not at my ironing board.

Sew Far, Sew Good

Follow these silk suggestions so the sewing is easy:

➤ For sheer silks, use a French seam. For crisper fabrics, keep a look out for ravelling. Use a flat fell seam.

➤ Use a standard presser foot for mediumweight silks with some substance. Use a straightstitch/jeans foot for slippery silks.

➤ The needle can range from a 60/8 to 80/12, depending on the silk weight.

➤ *China silk:* This is a very lightweight silk that's used almost exclusively for lining.

➤ *Brocade:* A textured silk with some stiffness; dry-clean only.

➤ *Chiffon:* Lightweight, very drapey silk that can be used on all sorts of garments—pants, tops, dresses, and so on. This is a fabric that goes with the flow. Dry-clean or hand wash, depending on test results.

➤ *Charmeuse:* A slinky, satiny, supple silk that works well as a 1940s redux dressing gown (or regular lingerie), dresses, and blouses. Be careful to use the right side—one is very shiny and the other isn't. Usually can be hand washed.

➤ *Crepe de Chine:* A light- to mediumweight silk for making the full range of garments. Crepe de Chine comes in two-ply, three-ply, and four-ply weights, with four-ply the heaviest.

➤ *Dupioni:* A stiffer and crisper silk that has telltale slubs and raised yarn on the fabric. Whether making Capri pants or a fancy room divider, dupioni is an easy-to-sew silk that adds a lot of fashion flair. Dry-clean only.

➤ *Georgette:* Lightweight silk with a barely visible nubby weave. Hand wash.

➤ *Raw silk:* This is a rough-looking silk with a dull finish. It's actually made from short silk filaments that are discarded as waste. But this is not silk's poor cousin—it's a fabric that's easy to sew and has a distinctive look. Dry-clean.

➤ *Washed silk:* The washing process makes this silk creamy and soft to the touch. It also makes this a great travel fabric that isn't as wrinkly as regular silk. I like it for flowy dresses. Usually can be hand washed.

➤ *Shantung:* An especially crisp and shiny silk for special occasion uses. Dry-clean.

➤ *Taffeta:* A crisp silk that's used for special occasion clothing. Taffeta wrinkles and swishes when you move. Dry-clean.

Wool

Wool is, in a word, wonderful. Made from the coat of sheep, wool is perfect for tailoring because of its "shapability," versatility, resilience, and resistance to wrinkling. The types and varieties of wool are mind-boggling. Here's a hit list:

➤ *Boiled wool:* Boiled wool is made in a similar fashion as felt, but has a much richer and more supple look and feel. The great thing about it is that, like felt, it doesn't ravel at all. There's no need to finish the seam edges, making it extremely versatile.

➤ *Boucle:* This wool has a really distinctive sweater-like nubby surface that's created with little loops. Perfect for soft shaping in coats and jackets.

➤ *Challis:* This is a medium- to lightweight wool with enormous drape and ease of use. It's hand washable, perfect for all types of garments (tops, skirts, dresses, and so on), and doesn't wrinkle much.

Noteworthy Notions

A wool rule: Always use a press cloth when pressing on the right side of wool. This prevents ugly fabric shine, an amateurish addition to any wool outfit.

➤ *Crepe:* Crepe can be composed of wool, silk, cotton, or synthetics. It varies a great deal in quality—expensive wool crepe is a beautiful fabric that drapes well and is extremely wearable. Dry-clean.

➤ *Gabardine:* This is a twill-weave fabric that works well on tailored and constructed garments. It's hand washable and does have a tendency to wrinkle.

➤ *Melton:* A thick, bulky wool with a soft napped surface. Use for coats and avoid any fussy details—this fabric is too thick to handle a lot of detail work. Use a Teflon foot and dry-clean.

Sew You Were Saying ...

More of the name game ... if you run across **viscose** on the fabric tag, don't get confused. This is just another name for **rayon,** an all-purpose synthetic.

➤ *Merino:* A very fine, expensive, closely-woven wool made from Merino sheep's coats.

➤ *Worsted:* A lustrous wool in a variety of weights that can be used for tailoring jackets, skirts, and pants. Dry-clean.

Fabulous Fakes: Synthetics Worth Clinging To

There used to be a snobby and biased attitude toward natural fibers: People just thought they were naturally better. But that's not the case anymore. Rayon, for example, is a great fabric, with flexibility, drape, versatility, and absorbency. There's no need to be standoffish around synthetics; it pays to get acquainted with their properties because there's a real payoff.

Synthetic fibers are processed either from natural materials, such as cellulose or protein, or from completely man-made chemicals, and forced through tiny holes called spinnerets. The material forms filaments that are twisted and turned into fabric.

Sew Far, Sew Good

Do the breathe test! Dampen a swatch of synthetic fabric—does it dry as stiff as a board? If so, chances are that this is what'll happen when you perspire.

Synthetic fabrics are classified by their generic names, like rayon or polyester, and further broken down into brand names, like Lycra, a kind of spandex made by Du Pont. There are a zillion synthetic fabrics (okay, maybe a million) including all the new microfibers that are on the market, so it helps to know the general categories that you'll run across: acetate, rayon, nylon, spandex, and polyester.

Blends are just that: two or more fibers that have been combined to create a new, and one hopes, better fabric. This is the case with many Lycra combinations. I used to do gymnastics in the '70s, and can certainly tell you that the addition of Lycra to cotton has changed exercise wear (my old photos of bottom-baggy leotards are enough to make anyone cringe).

Fabric Foilers: Some Special Fabric Instructions

Some fabrics are just harder to work with than others. That's a fact. Silks, stretch knits, and piled fabrics need special care if they are to be constructed properly. Beginners and those just sowing their sewing oats should stick to stable woven fabrics like cotton and wool before moving on to harder fabrics. Knits, very sheer and slippery fabrics, and napped fabrics all need a little know-how and experience. Following are a few tips for taking the plunge with more challenging fabric.

Knotty Knits

A very stable knit can be treated like wool. Some knits, however, stretch every which way, including loose when you sew them. Determine the fabric's stretch factor before you buy and handle accordingly. Follow the pattern instructions carefully regarding fabric recommendations for stretch knits or two-way stretch knits.

The ideal way to sew knits is with a serger. Knits have a tendency to stretch when being stitched on a regular machine. They also run an enormous amount. The serger solves both of these problems, finishing the edges with looping to prevent running. Some knits, however, react well with a regular machine, especially when you use a zigzag or stretch stitch. Here are a few more tips:

➤ You must preshrink knits by washing them the same way you will when they're sewn into a garment or project. For cotton and jersey knits, hand or machine wash. Wool jersey should be professionally steamed before use.

➤ The fabric should be cut so that the most stretch goes around the body.

➤ With nubby knits, use ballpoint pins for cutting and pinning.

➤ Always use a ballpoint needle. Instead of slicing though the fabric, this dull bulb separates the fibers. A regular needle will cause snags and pulls, so avoid it at all costs.

➤ Be careful when stitching—if you stretch a stretchy fabric, it will have a tendency to curl even more, making the hem or seam really wavy.

➤ Certain seams need stabilization while using stretchy fabrics. This is especially true of shoulder seams. The way to "stay" the seam is to use seam tape, sewn into the seam. You may want some stabilization and stretch in some seams—try clear elastic in these seams.

➤ Hang knits for 24 hours before hemming; clearly, they stretch!

➤ Always use steam heat; always use a press cloth on the right side of the fabric.

Plush Piles

Any fabric that has a piled surface, such as fur, mohair, terry, velvet, chenille, velour, and even cashmere, has a *nap*, or a raised fabric surface. The nap runs in one direction, reflecting light differently.

Sew You Were Saying ...

Napped fabrics have a raised surface. Any piled fabric—terry, velour, velvet, fur, fake fur, some cashmeres and knitted fabrics, and corduroy—has a **nap.** You can determine whether a fabric has nap by running your hand along the surface. Does it change appearance when you rub it up and down? The fabric should lay smooth when rubbed along the same direction. When you go against the directional pull, the fabric will have a different appearance.

You can spot the directional pull of the fabric by running your hand across it; if the fabric lays smooth when you stroke it, you are going with the nap. If the fabric stands up from the surface, is rough and has a different look, then you have brushed the nap against its direction.

➤ Napped fabric must be laid out and sewn in one direction; whether you choose with the nap or against it is a matter of looks and preference. Follow the "with nap" layout on the pattern directions (and see Chapter 13 "Tissue Issues: Understanding Commercial Patterns," for more info on laying out piled fabric).

➤ Be spare with pins on piled fabrics—they sometimes leave holes.

➤ Follow the special pressing instructions for piled fabrics in Chapter 12, "Pressing Matters: Ironing Out the Wrinkles."

Pelt Perfection: Working with Leather and Suede

If you decide it's time to make those skin-tight black leather pants, read on. Leather and suede are sold in specialty stores, and you need some skin savvy to tackle a leather project. Leather comes from animals like pigs, cows, and goats; it's sold by the "skin," rather than by the yard. You need to examine each skin before you buy it; because it's "natural," it often has holes and areas that are thicker and thinner. All of this comes into play when working with it—make sure if you buy a skin with a hole dead center that the pattern will work around the hole.

The cost of the skins is calculated by the square foot rather than by the yard. Always add enough for the seam allowances and for any piecing that needs to be done. For example, pants are usually pieced together at the knee because the skins aren't long enough to construct the legs.

A few more pelt pointers:

➤ Use a leather needle.

➤ Use a Teflon presser foot.

➤ Don't use pins while sewing, or you'll create permanent holes—here's where double-sided seam tape comes in handy.

➤ Stick to polyester thread—cotton thread is weakened by the tanning chemicals.

➤ Glue the seam allowances. Use a good fabric glue, such as Sobo or Magna-Tac. There's no need to finish the seam allowances for leather—skin doesn't ravel.

The Rules of Fabric

No matter what the fabric and how it's made, I always ask the following six questions to determine if it's right for me and my project:

1. *How does it look?* Obviously, a biggie. The first thing that catches your eye is the look: the sheen, the stripe, the gloss, the print, the border, the color, the nap …

2. *How does it feel?* Touch it. Rub it on the back of your hand. Will you like it against your body? Or does it need to be lined? Is it sturdy enough to make bedroom curtains, or will it wilt? Does the stripe entice you, but the scratchiness repel you?

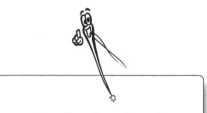

3. *How does it last?* Hard to judge on a first look, but durability is key to some projects. If you need a fabric to have some staying power, hold it up to the light. Does it look closely woven like it will last? Or is the fabric equivalent of pressboard, not concrete?

4. *How do I have to care for it?* Does it need to be dry-cleaned? Or hand washed? Or is it your very lovable machine wash, tumble-dry variety? What about ironing: Crisp cottons need a lot of attention, linens practically need a commitment right from the start, and my faves, rayons, give you a break and lots of space. How much time do you want to spend with your iron?

> **Sew Far, Sew Good**
>
> Don't wing it when it comes to your fabric choice for a commercial pattern. Stick to the suggestions on the back of the pattern envelope. Now is not the time to be a rebel; if it says for double-knits only, believe your mighty pattern master.

> **Noteworthy Notions**
>
> Want to see how your fabric wrinkles? Subject it to the crunch test! Grab a hunk of it, crunch it up in your fist, and let go. Has it held on to the wrinkles, or has it returned to its uncrunched state? This is the best test of how it will react, both on your body and off. Any fabric that holds the crunch won't make it through a day of wear, nor will it travel well.

5. *How does it breathe?* Polyester is the bad boy of breathability; the other synthetics, like acetate and nylon, less so. Rayon is the best, but breathability increases as you climb the natural fabric chain, with cotton at the top. This is why

cotton is used for underwear and exercise wear. Have you ever worn a synthetic top, only to find out that awful sweaty smell never, ever comes out of it, whether it's washed by hand, machine, or dry cleaning? Ugh!—the fabric equivalent of a loser.

6. *Is the weight compatible with the project?* Thick, bulky fabrics need a lot of room to sew and won't work when making tailored garments with a lot of details. Ditto for thin fabric—you can't cover your couch in silk challis. Weigh your options with the fabric weight.

How Wide Can You Go: Fabric Width

When you've put your finger on your fabric choice, how much do you need to buy? The first thing you need to figure out is the fabric width. Every fabric that's sold in bolts has its own width measurement, which will determine how much you need to cut off and buy.

The standard widths are 35", 45", 54", and 60". Cottons, like shirting, are usually sold in 45" widths, while wool, tailoring, and decorating fabrics often come in 54" to 60". Some drapery fabric and wedding satins, lace, and netting are sold in extra-wide widths to accommodate a long train or a wide window.

Stymied about how to convert the yardage for fabric that's a different width than your pattern indicates? Throw away your calculator and stop counting on your fingers—use this handy chart.

Yardage Conversion Chart

Fabric Width:	32"	35-36"	39"	41"	44-45"	50"	52-54"	58-60"
Yardage	1 7/8	1 3/4	1 1/2	1 1/2	1 3/8	1 1/4	1 1/8	1
	2 1/4	2	1 3/4	1 3/4	1 5/8	1 1/2	1 3/8	1 1/4
	2 1/2	2 1/4	2	2	1 3/4	1 5/8	1 1/2	1 3/8
	3 3/4	2 1/2	2 1/4	2 1/4	2 1/8	1 3/4	1 3/4	1 5/8
	3 1/8	2 7/8	2 1/2	2 1/2	2 1/4	2	1 7/8	1 3/4
	3 3/8	3 1/8	2 3/4	2 3/4	2 1/2	2 1/4	2	1 7/8
	3 3/4	3 3/8	3	2 7/8	2 3/4	2 3/8	2 1/4	2
	4	3 3/4	3 1/4	3 1/8	2 7/8	2 5/8	2 3/8	2 1/4
	4 3/8	4 1/4	3 1/2	3 3/8	3 1/8	2 3/4	2 5/8	2 3/8
	4 5/8	4 1/2	3 3/4	3 5/8	3 3/8	3	2 3/4	2 5/8
	5	4 3/4	4	3 7/8	3 5/8	3 1/4	2 7/8	2 3/4
	5 1/4	5	4 1/4	4 1/8	3 7/8	3 3/8	3 1/8	2 7/8

Noteworthy Notions

This chart comes in handy whenever you're fabric shopping, To keep it nearby, copy it from the book, reduce it, and laminate just like your credit cards. You'll thank yourself when you buy exactly the right amount of cashmere—not a smidge too much.

No need to bolt from the fabric store in fear anymore—armed with all this info, choosing fabric can be a pleasure, one that stimulates your senses and opens a whole new world of fabric creations. I used to love clothes shopping; now I love fabric shopping because it's filled with the endless possibilities that come from knowing how to choose and use fabric.

Don't Shrink from Preshrinking

After you've made your fabric choice, the first rule about raw fabric is that it needs to be pretreated, which means that you have to put it to the cleaning test right from the start. This is the pretreating rule: However you plan on cleaning the finished garment—by hand, machine washing, or dry-cleaning—you need to take it through that process before stitching. I know this seems like a huge waste of time and money—who wants to dry-clean a few yards of fabric? Well, the key to overcoming pretreating jitters is to realize that you will save much aggravation, puckered seams, shrunk garments, and just general sewing wear and tear by pretreating.

Noteworthy Notions

Pretreat, iron, and fold your fabric as soon as you come home after buying it. Store it in plastic bins. You'll be absolutely thrilled beyond belief next time you spot that beautiful gray flannel peeking through the side of the bin ready, or as they say, "ready for the needle" for whatever you have planned, be it a scarf, a blanket, or a terrific pants suit.

You need to anticipate the cleaning stress of a garment's life, to prepare for it ahead of time, so that the first wash doesn't produce a lifeless, formless blob. Almost any kind of washing creates shrinkage, especially in woven or knit fabrics. Cotton can shrink to one-fourth of its size (sounds almost alien, but it's true!) after several washings. The point is that pretreating saves much sewing grief, and it's worth the effort.

The Least You Need to Know

➤ Know the fabric facts; figure out the basic constructions, how the fabrics feel, drape, move, and react to the needle. Pick a fabric that's appropriate for each use: Remember, you can't make spandex curtains!

➤ Before giving any fabric a permanent place in your home or wardrobe, subject it to a few basic tests: how do you clean it? Will it last? Does it breathe? Be picky.

➤ Follow the fabric recommendations on the commercial pattern; don't be a rebel for absolutely no cause and end up with a straightjacket jacket instead of a free and easy jersey top.

➤ The standard fabric widths are 35", 45", 54", and 60". Always check the width of the fabric before it's cut from the bolt—you need to determine the necessary yardage based on the width.

Part 2
No More Hemming and Hawing: Getting Set to Sew

Just like so much of our electronic world, sewing machines have become computerized wizards, capable of taking care of all your sewing needs. But they aren't robots—you still need to know your machine inside and out to take advantage of everything it has to offer. This section takes you on a tour of all those buttons, knobs, and gizmos so that you know all of your working parts. Once all systems are go, it's time to thread your machine and hand needles and start stitching.

Take a seat at your sewing machine and take note of your sewing environment. All the equipment, from the cutting table to the pressing station, needs to be accessible so that you can sew efficiently. In this part I'll let you know how to set up a sewing space that makes sense.

When you're comfortable with the whir of the machine, you're ready to prep the fabric. All of this do-ahead preparation actually saves time and prevents fatal fashion errors later—proper blocking, layout, and cutting of fabric are essential to any sewing project.

Chapter 5

Man vs. Machine

In This Chapter

➤ Grappling with your machine's gizmos

➤ Guiding the thread and bobbins without any snags

➤ Deciphering stitch selection and length

➤ Demystifying thread tension

➤ Handling hand stitching and repairs

"Let your fingers do the walking" may sound like a good idea when you need a phone number, but when you need to do some serious home sewing, give your fingers a rest and let your machine take over. Your sewing machine (and serger) can work wonders, saving your delicate digits from the wear and tear of hand sewing. The machine is, indeed, mightier than the needle-wielding hand.

Machines have become so simple, easy, and stress-free that you can use them for most of your sewing needs. But they're not robots—you have to understand how they operate. That's why it's crucial that you get acquainted with every knob, button, wheel, and gizmo so that you can take full advantage of your machine, whether it's a 1940s metal model with a treadle or a brand new computerized wizard fresh from the factory. If you've been too intimidated to turn on your machine, this chapter will encourage you to take it out of the box (or the basement) and get your motor going, gizmos all in place and accounted for, so that you can ride down sewing easy street.

As much as I love using my machine for almost everything—a two-second bar tack or a two-week evening gown—there are times when hand stitching is the only way to fly. Hand stitching (which involves threading a needle, tying the knot, and working the needle and thread through the fabric) is useful for hemming, sewing on buttons, detail work, and a lot of repairs. If you're a needle novice and think you're all thumbs, this chapter will introduce you to your inner seamstress, from threading a needle to taking your first stitch. And, most importantly, it tells you when to ditch hand stitching in favor of the machine and when good old-fashioned elbow grease is the only answer.

Machine Make-Up: Know Your Working Parts

When you first used a computer, you were probably like me—completely cowed by all the seemingly incomprehensible bells and whistles. Now you probably can't imagine life without your computer. Well, sitting down at your sewing machine for the first time is usually a similar experience, but let me assure you that practice will change your sewing machine from an alien creature into a creature comfort. This chapter just gets you going; refer to Chapter 3, "Power Stitching and Steam Heat," for guidelines on which machine to buy and how big of an investment you need to make.

All machines are different, and therefore need to be used, threaded, and serviced differently. Even with all the advances made in machines, which are now computerized, some things remain the same—the basic inner workings never change. To illustrate all the knobs and working parts (see the following figure), I've picked a midlevel electronic model that does almost everything you need to make a couture creation. You don't want to get tangled up before you've even turned on your machine!

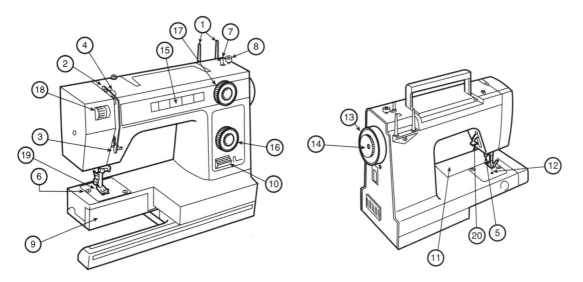

Sewing machine.

1. *Spool or thread spindle:* This is where your spool is placed, so that it unravels with ease.

2. *Thread guide:* Usually a metal loop that keeps your thread in line before it enters the tension mechanism or take-up lever.

3. *Thread spring guide:* The spring has some give so that the pull of the movement doesn't snap your thread.

4. *Thread take-up lever:* As your machine turns, the thread take-up lever moves up and down, precisely synchronizing the movement and the amount of thread needed for stitching.

5. *Needle and needle clamp screw:* This holds your needle in place, unscrewing so that you can remove it.

6. *Throat or needle plate:* This is the metal plate that fits over the bobbin case and feed dogs (more on those later). The needle slips in and out of the hole in this plate, which must be in alignment so that you don't break your needles.

7. *Bobbin winder spindle:* This is where you place the bobbin to wind it.

8. *Bobbin winder stop:* You press the bobbin against this to wind it. It will usually "pop" and stop automatically when the bobbin is fully wound.

9. *Bobbin case:* The bobbin snaps into its own case, which in turn snaps into place under the needle.

10. *Reverse button:* A quick press on this button switches your machine into reverse. This backstitching secures the beginning and end of your stitching so that your seams don't come undone.

11. *Free arm:* This is a great convenience; by removing a portion of the body of the machine,

Stitch in Your Side

If you ever thread your machine wrong, you'll find out—fast—that if you bypass the thread take-up lever, you'll end up with a snarled mess. Don't worry, though; threading your machine will soon become second nature. Before it does, however, you want to check every contact point, especially the take-up lever, so that you don't end up frustrated.

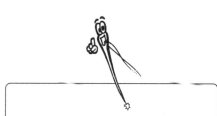

Sew Far, Sew Good

Check your throat plate for some guidelines—seam guidelines, that is. Most plates have notched lines at $1/4$-inch increments to gauge your seam allowance. Just like the center and side lines on a road, these will steer you through many a hem and a difficult curve, keeping you on the straight and narrow without any fender benders.

you expose the free arm, which is the narrow strip that holds the needle and bobbin works so that you can sew circles around things (pants cuffs, sleeves, small clothing, and so on).

12. *Feed dogs (or feed teeth):* The metal teeth that move your fabric forward or backward as your machine stitches are called feed dogs. You can usually adjust the feed dogs. I keep them in the highest, or most "up" position almost all the time unless I'm working with especially thick and piled fabric; in that case, I move them down a bit so that my fabric doesn't move too slowly through the machine.

13. *Handwheel:* In the olden days, before motors, this wheel was controlled by a rubber band conveyer belt that turned the wheel and drove the motion of the machine. Now that it's electric, it moves with great speed, but you can always move the handwheel (or balance wheel or flywheel as it's sometimes called) by hand.

14. *Stop motion or clutch wheel:* This stops the machine from stitching while still allowing the wheel to move. It's used only when winding the bobbin.

Noteworthy Notions

I always noticed my seamstress grandmother moving the handwheel around whenever she started or stopped the machine. She knew what she was doing—it's great to grease the wheels when you're just starting to stitch by turning the wheel slightly, and then letting the motor take over. Ditto for stopping. The top and bottom threads can often get caught up when you finish; let them loose with a little jiggle of the handwheel and you'll be set free, a flywheel fly girl.

15. *Stitch selector:* Old machines just stitched a straight line. Now, you can touch a key pad for computerized monograms and preprogrammed stitch witchery. Check the manual for everything your machine has to offer.

16. *Stitch-length selector:* This selector determines how long your stitches are. This is a complicated choice, ruled by a few factors that we'll sort out later in the chapter.

17. *Stitch-width selector:* How wide do you wanna go? This selector is especially important when you are zigzagging.

18. *Tension selector:* Thread tension is crucial! We'll take the knots out of tension selection later in this chapter.

19. *Presser foot:* This foot holds your fabric in place, guiding it through the stitching process so that it doesn't fly right off the table and into your face. Unlike you, your machine has more than one kind of foot; special presser feet are slipped in place for different uses. The most common type is a zipper foot, which makes inserting a zipper a snap. We'll cover some other feet if you keep on walking—oops, I mean reading ….

20. *Presser foot lever:* This raises and lowers the foot so that you can change it and move fabric in and out.

The Long and Winding Thread Road

You've decided to take the sewing plunge. You sit down at your machine, plug it in, and turn it on. If you're in luck, the light goes on, and you think you're ready to roll, right? Wrong! You've got a few hurdles to clear before you're stitching away. The first obstacle any sewer faces when sitting down at the machine is how to thread it. Sounds simple, doesn't it? This is where your machine's instructions come in handy. But what if your Aunt Tillie's machine came complete with a cache of thread from the 1920s, but no booklet? Following are a few threading do's and don'ts to take the mystery out of machine threading:

➤ Always raise the thread take-up lever to its highest point by turning the handwheel. You need to do this in order to thread the machine and to change or insert the needle.

➤ After you've matched your needle to your sewing needs (see Chapter 2, "The Eyes Have It: Needles and Thread," for the details), you need to put the needle in. Drop the presser foot lever, and then loosen the needle clamp screw. Grab your needle and take a good look at it—there's a flat edge and a notched edge; the flat edge should face the machine, regardless of whether your machine needle faces front or side. After inserting it, tighten the clamp.

Sew Far, Sew Good

Sewing machine makers are pretty crafty—it took me a while to figure out that most thread guides aren't completely circular loops that need to be threaded. They usually have openings or slits so that you just slip the thread into place instead of laboriously threading the loop. Take a good, hard look at your machine and see where you can save seconds while threading … they add up!

➤ Place the thread on the spindle. This is the usual machine thread course: Slip it through the thread guide, through the plates that control the tension, around the thread spring guide, into the take-up lever hole, and through lower thread guides until you reach your needle. Thread from front to back or from right to left, depending on your needle placement.

Bob-Bob-Bobbin Along

Stitches are formed by the intersecting looping of the top thread and the bobbin thread. *Bobbins* are plastic or metal minispools that you wind your thread around and pop into place under your needle. Winding a bobbin is a breeze. Just follow the instructions for your machine, and keep the following key bobbin tips in mind:

➤ Always loosen the stop motion or clutch wheel before bobbin winding. The same motor that drives the needle turns the bobbin, and you don't want to do both at once. To prevent this, loosen the clutch wheel; this will stop the needle from working up and down while you're winding the bobbin.

➤ Wind at top speed. It's scary at first, but you'll get used to high-speed driving, and you'll sure save time.

➤ When putting the bobbin back in its case, make sure the thread moves in the correct direction. The following illustration shows the most common way to wind.

➤ Make sure you hear the telltale "snap" when you insert the bobbin into its case. That way, you know it's really nestled, snug enough to withstand machine tugs.

Sew You Were Saying ...

A **bobbin** is a plastic or metal spool that holds thread; it's inserted in the bobbin case, usually under the machine, where it loops with the needle thread to create the stitches.

Common thread place-ment in a bobbin.

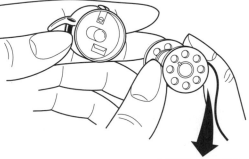

Bobbin Thread Direction

Noteworthy Notions

Keep bobbins from becoming the bane of your existence. Wind up a storm of black, white, and "invisible" thread bobbins and keep 'em in your spool pool at all times. You'll be ready for any quick fix at a moment's notice.

Tense About Tension?

If you have a computerized sewing machine that calibrates tension for you, you can skip ahead to the next section. But if you're like me, you may have tension anxiety! Since sewing involves two threads—the top and the bobbin—that loop together to form knots or stitches, the threads must have the same resistance to "pull" them when they reach the fabric or else they'll be out of whack. Ideally, the knot that forms the stitches should be balanced in the center of the fabric, rather than lying on the top or bottom of it. When the tension goes haywire it will be obvious because the stitches will become loopy, snarled, and uneven.

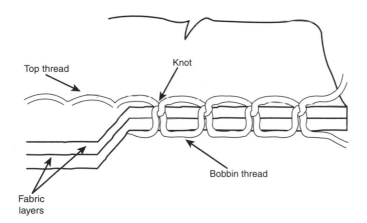

Perfect thread tension.

But not to worry! Both the top and bobbin threads can be adjusted. The bobbin's the easy one; it's controlled by a small screw on your bobbin case—go ahead, take it out and look at it right now and you'll see what I mean. You increase the tension by turning the screw to the right, and loosen by turning it to the left. But be careful! Turn in

61

very small increments—no more than one-quarter of an inch. Even the smallest turn of the screw will affect the tension dramatically. Usually, once it's set to a tension that works, you won't have to change it again for some time.

The top tension is more important, more variable, and—of course—more complicated. As the thread moves from the spool, it enters two plates that are tightened or loosened to control the tension. Depending on your machine, you can alter the top tension by turning a knob or screw, or by pushing a button. However, it's important that you know that just setting the tension at a certain number won't necessarily guarantee success; there are a lot of other variables. Following are a few of the things that will affect top thread tension:

➤ Fabric weight

➤ The feed dogs, and how they connect to the fabric

➤ Stitch length

Without getting an advanced degree in tension—which I already thought I had as a New Yorker—the only real rule is experimentation and practice, with your machine and with different fabrics.

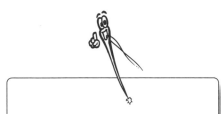

Sew Far, Sew Good

There's an easy rule for telling whether it's the top or the bobbin thread that's off: If the problem is on the underside of the fabric, you need to fix the top thread tension; if you see loopy or "off" stitches on the top of the fabric, you know that the bobbin needs some work.

Stitch in Your Side

Leftover fabric scraps are perfect for testing tension. Too many sewers start stitching on their 100-percent cashmere, only to get it tangled up with tension trouble. Test first on a sample scrap of the fabrics you'll be using so you can take care of the fine-tuning.

The Long and Short of It: Stitch Length

All those buttons on your machine actually make a difference, especially in stitch length. Stitch length is usually measured in millimeters per inch, ranging from 0 to 4, where 2.5 is the standard for medium-weight, firm fabric. Some machines may use stitches per inch, called *spi*.

This is when your feed dogs come into play, so now is the time to explain their importance. The feed dogs are the metal teeth on your machine plate that move the fabric as the machine stitches. They rise and move a certain length, which is determined by your stitch length setting. Even if you never change your setting, however, different fabrics will move at different speeds. Thick, heavy, and rough fabrics move slower than thin and slippery ones.

The slower the fabric moves, the smaller the stitch—no matter what your setting is. So set it accordingly. As a general rule, sheers, organzas, and silks need shorter settings (from 1.5 to 2 mm), whereas thicker fabrics need longer settings (from 2.5 to 3 mm).

I like to follow this rule of thumb: Any time you do a stitch that shows, such as top-stitching, shorten your stitch length a tad. In general, tighter stitching looks tidier.

These Feet Were Made for Sewing

Don't let presser foot pressure get you down; learn how to change your feet with ease to suit your many sewing needs. You'll find that the all-purpose presser foot is in place most of the time when sewing, but when you need another foot, you really need it. For example, the zipper foot is a sewing life-saver, not only for zipper application, but also for cording and other bulky sewing projects. Here's a walk down presser foot lane:

Sew Far, Sew Good

You may think I sound like a test fanatic, but here we go again: When you're testing tension, test your stitch length at the same time. Make sure your fabric scrap moves through without a hitch before you get started on the real thing!

➤ *All-purpose foot or zigzag foot:* Made of durable metal, this is the work shoe equivalent of the presser foot world. This foot has a 4–9 mm opening that can accommodate the sideways movement of your machine's zigzag stitch.

All-purpose or zigzag foot.

➤ *Zipper foot:* The zipper foot is exposed on one side so that a zipper, cording, or other bulky material can move with ease. Some zipper feet slide back and forth to accommodate a right or left application.

Zipper foot.

➤ *Blindhem foot:* Check out Chapter 11, "The Bottom Line: Hems," for instructions on how to use this handy dandy foot.

Blindhem foot.

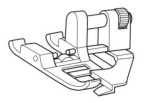

➤ *Buttonhole foot:* This foot enables you to sew perfect, symmetrical buttonholes with identical stitching. The foot moves to and fro in a sliding tray that attaches to the machine.

Buttonhole foot.

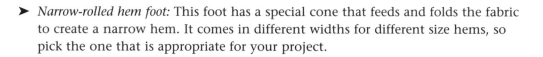

➤ *Narrow-rolled hem foot:* This foot has a special cone that feeds and folds the fabric to create a narrow hem. It comes in different widths for different size hems, so pick the one that is appropriate for your project.

Narrow-rolled hem foot.

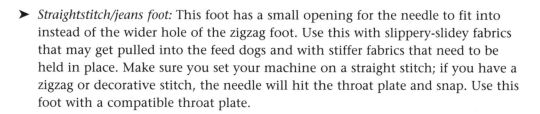

➤ *Straightstitch/jeans foot:* This foot has a small opening for the needle to fit into instead of the wider hole of the zigzag foot. Use this with slippery-slidey fabrics that may get pulled into the feed dogs and with stiffer fabrics that need to be held in place. Make sure you set your machine on a straight stitch; if you have a zigzag or decorative stitch, the needle will hit the throat plate and snap. Use this foot with a compatible throat plate.

Straightstitch/jeans foot.

➤ *Button foot:* This foot holds a button in place so that it can be zigzag-stitched in place. If your machine comes with a tailor tack foot, that will also work well for sewing on buttons.

Button foot.

➤ *Serger feet:* Just as your traditional sewing machine has a variety of detachable feet, so does your serger. Check out what's available for your machine.

Sleight of Hand: Hand Stitching

No matter how much we're a product of the machine era, there's no escaping hand stitching. Whether you're faced with stitching a quick hem, fastening a button that's gone astray, or creating a fringed finish to a scarf, you need to know how to put the old standards—thread, needle, and your nimble hands—to work.

Needle Threading Knowledge

I know you're out there—the kind of person who takes out your travel sewing kit (the one you took from the last hotel you stayed in), makes a few frantic stabs threading the needle, spits on the end of the thread a few more times in an attempt to get it right, and then just gives up, right? First the concentration, followed by the frustration, and then the decision of whether to spend the bucks and take your favorite shirt, which is a little frayed around the edges, to the tailor, or toss it into the trash heap. Believe it or not, you can master this relatively easy fix, and then move on to more advanced hand-stitching tricks.

First, take a deep breath. Enter a Zen-like sewing state. You are a thread master. Choose your needle carefully (use the guidelines in Chapter 1, "Shear Essentials"). Unravel the thread from the spool about 18 inches, cutting it with sharp scissors. Then, thread the needle, leaving the shorter strand hanging a few inches. Knot the longer strand according to the following illustration. Now you're ready to take the plunge.

Sew Far, Sew Good

Cut your hand-stitching time in half by doubling up on your thread. Thread the needle, pull the strands to an equal length, and tie the ends together. Use this technique for heavy-duty stitching or buttonholes.

Tying a knot for hand stitching.

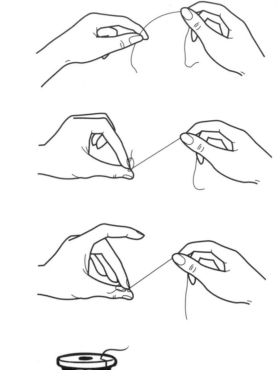

Noteworthy Notions

Having trouble with raggedy ends when threading? Try this trick: Cut your thread on an angle rather than straight across. Keep clipping until you have a clean sweep. If all else fails, wet the ends with God's gift to sewers: your saliva.

Simple Stitch Magic

The only time you ever need to make clothing completely by hand, without the benefit of a machine, is if you become a couture designer or a bespoke tailor, employing the Saville Row school of hand tailoring. Needless to say, there are very few people who feel the urge to spend so many hours sewing by hand—and for good reason. Machine stitching produces even, neat, strong stitches, the kind that keep a pair of pants on and going strong. But there *are* times when hand-sewn is the way to go. Following are some of the cases in which your hand needle is necessary:

➤ *Button fastening:* Buttons with a shank (rather than "sew through" with holes) must be sewn by hand. See Chapter 9, "Buttons in a Snap," for the surest ways to secure buttons.

➤ *Hemming:* When you want a blind hem discreetly stitched into place with nary a telltale stitch, blindhemming by hand is the way to go. Chapter 11 gives you the details.

➤ *Astray seams:* A neat slipstitch will fix even hard-to-reach seams that have started to unravel.

➤ *Attaching lining:* If you need to line a garment, you can't machine stitch it all into place because it will show on the outside of the garment. Instead, get out your needles and settle in for some hand stitching.

➤ *Closure:* Whenever you need to turn something (such as a pillow) inside out and stitch it closed, hand stitching will do the trick.

➤ *Finishing touches:* For tacking down facing, stitching on snaps, keeping a flap in place, and other last-minute details; when you're so close to finishing, you won't even mind doing some handwork.

➤ *Hand basting:* For a quick, easy, temporary way to hold some fabric together, nothing beats basting. You can even be as messy as you want because you'll take the stitches out later on.

> **Sew Far, Sew Good**
>
> Keep your fingers nimble with a thimble. Used on the second or middle finger of your sewing hand, a thimble pushes the needle through the fabric without poking a hole in your finger. Thimbles have come a long way from the simple metal caps of the past. Check out the new, snug varieties at your notion store—they fit almost as well as a Band Aid, and prevent the need for one after sewing! I like the leather sleeves that have a small metal coin for easy pushing; you'll have to find what works for you.

Hand Stitching How-To

Now that you know when to hand stitch, it's time to learn how. Here are the basics: Move from right to left; take small stitches; don't pull too tight (your fabric will pucker); and—the most important rule of all—don't lose your patience. Overeager stitching is the root of many a sewing disaster. To get started, check out the following list of stitches:

➤ *Running stitch:* This is the most basic of hand stitches. Take a few very small (from $1/16$ inch up to $1/8$ inch long) stitches in a straight line.

Running stitch.

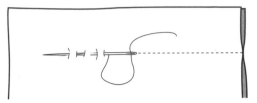

➤ *Backstitch:* The strongest hand stitch, this is as close as you can get to machine stitching using your hands. After making a stitch, back up halfway through your stitch and do another stitch (see the following figure). Bear in mind that the bottom stitches will be twice as long as the top stitches.

Backstitch.

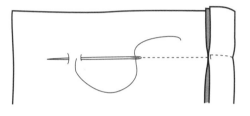

➤ *Slipstitch:* This stitch is perfect for those places you don't want a lot of stitching to show—hems, pockets, and so on. Follow the illustration, taking a tiny piece— just a few strands—from the bottom fabric, and taking a small stitch in the top fabric.

Slipstitch.

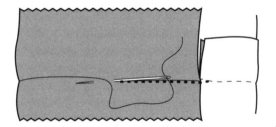

➤ *Blindhem stitch:* Check out Chapter 8, "The Ace of Baste: Seams," for the scoop on how to stitch without a smidge of it showing.

Blindhem stitch.

Tying the Knot

When you've reached the end of your hand-sewing rope and stitched your last stitch, how do you finish things up and not leave any threads hanging? You can simply do a couple of short stitches in place, or you can tie a knot. A knot is formed by making a loop and drawing the thread through the loop twice. Then pull it taut. Then, simply snip the thread and be on your merry way.

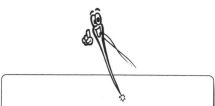

Darn It!

The other use for hand sewing is to repair those holey messes—worn out socks, done-in dungarees, and damaged workout wear, among other things. The first rule in repairing is take it to a pro if it's a prized possession. For example, my cashmere wrap met with a moth one summer. Rather than running the needle and thread through it, crisscrossing around, I took it to a professional weaver who treated it with the care it deserves. Know your garment—and your limitations.

> **Sew Far, Sew Good**
>
> When you know that hand sewing is on the agenda, make yourself comfortable. Settle into an easy chair, put on some of your favorite music, and switch on the best light you've got. Make it a treat rather than a chore, and you'll come back for more.

On the Mend

If you need to mend a hole, the easiest way to repair it is to crisscross stitch through it, creating a meshwork effect with your stitches. If the hole is too large for that, you'll have to patch it in some way. A small hole can be treated with an interfacing patch, a type of temporary Band Aid that can stay you for a while. Always trim stray threads, making the material as flat as possible. Trim a piece of interfacing that is of a similar or lighter weight than your fabric, making sure that the interfacing patch overlaps on the edges. Secure the interfacing in place with a zigzag stitch.

Dodging with a Dart

I once spent hours toiling over a tailored shirt only to make a tiny tear right in the center of the back. Rather than scrap the whole shebang, I decided to add a new detail: a dart. If your tear is small, you may want to correct it with this quick fix. Make a tuck in the fabric, tapering it to a disappearing point equally on each side. Sew the dart (see Chapter 7, "Ready, Set, Prep!" for some dart pointers). If you want to add to the illusion, make a matching dart on the other side of the garment, wherever it may be. In this way, you can make your errors your design strengths!

Noteworthy Notions

Rather than spending time sewing up a ripped running outfit, why not use an iron-on patch? It might not be the most elegant solution, but it takes only as long as it takes to heat your iron, and it saves that workout wear from the rag recycling bin.

Sewing machines are a great invention, a keenly calibrated machine that works wonders. Spend some time with your machine and get to know it; soon, sewing will be second nature. You'll be gratified to see how quickly your machine's mechanisms become your friend, with the thread, tension, and bobbins all falling neatly into place. But remember, your machine never replaces certain hand-stitching and -sewing tasks.

You need to make way for all your sewing supplies—man and machine—in the next chapter when you set up your sewing space. So get rid of the clutter and clear a clean, well-lit space for some serious sewing.

The Least You Need to Know

➤ Follow this simple rule for feet (presser feet, that is): Always have zigzag and zipper presser feet available.

➤ Follow this simple rule for stitch length: It's usually measured in millimeters per inch from 0 to 4, with 2.5 mm being the average stitch length used. The standard stitch length is 2.5 mm.

➤ Follow this simple rule for correct tension: If the loops on the underside of the fabric are off, it's the top tension; if the loops on top of the fabric aren't right, you need to adjust the bobbin tension.

➤ Follow this simple rule for hand stitching: Take it slow and easy and never pull too tight.

Chapter 6

Room to Sew

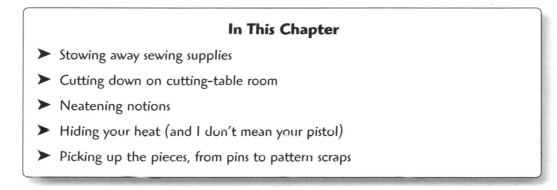

In This Chapter

➤ Stowing away sewing supplies

➤ Cutting down on cutting-table room

➤ Neatening notions

➤ Hiding your heat (and I don't mean your pistol)

➤ Picking up the pieces, from pins to pattern scraps

Whether you live in a five-bedroom house or a studio apartment, you may not have unused space just waiting for your sewing machine and notions. Don't fret! You can integrate sewing into your stunning home decor with hardly an out-of-place pin or piece of fabric giving away your part-time passion.

How can I say this so confidently? Picture this: I live in a tiny Manhattan apartment and value good looks and utility. Just like in a professional kitchen in a ship's galley, I've come up with ship-shape ideas to convert my space into a sewing place in no time! The key is to assess your space and sewing needs, and then put yourself into superorganization overdrive.

Just like some people who have loads of time on their hands yet never seem to be able to finish anything, too much space in a sewing area can actually be a hindrance. It's important to have everything you need—notions, cutting table, sewing machine, and ironing stations—all within arm's reach so you're not wasting time running from place to place.

I also believe that everything has to be handy or you'll put off that sewing project in favor of the TV movie of the week. When you have to push Christmas ornaments out of the way to find the fabric—after moving the luggage to get to the ironing board—it's all too easy to give up. But, when your essentials are easily available, albeit cleverly—and neatly—hidden, you'll actually look forward to setting up your machine and get cracking on those new cushions. If you set yourself up right, you can still have that TV movie on in the background, adding to the ambience! What better way to spend a rainy Saturday afternoon?

One of the best benefits of a well-organized sewing space is that it cuts down on the cleanup time. Sewing creates quite a mess—any serious session leaves thread wreckage in its path, strewing stray fabric pieces and leaving pesky pins all over the place. With a few neatnik tips, you can clear the mess in a sec, returning your space to its pristine state.

A Cut Above: Your Cutting Table

Contrary to common belief, the center of any sewing space isn't your sewing machine, it's your cutting table. You'll need a table totally devoted to sewing (or other craft work). Your beautiful dining room table is just not suitable for cutting, sewing, and generally nicking and scratching. Not only will this ruin your table, it'll also ruin your desire to sew—or to have a dinner party where anyone can see your table top!

The best table is large—at least 60 inches long and 30 inches wide—and around 35 inches tall so that you don't have to bend over constantly. I had many obstacles to overcome in creating a sewing area with a large table in my limited space, so the first thing I did was go to Hammacher Schlemmer (a national mail-order store) and buy the largest, sturdiest folding table I could find. It's durable metal with a Formica top, and the best thing is that it folds out to a neat $60 \times 30 \times 5$-inch surface, and slips right into my closet when folded up. It sets up in a snap, and has lasted through years of moves, dropped shears, nicks, and cuts, with hardly a hint of any wear and tear.

Noteworthy Notions

If you don't have the space or money for a separate sewing table, why not invest in a custom-made cover for a table you do have? These padded tops will protect your finish—both from sewing damage and spilled liquids at your next dinner party (if you add a tablecloth first!).

A Hard Decision: Hard vs. Padded Tops

Some sewers feel that a padded cutting surface works much better than a hard one. It prevents the fabric from slipping and sliding and you can stick pins directly into the surface rather than laboriously pinning only the fabric and/or the pattern pieces. I personally like cutting on a hard surface, and don't use pins at all when cutting as I find them to be a real time-waster … but I'll get to that later! I also don't like any utensil that serves only one purpose. I use my hard Formica table for cutting, but also as my machine work station.

Rolling Along: Rotary Cutting Mats

Another cutting table solution is to permanently attach a large rotary cutting mat to a table so that all your cutting is done with a rotary cutter, rather than shears. Again, why have a space waster for only one purpose? I've solved this problem by taping two large mats—both 30 × 35 inches—to the back of my table, and placing them on the floor when I need to use them. When I'm done, I just slip them back into the closet where they're hardly noticeable!

> **Sew Far, Sew Good**
>
> Try to have your machine out and ready to use at all times. If you don't have a space where it's convenient or looks nice, look for an attractive alternative, like keeping it in a cabinet or armoire.

Cardboard: After All, It Works for Card Tables, Right?

Why not use cardboard for a sewing table? Large cardboard tables are premade to be set up in seconds and disassembled when you have to make space for a crowd. Sew/Fit makes them in two heights—short and average—and with a gridded top for easy measuring.

> **Noteworthy Notions**
>
> If you don't have the luxury of a separate sewing room but still want a good-looking way of keeping your machine out at all times, try my solution. I had a carpenter friend make a special wooden cover that matches my wooden shelving. It's always there, ready to use, and fits beautifully and unobtrusively into my environment.

Stow Away Sewing Supplies

Now that you've set up command central, it's time to turn your attention to the details. You've gathered an impressive array of notions and tools, but where do you put them? Many of them are small—pins, hooks and eyes, buttons, and so on—and many are unwieldy, like pattern pieces and interfacing yards. The key is to tame the loose ends and put them in manageable units. Here are some tips on getting a grasp on the task.

Neatness Is Becoming a Pattern

Patterns can be cumbersome to store and difficult to keep organized and neat. Here is the pattern I follow for keeping my patterns at easy reach.

➤ *I keep all patterns that I haven't opened or used in a file cabinet.* It's just your garden-variety file cabinet, only for me there are two drawers filled with patterns (instead of tax info) that have been sorted by garment type. You can use whatever storage unit works for you, like a plastic box or shelving, but a cabinet you can shut hides the mess beautifully!

Sew Far, Sew Good

While working with a pattern, I hang it in the closet just like a garment. Press the pieces, fold them neatly over a pants hanger, pin the smaller pieces together, and hang them in the closet. This saves time folding and refolding, as well as ironing. It also keeps things out of the reach of my cat, who considers tissue patterns to be the perfect resting spot!

➤ *Once you've used your pattern and cut the tissue, don't even bother trying to squeeze it back into the package it came in.* Just store it in a large, clear, plastic Ziploc bag. I put the photo or drawing of the garment from the package facing out, and keep the instructions and pattern pieces neatly folded behind it. That way I can immediately identify what it is, and I even have space to include a fabric swatch that I found worked well for that pattern.

➤ *Almost all patterns contain multiple garments.* Say you buy a pattern to make a certain type of pajamas with a robe, camisole, and two different styles of pajama bottoms, but never plan to use the pattern for the pajama bottoms. Throw it out! Be ruthless! There's no point in wasting space on stuff you'll never use.

➤ *I have a rule for my clothes: If I haven't worn a garment in a year, it goes to charity.* The same goes for patterns: If you haven't used it in a year, or reused it within two, chuck it. Or better yet, recycle it! Maybe a friend will find a better use for it.

Organizing Notions

There are many ways to store notions, especially thread and bobbins, so find what works for you. Many sewers have come up with creative solutions for ungainly spools and sewing box messes, so keep an open mind. One of the most common ways of storing thread is on a thread rack that hangs on the wall. Simply slip the thread spools onto the pegs and they're within eyesight and easy reach.

I personally don't like the way a spool rack looks; instead, I store my spools of thread in clear plastic bins. I have two bins that are slightly larger than a shoebox that I bought at a storage supply store—Hold Everything is a national chain with a lot of variety. I slip these boxes into the bottom drawer of my filing cabinet where they're always handy. One box holds all-purpose thread; the other, specialty threads like top-stitching and silk buttonhole twist. Needless to say, I don't put the tops on the bins, so I can just reach in and grab a spool when I need one.

Smaller, catch-all notions such as pins, tailor's chalk, buttons, and bobbins are organized in the top two drawers of my filing cabinet. They're fitted into an office supplies organizer that has lots of separate compartments.

The essentials—my shears, seam ripper, extra needles, sewing gauge, and tape measure—go into a special box that I keep out on the table as I sew. I found mine at a flea market; it's a teal metal box from the 1950s that says "Sewing Supplies" on the top, and I just love the way it looks. You should find something equally pleasing to you because it will be out and about all the time you're sewing. These essentials can't be filed, hidden, or stored; they must be handy!

Stitch in Your Side

Label your sewing shears and sewing scissors so that your mother doesn't use them for her flower arranging class, your husband doesn't repair his tennis shoe sole with them, and your kids don't use them for their latest school project.

Noteworthy Notions

Although I don't use it, one of the most ingenious notions holders I've ever seen is actually a professional make-up case. It has all sorts of small compartments that unstack and fold out like an accordion, revealing a larger bottom container that's perfect for holding shears, rulers, and so on. The best thing is that it folds right back into a small, attractive unit!

Don't Bolt: Storing Fabric and Interfacing

Of course, now that you've found fabrics and interfacing that you're all excited to use, you need to find a way to keep them safe until you're ready to start your next project. What to do? Read on!

➤ Because fabric is so bulky, it's one of the harder things to keep on hand and store. The same rules that apply to your linen closet apply here: Preshrink and fold fabric carefully, and—I hate to say it—iron it before storing. It reduces an enormous amount of bulk.

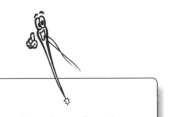

➤ While some sewers prefer shelving for fabric storage, I stick to my plastic containers. I buy them in large sizes and stack them on the shelves of my closet. If you fold the fabric carefully, the clear plastic allows you to see exactly what fabric is in the bin. You can also apply an adhesive label to the box, jotting down the different fabric as you add it to your stockpile.

➤ I also keep interfacing in a plastic bin, with the black on the bottom, and the white and gray near the top. The medium-weight fusible white, which is in constant use, is always right on top. Some sewers suggest storing interfacing on rolls so that it's ready to use and wrinkle-free, but I find that solution a little space-consuming.

Sew Far, Sew Good

Make a date to go through your fabric every few months. Sometimes your taste has changed since you bought a bolt or two, and it's time to clear it out. Other times, you've forgotten how beautiful that wool really is, and will be inspired to get cracking on a coat.

Hideaway Heat

Okay, we've established the absolute necessity of the iron and a good ironing board, but what the heck should you do with them when you're not using them? Good question—we're not talking about small items, so it's definitely a challenge. Here are some ideas.

➤ The back of a door is the ideal place to install a hanger for both your iron and ironing board. You can find heavy-duty hangers in most hardware stores or special-order them from catalogues.

➤ You can alter other pressing equipment—such as a press mitt, tailor's ham, and sleeve roll—by sewing a loop on the edge and hanging them on a hook on your closet door. This means all your pressing supplies will be on the same door.

If you've been reading carefully, you'll have figured out that everything I need to sew is in one closet: my folding table, my filing cabinet with threads and notions, my plastic bins with fabric and interfacing, and my ironing supplies on the inside of the door (and it doesn't even take up the whole closet!). My machine is placed on a bookshelf. So within minutes, my living room is a sewing room, and it can all be put away in the same short time.

Setting the Sewing Mood: Lighting

While I'm an aficionado of mood lighting and candles, they have no place in a sewing room. Utility is so much more important than looks when it comes to the lighting in your sewing space. Opt for warm, bright light throughout the room. Steer clear of spotlights aimed directly on your machine; the glare often makes it hard to see anywhere but right below the light. Any straining to see is a total waste of time and energy on a sewer's part.

Tying Up the Loose Ends

The great thing about a well-organized sewing space is that when you're done working, everything practically jumps back into place with very little effort on your part. Like a well-trained dog, your notions know where to sit, your fabric knows where to lie, and your machine knows where to sit up! But no matter how you've planned, you're still going to create your own kind of mess while sewing, some of which can't be avoided, but a lot of which can be tamed. Really!

I knew that I needed to take a stand on stray threads when I was at a dinner party with my fiancé. He regaled his dinner partner with my sewing exploits and said he was sure he could show just how integral sewing is to our lives by finding a stray thread on his pants cuff. Well, he reached down and pulled up a 6-inch white thread from his black wool pants. Needless to say, he proved his point!

Luckily, he's not a "neatnik," but I knew then and there that it was time to cut down on the cutting detritus and sewing straggles. I've learned how to reduce the post-op mess with experience, lots of reading, and tips from my ace sewing teacher. Here's the best of what I've gathered, divided into before, during, and after the sewing process.

Before: Sew Up the Loose Ends

A little foresight before you even begin sewing can shave time off your cleanup! Just follow these steps, and you'll leave your space in its pristine state.

Creating a Catch-All

First off, save your old sheets. I tear off pieces to test tension, but they also come in handy for quick clean-ups. I sew in a carpeted room, and no matter how careful I am about thread spread, snippets always end up embedded in my carpet. Even repeated vacuuming doesn't always get rid of them.

When I know I won't have the energy for post-sewing cleanup and don't want to get down on my hands and knees looking for stray threads, I throw a sheet on the carpet under my sewing table and where I'm sitting. It catches almost every stray thread, and I just have to roll it up and shake it out outside or in the bathtub. Just be sure that if you shake it outside it's not filled with throw-away fabric pieces. Littering just isn't allowed!

Another option is to make a special holder that can be attached to your sewing table for tossing spare threads and fabric scraps. It can be as simple as a brown paper bag that's taped to the table. If you're handy with hand tools, drill a hole in a metal canister and attach it to your table with a removable screw.

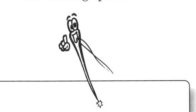

Sew Far, Sew Good

I like to sew unencumbered by jewelry such as bracelets and rings, but many sewers swear by their wrist-attached pincushions. Give one a try and see if it works for you!

Stitch in Your Side

While a Grabbit is a great gadget, never put it on the bed of a computerized sewing machine. The magnet may erase some of the stored stitching in the memory.

Pinning Down Those Pesky Pins

Pins are not only a pain—quite literally—they can also be dangerous to your machine if they get caught in the inner workings. So, taking measures to secure your pins is not just aesthetic! Some sewers like to keep a pincushion handy, but I find that just putting it on the sewing table isn't making it handy enough.

Mary Applegate (see *Sewing Tips & Trade Secrets* in Appendix C, "Further Reading," for more info) suggests this solution: Make a 3 × 5-inch cushion from some leftover material and stuff it with Polyfil. Attach some Velcro to the back and glue the other side of the Velcro to your machine. Then you'll have a permanent pincushion attached to the front of your machine and you won't be nearly as tempted to toss your pins!

Magnetized pin holders are also a godsend, no matter how neat you are. The magnetized bottom will catch your pins and keep them in place. If you're not careful about pins, you could wind up living out your own sitcom! During a party, one of my guests jumped with a squeal and pulled a pin out of his pants. It's funnier now than it was then, of course, but I swore I would master this pesky—ouch!—element.

Another tack to try is to get a Grabbit (it's a magnetized little helper) from your local notions store—you'll be amazed at how the pins seem to jump right off the table and floor and onto this great little invention!

Noteworthy Notions

Put your Grabbit into your bag the next time you go notion-shopping and test your pins before you buy them. Stainless steel pins won't stick to a magnetized surface, which, of course, defeats the purpose of this handy little helper!

During: Steps to Stop the Mess Stress

As with cooking, cleaning as you go is the key to reducing a big mess at the end of your sewing time. If you're not careful, you could be stepping around a mountain of interfacing, dodging fabric mounds, and tossing around tissue patterns!

Ship-Shape Scraps

To preserve your sanity as well as your precious patterns, make sure they're folded and put away after you're done cutting and marking them. Whatever storage method you use, get your patterns out of the way while you're sewing. If they're out and about, they'll be ripped and destroyed by the time you finish. Besides, they take up way too much space—mentally and physically.

Noteworthy Notions

One of the few times it pays to save scraps is if they might lend themselves to a terrific scarf. I made my fiancé a silk-backed cashmere vest, and had enough left over to make a scarf for a friend. You could also use smaller pieces to make a patchwork design for a quilt or pillow.

Just as you do with your patterns, do with your interfacing: Fold and file this stuff away as soon as you finish cutting, and then toss the loose scraps. Interfacing can be a big problem if you leave it lying around, especially since it tends to fuse itself to the wrong things! Be diligent about gathering those scraps off your ironing board, especially if you use the same surface to cut and iron.

Neatening Notions

Notions really need to be handy from start to finish, so don't go nutso about notions until you're all done. The only exception to this is thread spools. After you've wound a cache of bobbins, put away any extra thread you're not using (see earlier in this chapter for ideas on storing thread spools). Nobody likes dropping spools, or, worse yet, stepping on them while moving from the machine to the iron.

Noteworthy Notions

No matter what you do to prevent stray-thread syndrome, you'll find that they'll straggle, so take this tip from Caroline Wallace (see *Sewing Tips & Trade Secrets* in Appendix C): Put a small dish filled with about one-half inch of water on your sewing table. If you drop your threads into the bowl as you sew they will stay there and stop migrating to the rest of the house!

After: Taming the Sewing Beast

No matter how careful you are, you're going to strew the fruits of your labor around while you sew. Here's how to stow away steam, pick up the castaways, and clean your machine.

One Step at a Time

I almost always sew in stages. I've found the best way to keep my projects in tip-top shape and reduce mid-project mess is to hang as much as possible in the closet. Treat your tissue patterns, fabric pieces, and half-made garments just like your finest clothing.

Fold tissue pieces over a pants hanger, and do the same for your fabric pieces. Hang garment shells and home sewing projects as carefully as you can. This not only hides them from view, it also preserves their original pressing so they'll be ready for the needle when you are. Repressing is a sure-fire time-waster, and who likes to do the same job two or three times anyway?

Simply Breaking Down

If you're lucky enough to have a separate sewing space that doesn't need to be disassembled when you stop sewing, more power to you. I, unfortunately, have to hide all traces of my sewing life when I'm done. Here's the drill:

1. My table gets folded and stowed in the closet.

2. My ironing supplies go back to their hanging positions on my closet door.

3. Notions go back to their designated drawers and dividers.

It's a good idea to clean your iron before you put it away, just as you would your sewing machine, especially if you've been using a lot of starch and interfacing. Just wipe it down with some professional iron cleaner—like Rowenta's Soleplate Cleaner—and it'll be ready the next time you need it!

Finally, it comes down to the sewing machine. Before I cover it up and stow it, I (almost) always clean it, oil it, and change the needle so that the machine's ready for the next time I need it. Take out the bobbin, clean out the lint from the bobbin area and feed dogs, and wind some new bobbins to make up for what you've used.

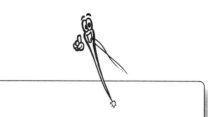

Sew Far, Sew Good

You know those plastic bags that dry cleaners use for your sweaters— the great ones with a snap? They're the perfect size for storing your small tissue pattern pieces on a hanger after they've been pressed and are waiting to be teamed up with your fabric. They also keep the small pieces from flying away and will protect them from tearing.

Odds and Ends

After all the tools, fabric, and machinery have been tucked away, all that should remain are the remnants. Even with great vigilance you will end up with tidbits of pins, thread, and flyaway fabric at the end of a project. A good vacuuming is now in order, leaving your room in the same shape it was when you started—the goal of any cleaning regimen!

The Least You Need to Know

➤ Find a great cutting table that suits all your needs, from cutting to pinning to sewing.

➤ Find a storage chest for your notions and stick to it! Choose a stackable box with a bunch of compartments—a make-up kit, a tackle box, a tool box—whatever works for you.

➤ Find a place for your patterns and fabric, taking time to both stow as you sew and stow for good.

➤ Find a way to clean as you go, picking up pins in a magnetized holder, tracking down throwaway thread, storing fabric and interfacing. You'll thank yourself for all of these finds!

Chapter 7

Ready, Set, Prep!

A friend of mine is a carpenter, and creates stunning handmade furniture and shelving. I first heard the phrase "measure twice, cut once" from him, and have learned that it applies to so many tasks in life, but especially to sewing. Just like wood cutting and crafting, fabric blocking, layout, measuring, and cutting are essential to creating a fantastic finished product.

This is a step that I used to skimp on in my rush to get to the machine to do what I considered the "real work." And it's one of the reasons that so many of my early projects—like that basic wrap skirt or those horrendous kitchen curtains that I made for my first apartment—didn't work out. It's simple: Improperly blocked and cut fabric will never come together properly. And it's simple to ensure that you'll never have that problem again.

Preparing fabric for sewing is one of the great time and energy savers. You solve so many potential problems in these early stages, and pave the way for simple stitching and effortless fabric ease. Here's how to do it.

The Straight and Narrow: Finding the Grainline

Fabric has a mind of its own, and you have to understand its mind to work on it. Its "brain" is its *grainline*, the direction of the fibers that are woven into the fabric. Any finished project, whether it's a complicated suit or a nice, breezy curtain, will never hang correctly unless you locate the grainline and lay out the pattern along the lines. Pants will bulge, dresses will sag, and table linens will be askew if they're cut improperly. All of which is to say that if you don't pay attention to the fabric, your effort will all be for naught.

Here's a basic course in understanding the grainline, and locating it so that your cutting and blocking is a breeze:

Sew You Were Saying ...

Grainline is the direction of the weave of fabric.

Stitch in Your Side

Knits are looped rather than woven, so you can never find their shifty grainline. But don't sweat it! Just try to align the fabric as straight as possible, draw a line across, and cut!

➤ *Selvage.* These are the two finished side edges of the fabric. The manufacturer tightly weaves together the edges, often printing a brand name or fabric make-up on the selvage edge.

➤ *Lengthwise grain.* Also known as the *warp*, this runs parallel to the selvage and is the all-important grainline. It's the strongest grainline and has the least amount of stretch.

➤ *Crosswise grain.* Also known as the *weft*, this runs from selvage to selvage and has more give than the lengthwise grain.

➤ *Bias.* This is the line that runs diagonally across the fabric. The true bias is always at a 45-degree angle to the crosswise and lengthwise grains and is the fabric's stretchiest point.

Okay, I know this seems like a lot of information to absorb, but when you've got a piece of fabric in front of you and are handling it, these terms make a lot more sense. If I've lost you, the best thing to do is to buy a few yards of muslin, which is a mediumweight woven fabric often used by beginners and fashion students because the grain is easily spotted, and the fabric is inexpensive. For these reasons, muslin is also used to make test garments, perfecting them before making the final garment with expensive fabrics.

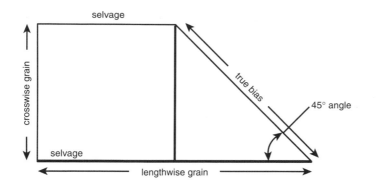

The grainlines.

The Rip Method

Grab a few yards of muslin and see if you can find the grain. Locate the two selvage lines and the crosswise grain that runs between them. Snip with your scissors into the selvage about an inch, and then rip it! That's right—rip it, don't cut it! It will rip exactly on the crosswise grainline, freeing you from using tape measures, grid patterns, and other measuring tools.

After ripping, place the fabric on a corner of the table and see how it lays. If the fabric aligns with the right angle of a table, the fabric is properly blocked (that is the grains are running straight). If not, you need to *block* it yourself by pulling with both hands in the opposite direction; that is, if the fabric leans to the left, you need to pull on the right bias line, and vice versa. Now that the fabric is blocked you can press and cut it!

The rip method of finding the grain only works on fabric that is "rippable." Here's a short list of fabrics that will rip:

➤ Cottons

➤ Light linens

➤ Some silks (be careful!)

➤ Very lightweight wools

Sew You Were Saying ...

Block fabric by locating the crosswise and lengthwise grains. They need to be aligned so that they run at an exact right-angle to each other. Check by lining them up at the edge of a table (or use a T-square), pulling at either end to straighten, and align them before laying out and cutting the fabric.

Straightening the grainline.

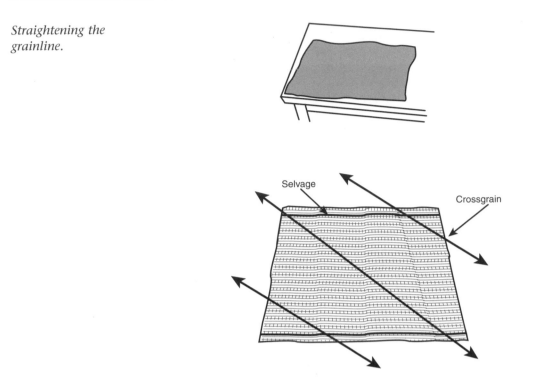

The Thread Method

Fabrics that have a raised surface, like corduroy, seersucker, velvet, and dupioni silks and other, heavier fabrics, must be cut along the grainline rather than ripped. Again, don't look for the grain by measuring; that will only lead to inaccuracy and error. Instead, snip with your scissors through the selvage and into the fabric. Pick a thread and pull it across the length of the fabric, puckering the fabric in a straight line. Now, you can cut across that line.

Using the thread method to locate the grainline.

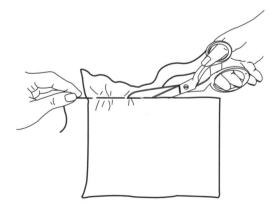

If you can't find the grainline by using either the rip or thread method (some fabrics just don't lend themselves to either approach), here's a last resort: Use a T-square to measure a right angle. Simply place the short end of the square along the selvage and square across a straight line, making sure that the fabric is blocked properly. It's more accurate than measuring, and certainly quicker!

Pretreated Precautions

When buying fabric, check to see if it's been treated with a permanent finish that will affect the way the fabric hangs. The giveaways are the terms "permanent press," "stain-resistant," "water-repellant," or "bonded." The resins used to treat these fabrics often make them not only permanent press, but permanently off-grain (that is to say that they will never hang right, not a good thing!). Do the table test before you buy: If you can't make the edge line up to the right angles of the cutting table, it will never line up to anything!

The Lowdown on Layout

Once you understand and have completed the preliminaries—pretreating, locating the grainline, and blocking—go on to laying out and cutting up. I always do the cutting for a project ahead of time rather than cutting and sewing on the same day. This way I'm fresh when I start sewing.

Pattern Puzzles

The first time I looked at a commercial pattern, I thought I was reading a foreign edition of *The New York Times!* I didn't know what any of the layouts, symbols, marks, or directions meant. If you're a pro at patterns, all the better—but if you're a beginner, skip ahead to Chapter 13, "Tissue Issues: Understanding Commercial Patterns," which will fill you in on what all these terms mean before you read on.

Once you get some sewing experience under your belt, the instructions that accompany these commercial patterns become less and less important. My sewing teacher never uses the pattern instructions. She just looks at the finished drawing, and imagines the garment as a puzzle with all different pieces that need to be fit together perfectly. She also advised me that you don't need to follow the layout religiously; you can often find better ways to fit the pattern pieces on your fabric piece. Just be sure to lay out all the pieces before cutting anything so that you're sure they fit, and always buy enough fabric!

Sew Far, Sew Good

If you're using a commercially prepared pattern to sew a garment, cut the pattern pieces roughly. Don't obsess and cut neatly around the edge. You have to cut the pieces again when they're placed on the fabric, so save the persnickety snipping for when it really counts!

Noteworthy Notions

Whenever you can, double up on cutting. Cut lining and interfacing at the same time that you cut the fabric. Put the thinnest, slipperiest fabrics on the top and the heaviest on the bottom.

Pressing Pattern Patter

This was a real shocker to me when I learned it: You must press all your tissue pattern pieces before cutting your fabric! Don't worry, the tissue can withstand the highest heat on your iron. It will make your cutting so much easier, and the heat creates static electricity that creates a bit of a bond between your fabric and tissue.

Noteworthy Notions

When cutting a slippery fabric like silk, use some of the tissue that you would use for gift wrapping as an anchor. Lay the tissue down first, pin the silk on top, and then place your pattern on top of the silk. Cut through all the layers and you'll have a much more accurate set of fabric pieces!

Weighty Measures

When I first started sewing, I laboriously pinned everything in sight, both during the cutting process and while sewing. Now, there's hardly a pin in sight unless I'm working on a tricky task like a sleeve. Even beginners should stay away from pins while cutting—really!

Use weights instead of pins, placed at the corners of the pattern pieces and along long stretches. Why? It's faster to put a few weights down than to struggle with pinning different fabrics to pattern pieces and interfacing. Plus, you'll completely avoid the risk of pin holes in the more delicate fabrics (sometimes, no matter how good the pin is, you'll still get a mark). My favorite weights are curtain weights, the kind that are sewn into the bottom of drapes to make sure they hang properly. They're perfect for cutting fabric, since they're small, heavy, easy to store, and cheap. My whole sewing class started using them when I whipped them out while cutting, and they never went back to using soup cans! You can also use commercial sewing weights—look for the brand Weight Mates.

Marking Up

Marks—notches, clips, placement lines, dart lines, and so on—are essential when you're putting together your material and making anything from a Roman shade to a shirt. The smart sewer knows that you don't have to transfer every single mark, but a few are indispensable to sewing anything that falls into place properly. Mark up your fabric while you cut—I mean, really, who wants to stop a sewing streak just to find out where that darned dart should go?

Many books and courses recommend that you transfer markings with tailor's tacks, a thread loop that is loosely sewn through the fabric and pattern pieces. When the pattern tissue is removed, the tacks remain in the fabric. I personally find tailor's tacks laborious and try to avoid them. Why sew before you sew? I transfer marks with a number of different tools, relying mostly on chalk and air- and water-soluble markers, making sure they're removable.

Here's a quick drill for transferring markings: If you have a small dot or line (for example, the tip of a dart, which is usually marked with a circle), take a pin and tear a small hole in the tissue pattern. Use a marker of your choice (I like tailor's chalk) to make a small dot on the fabric without moving the tissue pattern. I use this method for almost all of my markings. Just be sure that you don't tear too large a hole or line in the tissue piece. If you do, try tape. For a really big tear, you can always transfer the damaged tissue pattern to a new piece of paper. Try brown wrapping paper, or, if you want to look like a pro, pick up gridded pattern paper from a notions store.

Stitch in Your Side

If you're marking up your fabric with chalk or a water or air-soluble marker, test it first! You don't want it to show up on the finished garment. And be careful when snipping the fabric—deep snips translate into holes!)

Stitch in Your Side

Vee snips just won't cut it when marking fabric for serging. The serger will trim the seam allowance, snipping away your markings. Rather, make a mark exactly on the seam line so that you can see it when the serger blade cuts way the excess fabric.

Here's a brief description of the types of marks you should keep an eye out for while you're prepping and cutting your fabric:

➤ *Notches.* These are indicated on your pattern and are used to match fabric pieces together accurately. Rather than cutting a "vee" outward (as they're drawn on the pattern), snip notches about ¹/₄-inch into the seam allowance. Single notches always indicate the front of a garment, while double notches indicate the back.

➤ *Darts.* Instead of drawing all the lines of a dart on your fabric, snip the ends into the *seam allowance* of the fabric, and mark the point with a pencil, or water- or air-soluble fabric marker. If you do this first, it will be super-easy to pin the dart into place without any further marking!

➤ *Center points.* This is the mid-point or center of a piece of a garment, such as a collar or sleeve. Even if these points aren't marked on your pattern, snip into the seam allowance at the centers of your pieces—for example, the garment's front, back, collar, and sleeve center—and anywhere else that the center line is crucial for lining and matching pattern pieces. If the pattern does mark the center with a circle, dot, or other indication, it is much easier to do the snip in a snap than to laboriously transfer the markings.

Sew You Were Saying ...

The **seam allowance** is the amount of fabric added to your pattern to allow for stitching and trimming. Or, a little less technically, it's the space between where you've cut the fabric and where you stitch it. Almost all commercial patterns use a ⁵/₈-inch seam allowance, but you can vary it according to your sewing needs.

➤ *Buttonhole lines.* I never transfer buttonhole markings; I always wait until I get to the sewing stage before deciding on the buttonhole placement. It's rare that I don't alter the clothing in some way, and any alteration will change the button placement pretty dramatically. I also like to customize button placement so that I get the right fit, eliminating "gaposis" on a shirt or jacket. So, leave your buttonhole guide behind!

➤ *Circles, triangles, and dots.* You will often see these markings on many pattern pieces. Transfer these placement lines judiciously. A lot of them just aren't necessary. For example, the dots that are usually placed on a sleeve cap to indicate where you should start your ease stitch can be left out as long as you snipped your notches. So just use the snips as a place to begin and end your ease stitch.

➤ *Zipper placement.* Zippers are marked on patterns with a cross-hatched line that ends in a circle. No need to transfer all the marks—just mark the end point (the bottom of the zipper). The rest will take care of itself when you sew it.

If you're ready to jump into the driver's seat and start sewing, you've made it through some of the most time-consuming and peskiest parts of the entire job! Many sewers hate the presewing drill, but I've started to actually enjoy working with the fabric now that I know how to cut corners and break everything down into manageable chunks of time. The routines I've set down for you will let you sneak blocking, laying out, cutting, and the rest of fabric prep into a busy schedule, with just 10-minute tasks tucked in between work, picking up the kids, and even those few moments of free time!

Sew Far, Sew Good

When cutting the pattern pieces, take care not to lift the scissors from the table—keep the bottom blade fixed, gliding the top blade carefully. Don't use a choppy, sawing motion, and never cut all the way to the tip of the scissors—stop and move on before you get to the end.

The Least You Need to Know

➤ The first step in preparing fabric is locating the grainline, the direction of the threads that are woven into the fabric. The selvage is the finished edge; the lengthwise grain runs parallel to it.

➤ Second step: Block the fabric so that the crosswise and lengthwise grains are at right angles, meaning that the fabric hangs straight, not askew. You can block the fabric with a tug in either direction.

➤ Third step: Lay out the pattern pieces on the blocked fabric, following the grainline direction.

➤ Fourth step: Transfer the markings with the pattern pieces in place.

➤ Fifth step: Cut the pieces, taking care not to lift the scissors from the table.

Part 3

A Stitch in Time Saves Nine: Basic Techniques

My sewing teacher always taught me the importance of building a basic knowledge of sewing techniques that you can draw on, no matter what the project, no matter what the pattern instructions say. You start with the bricks and mortar of anything sewn— the seams, from the simplest straight seam to more complicated and versatile French and lapped seams. Once you've got seams under control, you learn how to handle buttons and zippers. They're the most common closures, but often require the most caution, cowing the beginning sewer. No need to be afraid—a few simple tips will have you zipping through them without fear. The same goes for hems, the finishing touch on anything sewn.

Before moving ahead to home-sewn fashions, it's time to brush up on your pressing skills. Be sure not to scoff at pressing. A little steam heat can actually "set" your seams and other sewn areas, preserving the proper shape of a project.

Chapter 8

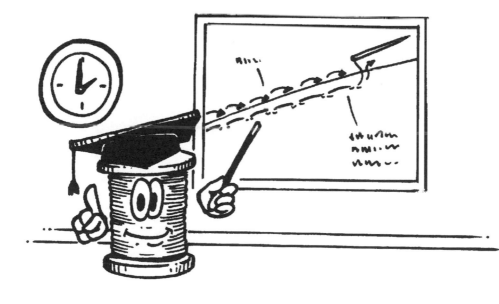

The Ace of Baste: Seams

In This Chapter

➤ Prep your fabric pieces

➤ Master simple stitches

➤ Conquer seam finishes

➤ Drive around curves

➤ Rip the ragged results

"I can't sew straight to save my life!" is a familiar lament I hear from many a wannabe sewer. Well, that's just because they haven't learned all the secrets that make straight seams not only possible, but impossibly easy!

Straight and finished seams are the building blocks of anything sewn, so once you've gotten them under control, you're on sewing easy street. First, you need to master the straight stitch. After that, it's around the bend to curved seams, and then switching gears into French seams and fancy finishings. This will make the inside of your clothes and home furnishings look just as good as the outside.

It's time for me to take you on a ride through the basics of stitching, from towing the line—the straight line—to the hitches and how to fix them so that you can master finished seams—the ultimate driving test of any home sewer. Once we've finished that, you'll be ready for the open road!

Before You Take Your First Stitch

Okay, you've got your fabric all ready—pressed and preshrunk—you've switched on your machine, the light goes on, and you hear that familiar whir. You've selected the proper needle and presser foot. You even thread your top and bobbin thread before sitting down. You're ready to sew, right? Wrong!

Before you take your first stitch, you need to get a few things straight. The first order of the day is thread tension. After threading your machine and inserting your bobbin, you need to test your tension on a swatch of the exact fabric and fabric thickness that you'll be using. (See Chapter 5, "Man vs. Machine," for detailed instructions on calibrating tension.) The two threads that loop together to form your stitches must fall almost exactly in the center of the fabric to stitch properly.

Once you've taken the tension stress test and passed, you can move on to stitch length. Again, Chapter 5 gives you more information on stitch length. The standard stitch measurement is in millimeters per inch, and is usually scaled on the machine from 0 to 4, with 2.5 being the average stitch length. Set stitch length at 0 mm to stitch in place; set it at 4 mm for a long basting stitch.

Sew You Were Saying ...

The **throat plate** is a metal plate on your sewing machine that surrounds your needle hole. It is below the needle mechanism and covers the bobbin mechanism. There are often different, detachable throat plates to accommodate different stitches. This is because the needle movement may swing wider from side to side in a zigzag manner, necessitating a larger or different hole in the plate. Check your machine's manual for the details.

Seam Allowances

You thought you were through with allowances, didn't you? Not quite! A seam allowance is the amount of fabric added to your pattern to allow for stitching and trimming. Or, a little less technically, it's the space between where you've cut the fabric and where you stitch it.

Noteworthy Notions

When people ask how I get my seams so straight, I tell them I cheat! I used a magnetic seam guide when I first started sewing. It sticks to the machine and forms a little shelf that you press your fabric against as you sew. If you don't want to buy anything, put some masking tape on your machine to mark your seam allowance and it will be easier to stay on track.

Almost all commercial patterns use a ⁵/₈-inch seam allowance, which is pretty big. They like to give you space for alterations and errors. Whenever I make something without a pattern—like pillows and curtains—or use my own patterns that I've made over the years, I always use a ¹/₂-inch seam allowance. It's a nice easy number, both to measure and to remember. Most machines have markings on the *throat plate*—the metal plate that surrounds your needle hole—at ¹/₈-inch intervals so that you can guide the fabric accordingly.

Prepare Your Pieces

Any time you sew, you're stitching two or more pieces of fabric together. The pieces must be aligned properly—whether it's just two pieces of straight fabric or a rounded sleeve and armhole section or even the complicated pin-tucked bodice of a dress—before you can sew them. Experienced sewers can manipulate the fabric with their hands, and have the ability to work with just the feel of the fabric. Beginning sewers have to work a little harder. Always align the fabric pieces, matching any notches, symbols, or other sewing guidelines before sitting down at your machine. Make sure to pin around curves, fitted areas or seams, particularly on slippery fabric, or anywhere you think you need guidance.

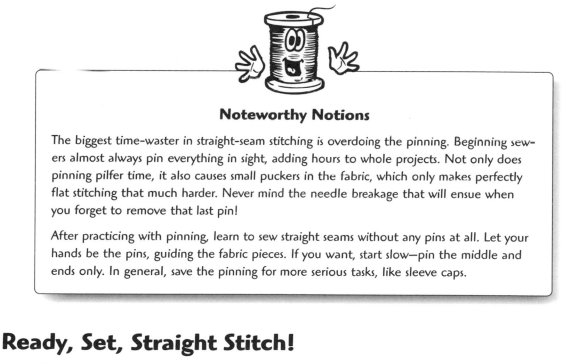

Noteworthy Notions

The biggest time-waster in straight-seam stitching is overdoing the pinning. Beginning sewers almost always pin everything in sight, adding hours to whole projects. Not only does pinning pilfer time, it also causes small puckers in the fabric, which only makes perfectly flat stitching that much harder. Never mind the needle breakage that will ensue when you forget to remove that last pin!

After practicing with pinning, learn to sew straight seams without any pins at all. Let your hands be the pins, guiding the fabric pieces. If you want, start slow—pin the middle and ends only. In general, save the pinning for more serious tasks, like sleeve caps.

Ready, Set, Straight Stitch!

All systems are go! Here's what to keep in mind to make perfect straight stitches, the most common seam in sewing:

➤ *Thread placement.* Pull the threads out a few inches and slide them behind the presser foot before starting, but keep the top thread going between the "toes" of the presser foot. You'll end up with two tails of thread in the back of your machine.

Pulling the thread tails before sewing.

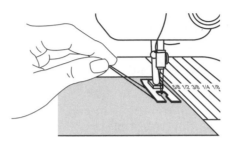

➤ *Fabric placement.* Now put the fabric in the "start" position: Align the right, raw edges of the fabric, place them on the throat plate with the desired seam allowance, and leave the rest of the fabric hanging off to the left. Drop the presser foot and lower the needle into the fabric with a manual turn of the handwheel.

➤ *Hand guidance.* My teacher always says that sewing is like driving. Your hands guide the fabric, steering like you would a car. Let your hands gently move the fabric as it's fed into the machine—don't push it, though, the feed dogs will take care of that—and certainly don't pull it from the back. Get used to working with different weights of fabrics and how they move.

Sew Far, Sew Good

When you start your first stitches, does your fabric sometimes get pushed down into the needle hole, dragging down your sewing? Try putting a separate swatch of fabric underneath your real fabric so that the two overlap slightly. Start sewing on the swatch and continue into your real fabric, and the problem will go away!

➤ *Beginning and ending.* How do you secure the thread at the start and finish of a seam? Never, ever, tie a knot by hand! Instead, as you begin a seam, stitch a few stitches forward, then a few back, and you're set. The backstitch, as it's called, will hold. Another method is to set your stitch length at 0, sew a few stitches in place, and your seam will stay put. Some machines have a bar tack setting on the machine that will do this for you.

If the seam you've just sewn will cross another seam line, don't waste any time with backstitching; the intersecting seam will take care of finishing it for you.

And again, practice, practice, practice! Practice is all you need to make the straight stitch second nature. Pick up some small pieces or remnants of different fabrics to practice stitching so that when you get to the real thing, your instincts will take over.

Stitch List

Here's an easy reference guide to the most used, simple, straight stitches:

➤ *Topstitch.* Stitch about $1/4$ inch from the seam or edge. This stitch can secure a seam, design element, or may just serve as a decorative touch.

➤ *Edgestitch.* Use this to keep finished edges flat, strengthen seams, attach pockets, or for a more polished look. Stitch about $1/8$ inch from the finished edge or seam. Used particularly on pockets, collars, jacket, shirt fronts and edges, and so on.

➤ *Backstitch.* To begin and end seams, just do a few stitches in reverse. Most machines have a button or tab for switching directions in a flash. I used to stitch back and forth quite a bit, thinking that was the only way the seam would hold. Well, all I did was add stitching bulk and mess. Remember, you only need to backstitch one or two stitches to secure the seams, so don't overdo it.

➤ *Basting.* This a temporary stitch to hold fabric in place while constructing your project. It's important to baste any time the sewing gets tough or you're unsure about the results, either because of your skill level or because you want to test drive before adding a more permanent stitch. The basting stitch, which uses the longest machine stitch length (4 mm on most machines), or a long hand basting stitch, is removed later, when the pieces have been permanently stitched in place. The long stitch makes it easier to cut and remove. If you can, use your weakest thread—cotton, rather than polyester—because you actually want it to break easily.

➤ *Staystitch.* Curved areas, like collars, necklines, and certain seams, have a tendency to stretch when stitched, so you need to "stay" the fabric with a staystitch. Straight stitch $1/8$ inch from the edge inside the seam

Stitch in Your Side

Now's the time to clip your thread—be very careful to just snip the stragglers, not the fabric itself!—that'll be left hanging at the start and end of any seam. Go ahead and clip the thread right next to the edge of the fabric.

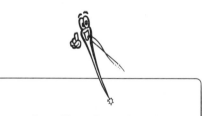

Sew Far, Sew Good

Want a quick way to keep a seam with a small seam allowance or a line of topstitching straight? Use your presser foot as a guide. Align the edge of the fabric with the right edge of the presser foot and stitch, keeping fabric in line with the presser "toe." Simple!

allowance. This stitch is not a seam; it doesn't sew together two pieces of fabric. Rather, it grounds one piece, providing a template so that the fabric stays put instead of stretching. I used to skip this step, thinking it was unnecessary since it wasn't a construction element. Well, when the front edge of my cashmere vest drooped, I saw the error of my ways. Follow your pattern instructions, and stay-stitch where needed. A good rule is that any fabric stitched along the bias (whether the true bias or not), has a tendency to stretch. Curb it with a staystitch.

Fancy Finishings

The first step—the straight seam—is under control. Now you need to take charge of finishing the raw edges of the seam, making its appearance as fantastic as its utility. And not just because it looks a lot better. Almost all fabrics, especially woven and knitted materials, will unravel, some an enormous amount, some not so much. But time and repeated washings usually bring straggly threads unless they're tamed with the proper finish. No one wants to look inside a pair of pants to see thread chaos. Here are a few options, from the simple to the fancy:

➤ *Pinking.* If you're using tightly woven fabrics that are pretty stable—silks, cotton, canvas, and the like—get out your pinking shears and trim the edges of your seams. This nice serrated set of shears keeps fraying in check within seconds. Don't use this on material that unravels easily, like knits, stretchy fabrics and linens, because it just won't make a dent in the disarray.

Sew Far, Sew Good

Want to take basting out in seconds? Use a contrasting color—like red if you're making white curtains—and it'll be clear that the red gets the ripper!

Sew Far, Sew Good

If you're planning on lining your garment, don't worry about seam finishes. The lining will cover a lot of sewing messes.

Pinking seam finish.

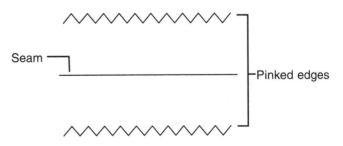

Seam

Pinked edges

➤ *Pinking and stitching.* If you need to crank up the hold volume on a pinked edge, sew a straight stitch on the inside of your seam edge and pink as close to it as you can without clipping into it.

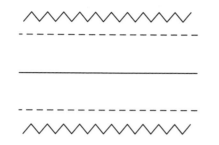

Pinked and stitched seam finish.

➤ *Zigzag.* If your machine has a zigzag stitch, use it! After sewing your straight seam, sew a line of zigzag stitching on the raw edge, stitching the zig in the fabric and letting the zag come right up to or fall off the raw edge. You're done!

Zigzag seam finish.

➤ *Baby hem.* This finishing, which has a silly but accurate name, takes a little more time, but is worth it for a fine finish. It is essentially a double-turned hem on each side of the seam. You should only use this on seam that has $1/2$- to $5/8$-inch allowance or more, but no less.

1. Turn in from $1/8$ inch to $1/4$ inch of your raw seam edge and press in place.
2. Turn again another $1/8$ inch to $1/4$ inch and press in place.
3. Now stitch this baby hem in place, using the presser foot as a seam guide.
4. You need to baby hem both sides of the seam allowance, and then press open so the seam lays flat.

Baby hem seam finish.

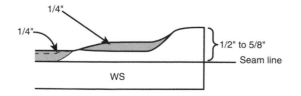

Noteworthy Notions

If you need to make bias tape from your fabric, try a Bias Tape Maker, a handy little metal gizmo that makes perfect single-fold bias tape from fabric strips.

➤ *Bias bound.* This is by far the most time-consuming finishing we'll cover, to be used when a fabulous interior look is more important than anything else. Bias-bound seams are particularly useful on an unlined coat or jacket. They're a sleek solution to bulky fabric, like coating, which can't be baby hemmed or French seamed, for example, because of the thickness of the fabric. The bias-bound finish is made with a strip of bias tape or bias material which is sewn around the raw edges of the seam.

You can make your own bias strip out of the fabric you're using, or you can do it the extremely easy way: Buy bias tape in a finished width of $1/2$ inch in a color that matches or complements your fabric. The bias tape has a preformed fold and turns under so that it's ready to go: no folding, measuring, or prestitching on your part.

1. Both seam allowances need to be bound separately, so start with one side.
2. Enclose the raw edge of the seam allowance in the bias tape, butting the edges of the bottom and top against the seam.
3. Pin into place.
4. Topstitch the bias tape into place, sandwiching the seam allowance into the bias tape, sewing all three layers at once.
5. Sew the next side. Now you're beautifully bound!

No matter what seam finish you use, always trim the excess from $1/4$ inch to $1/8$ inch. No one likes bulky layers, so grade them, or trim one $1/4$ inch and the other $1/8$ inch, when two layers lie against each other. You'll see the smooth difference it'll make!

Noteworthy Notions

To go the extra style mile on a bias-bound finish for the inside of a beautiful jacket, use a piece of satin fabric rather than the jacket fabric or bias tape. It adds an incredible sheen, and is worth the minimal investment.

Serging Ahead

A quick aside: A serger will finish seams with an overcast stitch, creating neatly encased seams that are cut and finished at the same time. If you're sewing a lot for utility, you should definitely get a serger and cut your seam finishing time to zero.

Beyond the Straight Seam

Variety is not only the spice of life, it's a sewing staple. While the straight seam is your all-purpose choice, there are other options out there that may better complement your fabric and garment. As you become comfortable with different fabrics and how they work, you'll notice that certain seams need extra care because they're bulky, are more visible, or need a splash of dash.

Experimentation in seams, as in all things, is the key to success. Even though almost all commercial patterns call for straight seams, bear in mind that you can use your creativity and know-how to improve on the pattern. Here's a sampling of my most-used seams, just a few of many!

French Seams

This is my favorite seam of all time. It totally encases the raw edges, adding a couture look to even the simplest of outfits. It's a great all-purpose seam when you want the inside of anything to look sleek and stylish. It definitely takes more care, including sewing two seam lines and extra pressing, but it's the ultimate in fancy finishings. The one place it really must be used is on sheer fabrics such

Stitch in Your Side

Make sure to trim enough of the seam allowance when sewing a French seam. Otherwise, those little straggles will show through on the finished seam. Yuk! Also, don't forget to leave enough seam allowance to start. This seam works beautifully with the commercial $5/8$-inch seam allowance.

as thin silks, organza, and chiffon. These see-through fabrics can be a dead giveaway of an extremely sloppy seam. Don't be scared off, though! French seams can actually become an integral part of your sewing regimen.

1. Match the right sides of your fabric together (that is, the finished sides of the fabric, not the inside or what's known as the "wrong side").

2. Sew a $^3/_8$-inch seam.

3. Trim a close $^1/_8$ inch.

4. Press the fabric flat with the seam allowance on either side.

5. Fold over the seam with the wrong sides out, encasing the raw edge, press again with the right sides together.

6. Sew a $^1/_4$-inch seam, press to one side. *Voilà!*

French seam.

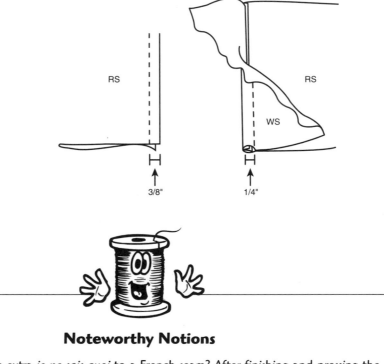

Noteworthy Notions

Want to add a little extra *je ne sais quoi* to a French seam? After finishing and pressing the seam to one side, edgestitch the free edge down so that it lays flat on the fabric. This finish is used in men's tailored shirts to make them look like a million bucks (or at least a few hundred!).

Mock French Seams

Don't use this stitch on anything too heavy—it'll create too much bulk. But for light-to mediumweight fabric seams—ooh la la!

1. Sew a straight ⁵/₈-inch seam with the wrong sides together. Don't press open.
2. Turn over each edge ¹/₄ inch toward the seam, press in place.
3. Edgestitch the pressed edges together. Press to one side.

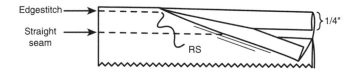

Mock French seam.

Flat-Fell Seams

This is a slightly breezier seam to sew than the French seam, with a slightly different look. Use it for heavy fabrics to reduce bulk while still adding style.

1. Sew a ⁵/₈-inch seam on the wrong side of the fabric.
2. Trim one seam allowance to ¹/₈–¹/₄ inch.
3. Turn the other seam allowance under ¹/₄ inch, press into place.
4. Place over trimmed edge, press, and edgestitch into place.

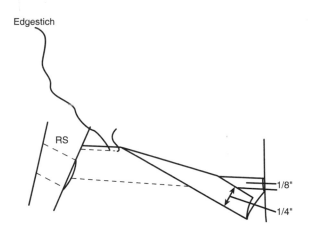

Flat-fell seam.

Noteworthy Notions

Why not try a reverse flat–fell seam; that is, put the right sides of your fabric together and stitch on the outside of your project? You can even use a contrast thread color to add to the decorative mix.

Seems Like It Will Never Fit? On to Curved Seams

The great thing about fabric is that it rolls with the punches. It moves with your groove, around necks, waists, shoulders—all your curved areas. How do these two-dimensional pieces of fabric do it? Sometimes it seems like a mystery, especially when you're stitching together two pieces of fabric that look like they'll never come together. Two good examples are collars and princess seams, which are seams that curve around waists and hips.

When two pieces of fabric fit together to form a curved area, there is one inner curve piece and one outer curve. For example, a princess seam is often used to curve along the waistline and hips of a jacket or blouse, creating contouring that follows the human shape. If you lay the two pattern pieces and corresponding fabric down flat, it looks like they could never fit. Follow these guidelines and you'll be able to create hourglass garments in no time:

Sew Far, Sew Good

If you're sewing two curves together, use the inner curve as the anchor fabric, pinning the outer curve to it. The inner curve should be on the bottom, against the presser feet, which is a more stable position. The outer curve will shift more while you guide it, giving you greater mobility.

1. Staystitch the curved edges right inside the seam allowance.

2. Clip the inner curved edge to the staystitching, making sure not to cut into the stitches. Cut small wedges into the outer curved edge at regular intervals.

3. Place the outer curved edge over the inner curved edge, matching your notches and pinning into place (this is one time you really need to pin at the key places!).

4. Stitch the seam, carefully guiding the fabric around the curve.

5. Proper pressing is very important for a curved or princess seam. The seam should be pressed over a tailor's ham, with the seam opened. Clip notches where necessary to allow the seam to lay flat.

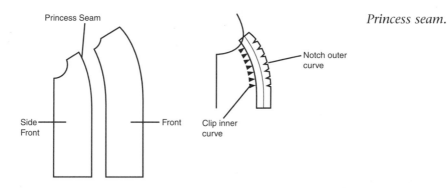

Princess seam.

Unseemly Seams: How to Rip Them Up

No chapter on sewing seams would be complete without telling you how to un-complete your seams. The familiar lament "As ye sew, so shall ye rip" will become second nature to you. No matter your level of expertise, you'll find yourself making mistakes and ripping out seams—a laborious process, but well worth it to make something that looks just so. My teacher is very fond of saying that if you leave a mistake in and just blithely sew on, your eye will always go straight to the mistake, ruining your experience as well as your sewing project.

Get used to your seam ripper. Find a way that's comfortable for you to hold the seam ripper and the fabric. Rip a few stitches at a time. Never, ever, try to rip straight through the entire seam in one fell swoop. Remove the threads after you've ripped the stitches. If necessary, use tweezers to pull out the threads rather than leaving them in when you restitch.

You have just learned to take your first stitching steps, and you're already off and running. Sure, there are plenty of other specialty seams and seam finishes, but the basic stitches and seams that we've covered allow you the opportunity to make almost any garment or home furnishing, from a simple pillow to a fancy jacket. The next chapter teaches you how to close up that jacket with buttons and buttonholes, one for the most common and, believe it or not, simplest of sewing skills.

Stitch in Your Side

Be patient when ripping seams—attack the ripper and you'll surely slice right through your fabric!

Using a seam ripper.

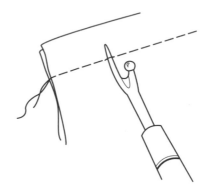

Noteworthy Notions

Suzen Weiner (in the book *Sewing Tips & Trade Secrets*) has a tip for all those little holes that are left in fabric after you've ripped a seam: Dampen a cloth with white vinegar, spread it under the fabric, and press.

The Least You Need to Know

➤ Before you start stitching, go over this quick list: Check your thread tension and stitch length, and prep your pieces, pinning where necessary and aligning properly.

➤ Before you get to the end of the seam, remember this: If you're crossing another seam, there's no need to backstitch.

➤ Before stitching, decide on your seam finish; make sure the seam finish is appropriate for the look and feel of the fabric.

➤ Before moving on, make sure your seam is straight and sewn properly; if not, rip it out rather than compounding the problem.

Chapter 9

Buttons in a Snap

When I was growing up, every time I said "So ..." my parents immediately shot back a hokey "Sew buttons!" I never seemed to heed their retort, though, and when I finally did, I sure made a mess of my buttons. They always turned out to be snarled with loops and knots, nothing like the neat, taut threads around the buttons on store-bought clothes or the ones that the tailor fixed faster than you can say "Sew buttons!" Or worse yet, I would sew on a button only to have it fall off after just one wearing, leaving me in the button lurch yet again. Sew buttons, indeed.

This was before I got some closure on closings. You can conquer buttons and button-holes with relative ease as long as you know how to get around the holey messes. There are plenty of little hints that make hand sewing buttons not only simpler but stronger, so that you don't waste time resewing. While I'm an advocate of machine stitching whenever possible, there are times when your button pops off on a trip, or just as you're about to run out to a business lunch, or two seconds before you walk down the aisle. Hand sewing can't be beat when you're beating the clock and are far away from a set-up sewing machine. A little button know-how goes a long way during these moments of button stress. But hand sewing is just the tip of the needle.

Even the cheaper machines can stitch a button on in no time. There are also everyday uses for your button skills—it really helps to know the ABCs of button application so that you can apply your skill at any given moment. We're going to tackle hand sewing first, and then move on to machine stitching, finally working our way up to creating, placing, and perfecting buttonholes, the yin to the button's yang. With a few fundamentals and fun facts, you'll be able to make buttonholes with a Zen-like calm. So put aside your safety pins and masking tape, because now you can be all buttoned up without losing your cool.

Noteworthy Notions

If one button out of four on your jacket has gone astray, instead of painstakingly trying to match the missing button, why not pick completely new buttons? They can update or change the look of a jacket, making it seem new for a fraction of the cost.

Getting Your Buttons Straight

There are two basic types of buttons: sew-through and *shank*. There are other, more exotic types, but these two are your all-purpose standards. Sew-throughs have two or, more commonly, four holes and lie flat.

Button varieties: sew-through and shank.

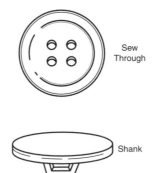

Sew Through

Shank

Shank buttons lift the button from the surface of the garment, making them especially useful on heavy clothes that give the buttons a workout, like overcoats. Both types of buttons, however, need at least a little space that gives them a lift, allowing for some give so that the button unbuttons and buttons easily: This space is called a shank as well, causing a little button confusion. Don't confuse your shanks. I'll let you know how you can get a sew-through button to have a shank, making it look like it's sewn on by a pro.

Buttoned Up: Hand Stitching

Although this is the most common sewing fix-it, it also seems to be the most dreaded. So many of us become all thumbs when it comes to buttons. It doesn't have to be that way. The simple rules for hand stitching on buttons will hold you (and keep your buttons on) for the long haul. First, we'll run through sew-through buttons, and move on to the shank button, covering all you'll ever need to stay buttoned up.

Sew-Through Made Sew Easy

Sew-through buttons are the most commonly used button type; they often lie flat and have a two or four holes for stitching right through the button to the fabric.

➤ Start with the needle: Use a sharp with a bit of a larger hole (say, a size 6 or an embroidery needle if you're using thick thread).

➤ Move on to your thread. Use heavy-duty, monofilament ("invisible"), or buttonhole twist thread for optimal strength for outerwear or jackets that get a lot of wear. All-purpose 100-percent polyester thread works on the majority of buttons that don't get too much wear and tear. Avoid cotton thread because of its tendency to snap under stress.

➤ To cut your sewing time in half, quadruple the thread. That is, fold the thread in half, pushing the center fold through the needle eye, fold in half again, and knot the end.

Sew You Were Saying ...

A **shank** means two things when referring to a button:

1. A shank button is a type of button that doesn't have holes through it; there's a metal ringlike projection on the back that's sewn on to the garment. Shank buttons are used on heavy coats, suede and leather jackets, and for closing other bulky materials that have a lot of stress and wear from buttoning and unbuttoning.

2. Since buttons need a little "wiggle room" to work properly, almost all buttons can benefit from a shank—a certain amount of separation between the button and the fabric. This is created by leaving some room, which means not pulling the threads too tight to secure the button, or encasing the thread connection between the button and the fabric with several winds of the end thread, creating a column of thread that lifts the button from the surface.

Sew Far, Sew Good

Here's a quick rule of thumb for figuring out the distance that the button should comfortably "lift" from the fabric, otherwise known as the shank height: It should be equal to the thickness of the garment fabric, plus about $1/8$ inch, for the proper "wiggle room." Measure the first few times; after a while your instincts will start to take over.

➤ Backstitch once over the button placement, and then sew on the button. Stitch only twice through each hole set (so you sew twice for a two-hole button and four times for a four-hole).

➤ If need be (and usually, you need to), create a shank, or a "lift" between the fabric and the button for ease of use. Simply place a toothpick, thick needle, or even a wooden matchstick across the button between the holes. Make five or so stitches over the toothpick and through the holes. After going through the hole the last time, toss the toothpick. Take the thread under the button and wrap it around the bottom stitches about five times, completely encasing the stitches in a neat coil of thread.

➤ Tie off the button by making a small knot on the right side or by making a bunch of very tight stitches in place under the button.

Creating a shank with a toothpick.

Noteworthy Notions

For button-stitching dazzle, use silk buttonhole twist. The beautiful sheen can't be beat. But bear one important thing in mind: Silk has a tendency to be slippery, so make sure you secure the ends with two knots rather than just one. Also, since buttonhole twist is thicker, there's no need to double or quadruple the thread when stitching; a single thread does the trick.

Frank Shank Advice

Hand sewing on a shank button is even easier. Simply anchor the thread with a back-stitch, stitch twice through the shank if your thread is quadrupled (four times if it's doubled), and secure the button with a few small stitches or a tiny knot.

Security Measures: Button Anchors

Some buttons need some extra strength, especially on overcoats, sportswear, outerwear, or children's clothing. An anchor, whether it's a button or fabric, placed on the inside of the garment does the trick. I realized how important this is after my fiancé's leather buttons on his hipster suede jacket popped off for the last time. The interior button anchor has stayed the course since.

➤ Use a flat button that's a bit smaller than the outside button. Often, a clear button is the best choice because it's unobtrusive, blending into the background.

➤ Follow the same steps for a sew-through button, but place the smaller button on the inside of the garment, directly behind the fashion button, aligning the holes, sewing straight through from one side to another.

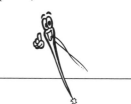

Sew Far, Sew Good

Because thread is twisted, both in its construction and around a spool, it gets as coiled as your old-fashioned telephone cord. Just like you, it needs to unwind to sew well. To cut down on thread snags, pull the thread off of the spool with one hand, letting it unravel over a finger from your other hand. Pull out as much as you think you'll need, and let it dangle and unwind before stitching.

Machine Button Magic

Nothing beats the speed and strength of machine-sewn buttons. Mastering this technique frees your thimble-ridden hands to do so many other things, and shaves minutes off your sewing projects. For example, I'm a fan of throw pillows with button closures on the back, but I used to balk at this extra effort before I learned the minute method of machine stitching. It's the fastest, so take the plunge:

➤ You need a machine with a zigzag stitch and a button presser foot (a tailor tack foot also works wonders, with the bar aiding in creating the shank).

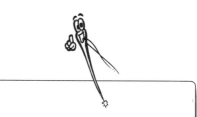

Sew Far, Sew Good

For lighter-weight fabrics such as silk, where you need some extra button oomph, instead of using a button anchor, use a small piece of the garment fabric or a square of interfacing, sewing through the layers and securing on the back.

Sew Far, Sew Good

To check that you have the right stitch width that matches the holes in your buttons, put aside your pedal and use your hand-wheel, giving it a good manual turn, making sure the needle drops right into the holes. This prevents broken needles and nicked buttons from the needle jamming into the button rather than the hole.

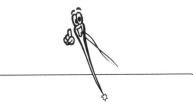

Sew Far, Sew Good

You can create a shank even with your machine-stitched but-tons. Use the versatile toothpick method. When you're done stitching, leave a long tail of threads (about 10 inches). Wind the thread tails around the shank and tie the ends (the only time I recommend hand tying!).

➤ It's crucial that you secure the button in place so it doesn't slip-slide away while sewing. You can do this with Scotch Magic tape, some Sobo glue, or a dab of a glue stick under the button.

➤ Drop the feed dogs, lower the presser foot, set the stitch length at 0, and set the stitch width that matches the holes in your button.

➤ Stitch about six times. Put the stitch width at 0 and stitch a couple of times in one hole to tie it off.

Take off the tape, and ta-da!—a perfect machine-sewn button!

Bungleproof Buttonholes

Machine-stitched buttonholes are God's gift to sewers. Back before the home machine revolution, button-holes were tailored with laborious hand stitching or even more laboriously bound (a couture technique that binds the hole in fabric, not stitches). Nowadays, even the simplest of home machines can handle but-tonholes, and with a little practice, this erstwhile im-possible task will take no time.

Button Boundaries: Placement

Ever try on a shirt and find that it just doesn't hang properly? The bust gaps, the vee neck is too long, or maybe there's just too much space in between the buttons, showing a little more skin than you're will-ing to show on one of your shy days? Sometimes the problem is in the cut, but lots of times, simply re-arranging the button placement can mean the differ-ence between a bust button flying off at just the wrong moment, exposing your new bra, and a spec-tacular entrance in a smooth-fitting blouse. The key is proper placement of the buttons, which is actually dictated by where you put the buttonholes.

Commercial patterns come with buttonhole placement guides so that you can mark your fabric. But almost no one I know is made like the tissue-paper person it's patterned on, so there's no way the pattern can tell you where the buttons should go. If you're short-waisted, long-waisted, voluptuous, thick-in-the-middle, barrel-chested, or thin-as-a-rail, you need to put the buttons where they'll do the work they're supposed to, which is to keep your clothes on, laying smooth, pucker-free, and without any stress lines. So chuck the buttonhole pattern, and follow these steps to make your buttonholes.

➤ *Up or down.* There are two kinds of buttonholes: horizontal and vertical. Horizontal ones are used more often on places where buttons are used more often, as well as on women's clothes, where curvy bodies create stress (and I'm not talking about PMS). Vertical ones show up on menswear, cuffs, in smaller areas, and wherever you want a clean, straight line. The nice thing is that you can decide what works for you and your garment.

➤ *Starting point.* Vertical buttons should be placed on the center front of a garment. Horizontal buttons should begin $1/8$ inch from the center front toward the edge of the garment. What does this mean in plain English? I boil it down to this: You should usually start a buttonhole $3/8$ to $1/2$ inch from the edge of the garment. Period. But play around with your garment while it lays flat and pin it in place. Try it on. See for yourself.

➤ *First buttonhole.* The first buttonhole needs to be placed at the bustline for a women's shirt or at the widest point of the chest for a guy's duds. After locating the starting point, place each button 2 to 3 inches apart, dividing as equally as you can so they are at regular intervals.

Stitch in Your Side

Instead of becoming an expert in snap-front jackets because you're afraid of your fancy-schmancy buttonhole settings, take time to learn your machine's capabilities. Whether you have a computerized machine that calculates the buttonholes and memorizes them, or just a standard buttonholer, know your machine. Embrace your inner buttonholer.

Sew Far, Sew Good

Button placement starts with the buttonhole, not the button. That's why I recommend that you mark and make the buttonholes first, and then sew on the buttons.

Buttonhole placement.

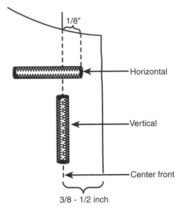

➤ *Marking up.* After you've decided where they go, you need to mark buttonholes on the front of your fabric. You can do this a couple of ways: Use a water- or air-soluble marker (which you tested first), or my favorite—place a piece of Scotch tape directly above the buttonhole, marking with a pencil or pen the end points.

➤ *Buttonhole length.* How long do you make the buttonhole? Use this rule: Measure the diameter of the button (which is very important if it's rounded or domed button), calculate the thickness, and then add $1/8$ inch for some give. This allows a longer length for thicker buttons and a shorter length for flat ones.

Still befuddled about buttonhole length? Try this easy test: Wrap a piece of string, strip of fabric, or even a ribbon around the button and mark where it meets. Divide this in half and add $1/8$ inch. It's foolproof.

Sew Far, Sew Good

Remember this easy rule for which side to place your buttonholes: Women's shirts have buttonholes on the right, men's on the left. But if you make a mistake and switch sides, don't sweat it; just pretend you're part of the gender-bender revolution and designed it that way!

Marking buttonhole placement with Scotch tape.

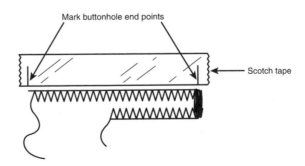

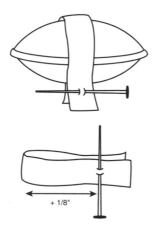

Determining buttonhole length.

Taking the Buttonhole Plunge

I'm sure you've been told to look before you leap, and buttons are no different! Here are some things to keep an eye on before you get in over your head!

➤ *Needle news.* Use a fresh, sharp needle. You need these stitches to cut right through, with no snags or pulls. Use a needle that works perfectly with your fabric: a Universal for everyday fabrics, a ballpoint for stretchy stuff, and so on.

➤ *Stitch standards.* This is a crucial buttonhole point. A buttonhole is formed by a zigzag stitch that goes up one end, crosses the breach, and then goes down the other end, finally connecting the two lines, or *beads*, as they're called in the trade. The zigzag stitches have to be just right; if they're too tight and packed in, they'll cause the fabric to pull and pucker. If they're too loose, the stitching has a tendency to unravel after the buttonhole is cut, defeating the purpose of binding the fabric. How do you find this middle ground? Start by setting the stitch length at .5 mm. See how tightly packed it is and how it looks. Trust your eye; does it look like your pro buttonholes, or a really lame version? Adjust, adapt, alter.

Sew Far, Sew Good

Always sew the lower buttonholes first. If you make a mistake at the bottom of a shirt or skirt, not too many people will notice. That bottom button wears an invisible sign that says, "If you can see any mistakes on this, you're too close."

117

➤ *Tension truths.* You actually want your buttonhole tension to be a little "off." That is, you want the knot to form on the bottom of the fabric, rather than in the middle or on the top. You can do this by loosening the top tension slightly and/or tightening your bobbin tension slightly. But ever so slightly …

Sew You Were Saying …

A buttonhole **bead** is the row of stitching on each side of the buttonhole that encases the fabric in zigzag stitches, preventing raveling when you cut the hole.

➤ *Directional direction.* You should start sewing the buttonhole on the left bead going toward your fabric edge. Stitch the left bead first. Stop at your end point. Set your stitch length at 0. Stitch five stitches that span the bottom of the buttonhole. Now you're ready for the right bead. This one has a tendency to look a little different because it's moving backward. Don't be alarmed; just adjust the stitch length a little if necessary and make sure to pull the fabric taut.

Noteworthy Notions

Does your fabric fail when you try to stitch a buttonhole? Don't want to add too much stiffness? Try one of these stabilizers: A liquid stabilizer, such as Perfect Sew, is applied to the fabric. After it dries, stitch the buttonhole and remove the stabilizer with water. A tear-away stabilizer like Stitch-n-Tear is applied and the remainder ripped. Avalon Soluble stabilizer washes away with water. All that's left is what's under the buttonhole stitches.

➤ *Reinforcement rules.* Buttonholes are almost always made somewhere where there's some reinforcement: a snappy (and stiff) cuff, a blouse front with facing and/or interfacing, etc. If you find that your fabric can't support the buttonhole, add some light interfacing or a stabilizer.

➤ *Now you're ready to test!* You know the basics, now test the buttonhole on your exact fabric; that is, if you have fabric with interfacing and facing, use that, test it, and see how it works. If you have problems, solve them on your test fabric rather than on your project.

➤ *Buttonhole bravery.* Go for it—buttonhole on your project. Conquer brave new button worlds.

Cutting In: Cutting Buttonholes

Your buttonholes are stitched, set, and ready to cut. Here's how to keep them intact:

➤ Use small scissors, a seam ripper, or a straight razor to open the buttonhole. To ensure that you don't clip over the end line, place your fingers on each end before clipping or place a pin on the end stitching—buttonhole insurance at no cost.

Try this groovy trick that I use almost every time I cut buttonholes. Fold them in half lengthwise, and then snip the middle with your scissors. No special tools needed, just a careful and steady hand.

Stitch in Your Side

Sewing buttonholes? Sew tight! No, I don't mean after a few drinks. This is one case where you should pull your fabric taut on the front and back side so your stitches lie flat.

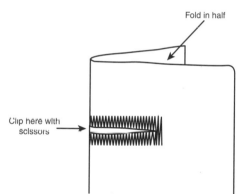

Fold in half

Clip here with scissors

Cutting a buttonhole.

Noteworthy Notions

Buy yourself a special chisel-shaped blade with a handle that just cuts buttonholes. You'll need to use it on a wooden cutting board or a cutting mat, but you'll never have to worry about snipping off the end of your hard-earned buttonhole labor again.

119

Stitch in Your Side

When it comes to buttonholes, do not wing it! Make sure you take the time to test your technique on a practice piece of fabric. You don't want to have spent 20 hours on a tailored jacket, only to ruin it with one off-kilter buttonhole right on the center front. Why, oh why, didn't you test?

➤ Use a little seam sealant, like Fray Check on the center of the buttonhole before cutting it. If it goes on too heavy, use a toothpick to apply it.

➤ Cut away and throw all caution to the wind.

Braving buttons has made you a stronger sewer. Hand stitching was just the start; now you know how to get some closure on all those jackets and tailored shirts that you've been avoiding. And now you see there was nothing real to fear: Buttonholes open a whole new world of garments and home furnishings that will leave you thirsting for more challenges. Lucky for you, the next chapter covers zippers, the other *bête noire* of the sewing world.

The Least You Need to Know

➤ Don't ever hand stitch buttons like crazy, zigzagging around the holes of sew-through buttons, pulling the thread too tight, creating button mayhem. A few neat and well tied-off stitches do the trick.

➤ When hand stitching a common sew-through button on to a garment, create a shank, or "lift," between the fabric and the button by stitching over a toothpick or matchstick.

➤ Buttonhole placement made easy: Vertical buttons should be placed directly on the center front line. Horizontal buttons should be placed $1/8$ inch from the center toward the edge.

➤ Accurate marking, correct tension, proper length and width of the stitches, and how tightly packed your stitches are will determine buttonhole success.

Chapter 10

Win One for the Zipper

In This Chapter

➤ Zipper preliminaries: length and type

➤ Zipper zones: inserting a centered zipper

➤ Advanced zipper course: the lapped and invisible zipper

➤ Zipper fix-its

Into each life, a few zipper mishaps must fall. Whether it's a torn zipper, nasty broken teeth, or a rotten pull, zippers have a tendency to give out long before your garment. But you can actually zip through zippers, from simple repairs to setting in an invisible zipper that barely shows except for the telltale pull.

Sure, sewing in a zipper can be scary, and often strikes fear into the heart of many a sewer. For some reason, zippers get a bad rap for being a difficult and dreary repair destined for failure. This needn't be the case; tailors know only a few more secrets than your average sewer, and I'm going to let you in on them. Soon, your zipper fear will disappear!

First, I'll show you how to insert a zipper so you understand zipper basics. Then we'll conquer invisible zippers, a nifty couture trick that's actually easier than inserting a regular zipper. And finally, you're ready for zipper renovation—replacing a broken zipper and putting in a spanking new one. Your tailor may not thank you for mastering this expensive little repair, but you'll be pleased to know that zippers usually cost between 99¢ and $2, less than a cappuccino at your local café.

From A to Z(ippers)

Zippers, like everything else, have changed over the years. Go to a flea market or used-clothing store—you'll find metal zippers in even the most delicate of garments, including your Aunt Tillie's old wedding dress. Now, plastic, nylon, or polyester is the favored zipper material except when used with heavy fabrics, outdoor wear, or crafts such as denim, patio cushions, and so on, where metal is still *de rigeur*.

There are a few terms you need to know to be able to talk about zippers, so check out the following figure.

Zipper terminology.

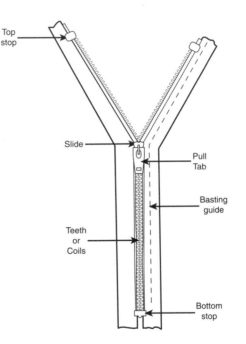

But what's the difference between metal and plastic? Metal zippers have teeth; plastic ones have coils. Metals come in limited colors (steel being the top choice), whereas plastics come in a huge variety of colors, so you should be able to find one that matches or complements even your wildest creations.

There are several kinds of zippers: standard zippers, invisible zippers, and separating zippers. I'll dive into the difference between standard and invisible zippers later in the chapter. Separating zippers do just that—split into two separate pieces. They're used on the front of jackets and with some craft items that need to open entirely.

The Long and Short of It: Zipper Length

Zippers are made in many lengths, usually from 7 inches on up. I used to check my pattern or my project to buy a zipper in the exact length needed. Believe it or not, this is actually a big mistake! Always buy zippers that are longer than the project calls for. That way, you can make the zipper any length you want with nary a care; it's a snap to custom-shorten any zipper from either the top or bottom, creating your own stops.

The other reason it's wise to insert a longer zipper (always use a minimum of 1 inch longer) is so the pull extends past the fabric when you're stitching it in place. By doing this, you can be sure that the bulky pull doesn't get in the way of the stitching, creating any unsightly skips or crooked stitching that will show on your garment. The zipper then conforms to your garment or project, instead of the other way around. Here's how to shorten a zipper:

1. To shorten a zipper from the bottom, figure out the length of the zipper you need. Stitch back and forth five times over that length (yup, right over the zipper coils) and back-stitch to hold it. Cut $1/4$ inch below the stitching, and it'll stop a running train (or at least a zipper pull). Don't try this on a metal zipper, though; it will snap the needle.

2. To shorten a zipper from the top—my favorite and easiest way of dealing with the top stop—place the zipper so that it extends a couple of inches above the fabric. Close the zipper. That is, pull the zipper pull up so that it's above the fabric. Sew in the zipper, pull the pull down, stitch across the top of each side, creating a stitched stop for the top of the zipper. Now you're ready to roll.

Sew Far, Sew Good

Why is shortening the zipper from the top the tops in sewing ease? This way, you don't have to sew around the pull, a difficult and bumpy ride that creates the most common zipper stitching complications. And who needs that?

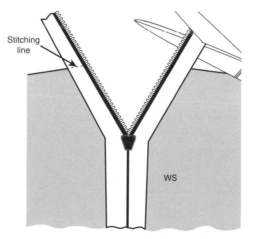

Stitching line

WS

Shortening a zipper from the top.

Zipper Zones: Centered, Lapped, Invisible

All zippers are not made alike. There are two distinct types of zippers you can purchase, and you need to decide ahead of time which zipper will work with your project before you start stitching (not only the zipper, but also the project's seams).

The standard zipper is sewn into a seam. The zipper coils are somewhat visible (depending on how it's inserted) and there is topstitching around the zipper that shows on the outside of the garment or project. A centered zipper is the easiest insertion: the zipper is aligned with the seam and stitched into place. Since the coils can be seen, it's a good idea to try to match the zipper color to the fabric.

A lapped zipper has a flap on one side that covers the zipper to a large extent. The invisible zipper is an entirely different beast. It's constructed differently and has a neat little pull. Use this kind of zipper when you want to tuck the zipper inside the seam, making it look exactly like a seam to the untrained eye. The only telltale sign is the pull.

Here's how to size up your zipper needs and pull on the right one.

Stitch in Your Side

This may seem like an obvious caution, but always check to see if the zipper pull is positioned out before inserting it. Have you ever tried to unzip your pants from the inside when you're wearing them? It's not pretty, and neither is removing the zipper and starting over.

Staying Centered: The Centered Zipper

The easiest way to insert a zipper is to put it in a seam. Whether on a back seam or a side seam, it's simple to drop in a zipper, which also makes it possible to remove your pants without doing the Watusi!

There are two kinds of seam zippers: centered and lapped, with centered zippers being the easiest and most common. I use this method all the time, and you will too!

First you've got to mark the zipper placement on the fabric. Commercial patterns always indicate the zipper with the markings in the following figure. But you don't have to transfer all the markings; when you cut your fabric, just mark with either a snip into the seam allowance, a chalk mark, or a disappearing marker where the end point of the zipper is (usually shown on the pattern with a circle). Now you'll be ready when you get to the zipper zone.

Zipper pattern marking.

Once you've marked the zipper placement, the next place to go is your foot—your zipper foot, that is. You need to replace the regular sewing machine foot with the zipper foot, which is thinner and sits on one side of the needle so that it can ride right next to the zipper teeth. Sometimes the zipper foot is made to swing from left to right so that you can position it properly around both sides of your zipper. Once that's in place, follow these steps:

1. Stitch the seam that will include the zipper. When you reach the exact point that's the bottom of the zipper (you did mark the placement, didn't you?), stop and bar tack or backstitch to secure the stitching.

2. When you reach the point where the zipper begins and you've backstitched, keep sewing the seam exactly as you would normally, but switch to a basting stitch. In practical terms, this means that you should change to your longest machine stitch and sew to the top of the seam.

3. Press the seam open from the wrong side.

4. Close, or zip up, the zipper and center it on the wrong side of the seam. Make sure that the pull is facing out. Place the bottom stop at the exact bottom point that you've indicated (or create a new stop with stitching).

5. You're going to have to stitch the zipper exactly into place so that it's perfectly centered. How do you do that? Definitely not with hand basting! There are a few tricks to keep a zipper from slipping and sliding when you're stitching. My favorite is $1/8$-inch basting tape, a double-sided sticky tape backed with paper. Place it on the edges of the zipper, peel away the paper, and position the zipper where you want it to stick.

Noteworthy Notions

Run out of basting tape? Or don't want to run out and get some? Instead, use some good ol' regular household tape (the Scotch Magic brand does just fine), placing it on the sides of the zipper and removing it later.

6. Now that the zipper is stuck, turn over the garment to the right side so that you can sew the zipper in place. This is where you need the stitching to be straight and perfect. Remember, topstitching shows. But how do you indicate the stitching lines on the right side of your project? Easy: Position $1/2$-inch transparent tape exactly centered on the seam. Use it as a stitching guide and stitch around it. Some people like to baste, others like to use water- or air-soluble markers, but I've found that tape is the easiest method of all—just tape on, stitch, and yank off, revealing perfect stitching results each time.

Sew Far, Sew Good

Want your zipper stitching to be smooth and flat? Always stitch across the bottom of the zipper first and then stitch from bottom to top on both sides. It'll produce a pucker-free zipper zone.

7. If the zipper is too long, pull the pull down and snip off the excess zipper sticking out on each side. Stitch back and forth right across the top of both sides to keep the pull from pulling right off. Warning: Always pull the pull down before cutting and stitching!

Scotch tape, basting tape, or Sobo glue can come in handy when getting a zipper to stay put, but it can sure gum up the works of your machine needle. Never sew over this sticky stuff, or you'll ruin your needle and maybe even get goo caught in the bobbin mechanism.

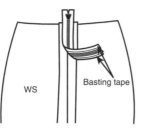

Sewing the centered zipper.

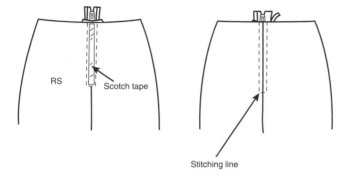

One last little tip if you've been having some problems: If your zipper moves with a start and a fit, buy a little bit of paraffin wax from the hardware store. Rub it across both sides of the zipper teeth and it'll slide with the greatest of ease.

Lapping It Up: The Lapped Zipper

Sometimes you need to shake things up a bit. So, instead of a centered zipper, you might want to try a *lapped* zipper. The term "lapped" comes from age-old construction speak: A lap joint is one where two boards or metal parts are pieced together with the edges overlapping slightly so the surface stays flat. It works just as well for fabric: The zipper is hidden under a flap that falls on one side of the seam and is stitched into place, leaving only one stitching line showing on one side of the seam (when you're wearing it). This differs from a centered zipper, which always has an equal amount of fabric on each side and a double row of stitching.

Sew Far, Sew Good

If you have to do a lot of altering, and your skirts or pants need taking in or letting out, place the zipper in the back seam rather than the side. Then your clothes can fluctuate with your ever-changing sizes without serious zipper alteration altercations.

127

Noteworthy Notions

If you're making pants out of Day-Glo fabric from the 1970s and can't quite find psyche-delic pink among your zipper choices, try changing your centered zipper to a lapped zipper. You won't see the zipper teeth and their color at all, and you can paint the pull with nail polish or craft paint.

1. Repeat step 1 for inserting the centered zipper, stitching and securing the stitches where the zipper will begin. Rather than baste all the way up to the top, turn and press the right side $^1/_2$ inch, then turn and press the left side $^5/_8$ inch. The left side will create the flap that laps.

Sew Far, Sew Good

Keep the machine needle down whenever you shift your fabric to start stitching in a new direction. For example, when you stitch across the bottom of the zipper, and then shift to go up one side, make sure to position your needle at the corner, put it down into the fabric, and then shift. Remember when your teacher said "Pencils down!"? Now think of it as "Needles down!"

2. You can open or close your zipper to do the next few steps. Most patterns say open; I say closure is best because it prevents puckers from forming when the zipper is closed later. Put the basting tape on the right edge of the zipper, sticking it in place. Switch to a zipper foot. On the right side of the garment, stitch from bottom to top as close as you can to the zipper teeth. You won't need a stitching guide because the seam will be open and you can see where you're going.

3. Put basting tape on the edge of the left side, then press into place over the right side where you've already stitched. Make sure the zipper is stuck. Here's where you need some stitching guidance. Position $^1/_2$-inch transparent tape on the right side of the fabric along the edge of the overlap. Stitch carefully around your tape, starting at the bottom, shifting, and then taking a turn up until you reach the top of the seam.

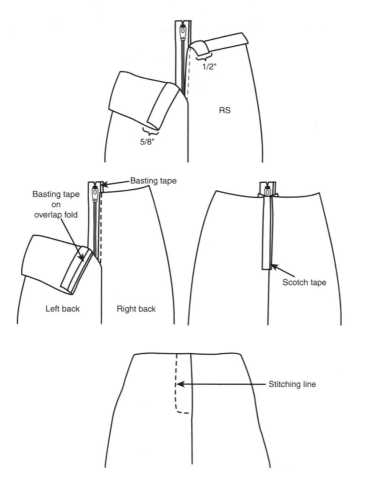

Sewing the lapped zipper.

4. Take off the tape, trim and finish the top of the zipper if it's too long, and be on your merry way.

On the Fly: The Fly-Front Zipper

The only traditional zipper that's not sewn on a seam is the fly-front zipper, a tailoring technique that you'll find on men's and women's trousers. I find that some jobs just aren't worth the investment, like remodeling your kitchen yourself, making puff pastry for a dinner party of 30, or rewiring your son's sound system for his garage band. I think fly-front zippers fit into this category if you're a beginning sewer. If you're determined to make tailored pants, take them to your tailor when you get to the fly front; save it for when your skill level increases.

The Amazing Disappearing Zipper: The Invisible Zipper

You're putting together a wedding dress; it's a simple white number with a beautiful V-neck. Perhaps you're making a complicated blouse with lots of top details. Or you want to make an envelope bag out of a fabulous vintage fabric. Where and how do you insert the zipper? The answer, with a resounding shout, is the invisible zipper! The reason it's called "invisible" is because there's no topstitching, no way to see the zipper coils, no nothing on the right side of the fabric until you get to the pull, the only telltale sign that it isn't just a seam.

The invisible zipper is sewn on the right side of the fabric, very close to the coils. When you pull the zipper closed, it turns the coils to the inside, pulling the fabric over them, closing it for a neat seamlike look. This may sound complicated, but it's actually easier than inserting a regular zipper because there's no outer stitching.

Invisible zippers are inserted in a completely different way than other zippers. You can use a conventional zipper foot to insert an invisible zipper, but you'll find that it's much easier if you have a zipper roller foot. This neat little hinged foot has a couple of grooves on the bottom that glide over the zipper coils and roll with all the invisible zipper punches and fabric bunches.

Here's how to make your zippers disappear:

1. Unlike other zippers that are inserted into an already-sewn seam, you sew in an invisible zipper first, and then sew the rest of the seam around the zipper. Start with the zipper and build from there.

Sew Far, Sew Good

Whenever you wash or dry-clean your clothes, remember to pull your zipper up. It'll prevent zipper tooth decay and coil spoilage.

2. Press the zipper on the wrong side so that the coils stand up straight, making it possible for them to fit into the presser foot groove. Avoid pressing the coils—they melt! This isn't one of those steps that makes something look nice; it's actually important to the construction process.

3. Open up the zipper. Position it, right side to right side of fabric, with the zipper teeth at the $\frac{5}{8}$-inch seam allowance.

4. Starting at the top, stitch down the length of the zipper side right next to the coils. This is crucial! For it to be truly invisible, you must sew as close to the coils as you can. Stitch as far as you can. There will be a few stitches that you can't sew because of the zipper stop. No worry. Go as far as you can and stop.

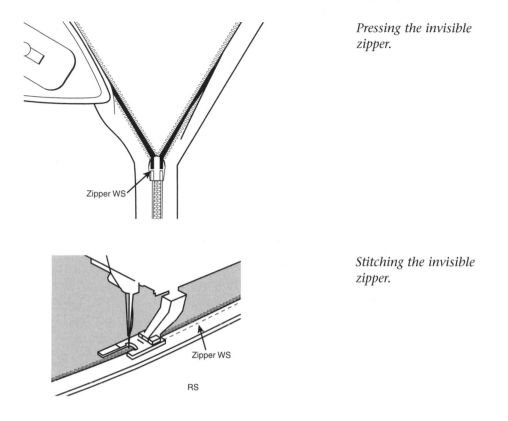

Pressing the invisible zipper.

Stitching the invisible zipper.

5. Close the zipper and pin the other, unsewn side to the top, making sure everything lays nice and flat, without any bulges. Open the zipper and sew the remaining side, again, as close as possible to the coils.

6. With your zipper perfectly in place, you can now sew the seam. Now you need to replace the regular zipper foot. Slip it on so that you can stitch the seam as close as possible to the zipper. Close the zipper, place the fabric right sides together, backstitch or bar tack, and then sew with the same ⅝-inch allowance until you've cleared the zipper by a few inches or so. Then switch to the standard presser foot and sew on down the line.

Each zipper is easy to insert; once you've played around with the different types and how to handle them, you can decide for yourself the best zipper and placement, creating the right look while making it easy to zip in and out of any garment.

Good as New: Replacing a Zipper

Now that you know how to put in a zipper, you can certainly take a broken one out and put a new one in. Removing the offending broken zipper takes a sharp seam ripper and some patience.

Noteworthy Notions

If you've just ripped out a zipper and can't catch all those stray leftover threads, try tweezers. It's easier and less painful than plucking your eyebrows.

Once you've gotten the zipper loose and removed all the straggly threads, make sure you mark the placement along the same lines. Baste the seam all the way to the top, and simply follow the directions for inserting the type of zipper—centered or lapped—you just took out. If you're removing an invisible zipper, take out several inches of the seam as well as the zipper so that you can resew it properly.

Every time a once-zipper-cowed sewer turns the tables on zippers and realizes how easy it is to insert, replace, and fix them, she's shocked at how silly it was to be scared of them in the first place!

The Least You Need to Know

➤ Always buy zippers that are at least 1 to 2 inches longer than the finished zipper length. You can create your own zipper stops on both the top and bottom, tailoring the zipper to you and your garment, rather than the other way around.

➤ When inserting a centered zipper, the topstitching lines are all important. These lines show on the outside, and need to be fair and square. Use a Scotch tape guide for easy sewing.

➤ When topstitching will ruin the look of a project, use an invisible zipper. Remember this important rule: When inserting a standard zipper, sew the seam first and then insert the zipper. When applying an invisible zipper, sew in the zipper first, and then sew the rest of the seam.

➤ Now there's no need to take zipper repairs to your local tailor. Get out your seam ripper, remove the zipper, and replace it, employing basting tape for the proper zipper positioning.

Chapter 11

The Bottom Line: Hems

In This Chapter

➤ Handling hand hemming

➤ Easing through ease

➤ Motoring through machine hemming

➤ Seeing through blindhem stitching

➤ Tacking like a tailor

I hate to hem. Or at least, I used to. Hemming is either the last touch on something that you've been making (meaning that you want to cut corners, rushing through it just to get it done), or the last-minute fix on that fantastic new dress you bought that would be perfect for tonight's party, but just happens to be too long.

What you need is a way to cut corners that doesn't create curvy hems, a way to finish off a project, whether it's a set of table linens or a ball gown, so that you actually do finish it, instead of putting if off because of the dreaded hem. Or worse yet, send it to the tailor because you can't cross the finish line.

To get you to go the distance, I'll give you some general guidelines for different hem finishes. Then we'll get into the specifics for specific projects—pants, skirts, sleeves, linens—just about anything sewn. And finally, we'll end with hemming tailored pants, one of the most common sewing repairs. Why make your tailor any richer and yourself any poorer? You can learn to hem faster than you can say "no cuffs, please."

Hemming Can Be Your Friend

Hems are essentially a way of finishing the raw edge of anything sewn. Usually, a hem is at the bottom of pants, skirts, shirts, jackets, and sleeves. But you also need to hem curtains, table linens, tablecloths, pillowcases, and so on. The rule is that if it doesn't have an enclosed seam, it needs a hem. Period. So there's no way of getting around hemming.

Hem success depends on a few things. The most important is picking the right way to finish your project, whether it's simply turning it a few times and hand stitching it into place, or using a more complicated finish that's better suited to your suit. The other biggie is measuring properly. You need to mark and measure the garment or project carefully, making sure the lines are straight. After marking the finished hem length, you can choose the type of hem from the different hem options.

Brass Tailor's Tacks: Measuring

When measuring for a hem, especially on skirts, pants, and dresses, it's important to keep the following in mind:

➤ Always try on the garment the same way that you will wear it; that is, if you plan on wearing high heels, a snazzy belt, and stockings with a swingy dress, put them on when measuring the hem.

➤ Make sure that the waistline of the garment sits properly—don't pull your trousers up to your rib cage and then measure the hem.

➤ Stand naturally. Don't slouch. Take your hands off of your hips and let them fall. Face front. Listen to your mother.

➤ Ideally, someone else should measure while you stand absolutely still. Have your helper use a wooden or metal yardstick and move around you while you stand still, just like the tailor does. Mark with chalk and then pin.

➤ Try on the garment while pinned. Make sure it hangs properly all the way around. Correct any dips or curves.

Stitch in Your Side

If you need to hem a garment that's cut along the bias, make sure you hang it on a hanger overnight (or at least 24 hours) before measuring and hemming. Any garment constructed along the bias will stretch as it hangs, sometimes in unpredictable ways. Why try to see into the future? Let gravity take its course, and then take over.

The Hand Is Mightier Than the Machine

Ugh! I can't stand sewing anything by hand, whether it's hems or buttons. But sometimes you can't avoid hemming by hand, especially if you have a machine that's incapable of a blindhem stitch (more on that later in this chapter). So let's get the dirty work over first.

Hand hemming has its benefits. When you don't want the hem to show at all on the right side of your fabric, hand hemming is the best. You catch only a tiny thread from the front of the garment, creating a couture look to even the simplest of outfits.

The best time to use this is on the bottom of skirts and other garments when you want a clean look, one without stitching lines, bulk, or added details. This hem goes by a few names: tailor's blindhem stitch, designer hem stitch, or just blindstitch. Here's how to hem the way fine tailors do:

1. Use a sharp needle—and when I say sharp, I don't just mean honed. This is actually a needle classification (for more on choosing the right needle, see Chapter 2, "The Eyes Have It: Needles and Thread"). Choose the smallest size that you're comfortable using that works with your fabric (sizes 7 through 10 are used on most medium- to lightweight fabrics). Thread the needle (single thread, not double) with a knot at the end.

2. Decide on the edge finish (see later in this chapter and Chapter 8, "The Ace of Baste: Seams," for more on seam finishes if you need some guidance). Turn the hem up the width you've decided is appropriate. Press into place.

3. Fold back the hem slightly. Working from right to left, catch just one or two threads from the front of the fabric, sewing short stitches. Make sure they're evenly spaced. Patience, please.

4. Every eight or so stitches, tie a knot in the hem, finishing the entire hem with a double knot. This prevents complete and total hem breakdown when you're out on a date. If you get your umbrella caught in your hem, only a tiny portion of it will droop, rather than the whole thing.

Sew Far, Sew Good

Once you've made the paper strips that you'll learn about in Chapter 12, "Pressing Matters: Ironing Out the Wrinkles," use them on hems to prevent pressing marks. Fold the hem over the strip, and press without worrying that you'll leave a mark.

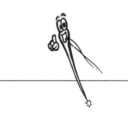

Sew Far, Sew Good

Use long-staple polyester thread for hemming. It's stronger and lasts longer. Save cotton for more decorative uses. For a really sturdy hem hold, turn to the monofilament "invisible" thread.

Hand hemming a blind-stitch.

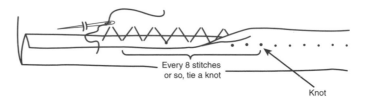

Every 8 stitches
or so, tie a knot

Knot

For blindstitch hemming success, don't pull the stitches too tight or leave them too slack. Too tight means that you'll see puckers on the outside; too loose means they'll droop. Find the balance that works for you and your garment, and stick with it.

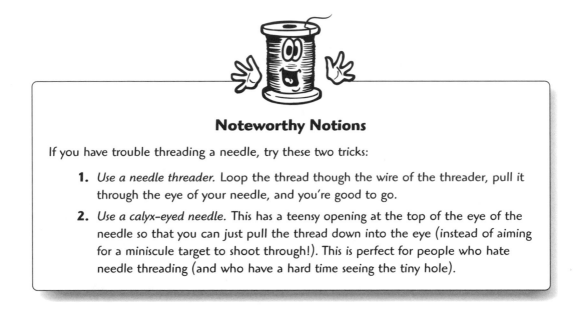

Noteworthy Notions

If you have trouble threading a needle, try these two tricks:

1. *Use a needle threader.* Loop the thread though the wire of the threader, pull it through the eye of your needle, and you're good to go.

2. *Use a calyx–eyed needle.* This has a teensy opening at the top of the eye of the needle so that you can just pull the thread down into the eye (instead of aiming for a miniscule target to shoot through!). This is perfect for people who hate needle threading (and who have a hard time seeing the tiny hole).

Ease-y Does It

Ease means a few things in sewing parlance. First, it applies to any time you need to fit a longer section of fabric to a shorter one. This almost always happens with a set-in sleeve, the cap of which needs to be eased to fit into the armhole, or a long hem where the folded fabric needs to be eased to fit the garment fabric. The extra fullness of the hem fabric fold needs to be carefully eased as you stitch so that you're not left, at the end of the hem, with a bulky bunch of fabric with nowhere to go. The top (folded) fabric also needs to be eased because the bottom (garment) fabric moves through the machine at a faster speed due to the feed dog pressure.

How to handle the bulk? Ease-y! Always pin the key points of a hem to make sure the hem fold lines up with the fabric—place one pin at each side seams to be sure. When stitching, carefully push the top piece of fabric with your fingertips toward the needle, feeding it at a slightly faster rate than it would naturally.

If you still have excess bulk, you can ease the fabric with a machine basting stitch. Set your machine at its longest stitch length (usually 4 mm), edgestitch $1/4$ inch from the edge of the fabric, leaving a thread tail. Pull the thread, gathering the material slightly. Fold over the hem, pin at the key places, and distribute the ease throughout the hem with your fingertips. Stitch the hem into place.

Motoring Through Hems

Machine-stitched hems are by far my favorite, and definitely the faster and easier option. Motoring through hems provides an even, unmatched appearance, and can save hours when you're working on large amounts of fabric, such as curtains and bedspreads.

There are a number of different hemming stitches to master, starting with the simplest turned and stitched hems to the more complicated double-needle and fused hems.

Turned and Stitched Hems

This is the easiest way to sew a hem. You simply turn the fabric over the desired amount and sew a straight stitch, or an edgestitch along the edge of the turn. Use this on fabric that doesn't slip or stretch a lot. That means that silky, satiny fabrics are out, as are knits, Lycras, etc.

Baby Steps: The Baby Hem

A baby hem is a turned and stitched hem with each fold a scant $1/8$ to $1/4$ inch. These tiny turns create a small, neat, and even hem on the sleeves and bottom edge of blouses, home projects, and children's and baby (naturally) clothes. I use a baby hem to finish seam allowances on many a tidy tailored garment.

Sew Far, Sew Good

Here's an all-important tip for sewing a clean, straight, turned and stitched hem. Decide on the finished length of your garment; mark it with tailor's chalk or a disappearing marker. Sew a straight stitch along the marked line. Use this stitching line as a stabilizer and guide so that you can turn the fabric cleanly. Make sure that the stitch line is just inside the hem so you can't see it from the outside.

Machine Blindhem Stitch

This accomplishes exactly the same hem that you did with the blindstitch, but you hum along at a much speedier pace with the aid of your trusty sewing machine. You need a machine that has a blindhem foot, which usually comes with your machine. In order to accomplish this stitch, your machine must be able to zigzag stitch; if it can, it can blindhem stitch.

1. Attach the blindhem foot to your machine according to the instructions. Set the stitch length to 1 to 2 mm (you may need to fiddle with this). Release the upper tension a bit.

2. Press the hem in place. Fold the hem according to the following figure so that there is a ¹/₄-inch overhang between the folded hem and the front of the fabric.

Folding fabric for a blind-hem stitch.

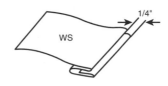

3. Place the fabric with the fold resting on the shelf of the blindhem foot and the ¹/₄-inch overhang moving along the feed dogs of your machine. Here's how it works: As the machine stitches, it zigzags every fourth or so stitch, so that the zigzag catches only one or two threads from the front of the fabric, while the rest of the hem is sewn with straight stitches. Stitch slowly and carefully, making sure that the stitches catch the edge of the fold.

Stitching the blindhem stitch.

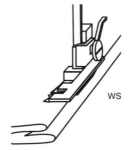

The finished blindhem stitch.

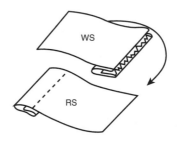

Rolling Along: The Narrow-Rolled Hem

This is perfect for anything that needs a very narrow hem that's evenly rolled and stitched. Sleeves, napkin edges, handkerchiefs, wide bias skirts—they'll look all the better with a rolled hem, especially if you're using lightweight fabric.

It's so frustrating trying to turn a tiny bit of fabric over, press it in place, and stitch it perfectly. But your machine will take care of it with a narrow-rolled-hem foot (which attaches to most machines, even the older ones). They even come in different sizes, depending on the width you would like the hem to be. The wider the funnel on the foot, the wider the hem, so be sure to use the right size.

The general rule is that the lighter and more sheer the fabric, the smaller the groove and the hem; the heavier the fabric, the wider the groove. But don't use this type of hem on heavy fabric—it just doesn't work because bulky or stiff fabric won't roll. Ditto for very sheer or lightweight fabrics—they don't feed properly into the funnel and can't roll right.

1. Attach the narrow-rolled hem foot. Set the machine for a straight stitch at a length of about 2.5 mm.

2. Place the fabric under the presser foot and stitch a few straight stitches in place. Create a thread tail by pulling on the needle and bobbin threads. The tails will be used as a guide to feed the rolled fabric into the curled foot.

3. Gently pull the thread tails so that the fabric moves into the funnel of the foot, folding over into a hem. Stitch.

Sew Far, Sew Good

If you're using a lightweight fabric that needs some extra help in rolling while narrow-rolled hemming, you may want to try some spray starch. The shot of starch will sometimes give the fabric what it needs to feed. Just don't try this on silks—they will be damaged by starch.

Stitch in Your Side

When rolling along with the narrow-rolled hem, don't be a control freak! Let the foot do all the walking for you. Instead of feeding the foot with an already rolled piece of fabric, let the foot turn the fabric while you pull from the back (and back off from the front).

The narrow-rolled hem.

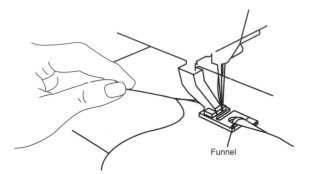

Funnel

Double the Fun: Double-Needle Hemming

This is one of those really smart inventions that make life easier for the sewer. A double row of stitches looks fantastic, hems like a dream, and lasts a long time. Wouldn't it be great if your machine could do this for you?

Well, if your machine has the capability for a zigzag stitch, it can double-hem with a double needle. These needles have one prong that fits into the sewing machine, with two needles that are attached to the prong. Each needle is threaded separately to sew an absolutely picture-perfect row of double stitching. The top of this double row of stitching is a straight stitch, whereas the bottom is a zigzag stitch that crosses between the two rows.

Sew Far, Sew Good

Got some stretchy stuff that needs hemming? Double-needle hemming will fit the bill—because of the zigzag bottom stitch, this hem allows for some give and take, retaining the stretch. Perfect when you don't want a hem to pull out when pulled!

These needles come in different sizes—the size indicates the width between the needles—translating into the width between the stitch lines. Use the ones made by Schmetz—by far the best, in my humble opinion—and try a 4.0/100 size for most hemming. The first number (4.0) is the width between the needles in millimeters, and the second number (100) is the needle size.

You'll need to thread the needles from two different thread sources. If you have a double spindle on your machine, great; if not, you can still double-stitch. Nancy Zieman (see Appendix C, "Further Reading," for information on her book) came up with this brilliant idea: Wind an extra bobbin with the thread you're using, and place it on the spindle first, and then place the spool on top of the bobbin.

To make sure that the threads move evenly through the machine, put each thread on one side of the tension disks, and then continue to the needles, threading them separately.

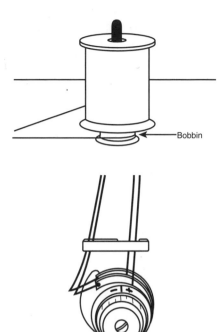

Place the thread spool on top of a bobbin to create two thread sources for double-needle stitching.

Bobbin

Double-threading the tension disks.

Tension disk

1. Turn up the hem the desired amount and press into place.

2. Set the machine for a straight stitch. Set the stitch length at about 3 mm.

3. Topstitch the hem on the right side of the fabric, leaving about $1/2$ to $3/4$ inch from the turned edge (depending on how you would like it to look).

You can multiply the multiple stitching fun by using a triple-needle stitch, creating three rows of even stitches.

Double-stitching a hem.

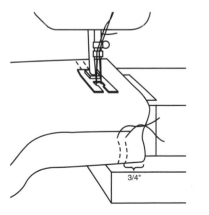

3/4"

Fusing: The Lazy Alternative to Hand and Machine-Sewing

If you really hate hemming, and hand and machine stitching has got you down, you can actually eliminate sewing (almost) entirely from hems. (Go ahead, let's hear some applause!) Just cut a strip of fusible webbing, which has adhesive on both sides, place it at the edge of the hem, and simply press it into place. Minimal sewing, minimal hassle! Use this for work clothes, shorts, casual skirts, children's clothes—anything where looks take a second place to speed and utility. Here's how to do it:

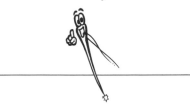

1. Decide on the hem width, then cut your fusible webbing $^1/_4$-inch thinner than the width of the hem.

2. Align the webbing with the hem, placing it $^1/_4$ inch from the edge of the fabric.

3. Fold the $^1/_4$-inch edge over, and then fold the hem in place. Fuse by using a damp press cloth. Using some elbow grease (pressure, that is), press with a steam iron for 10 lo-o-ong seconds.

> **Sew Far, Sew Good**
>
> When double-needle hemming, use the throat plate markings or a magnetic guide to help you keep your stitching on the straight and narrow. This is one hem that you really want to keep perfectly straight!

A fused hem.

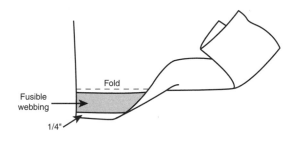

Fold

Fusible
webbing

1/4"

> **Noteworthy Notions**
>
> A fusible webbing is the way to go for fast hems. There are two main types: a double-adhesive webbing such as Stitch Witchery, which has resin on both sides and works with a range of fabric weights, and a paper-backed webbing such as Wonder-Under and HeatnBond, which can be used with more heavy duty fabrics. Just peel off the paper and press.

Want to avoid any fusing problems when fusing hems? Instead of turning the edge ¹/₄ inch, zigzag stitch (or serge) the interfacing to the fabric before turning the hem! You'll have finished the edge and prevented any sticky problems when pressing the fusible webbing.

The Finish Line: Hem Finishes

Just like finishing seams, you need to finish the edge of a hem so that it looks neat and tidy. When you're sitting at a dinner table and your red wrap-around skirt flips back, *you* don't want to turn red just because your hem is a mess! Hem finishes are very similar to seam finishes, with just a few extra touches:

➤ *Pinking.* Just cut the edge with your pinking shears! Use with fabrics that don't have a tendency to ravel.

➤ *Pink and stitch.* One more stitch, but still a simple finish.

➤ *Zigzag stitch.* Run a tight zigzag stitch along the hem edge, and it's secure.

➤ *Bias bound (or Hong Kong) finish.* Just like finishing a seam. (For a refresher, check out Chapter 8.)

➤ *Turn or double turn.* This is just a quick turn (or double turn) so that the raw edge is enclosed within fabric and won't fray or unravel.

➤ *Serge.* If you have a serger, go for the neat, finished serged edge.

Stitch in Your Side

For a quick fix, always use bias tape for bias-bound hems, not bias-cut fabric! Bias tape comes prepackaged and ready to sew.

How Much to Hem?

Decisions, decisions! How do you decide how much hem allowance you should have? It really depends on the type of garment or project that you're working on, the fabric's personality, and the way you'd like the finished project to look. Here are a few guidelines:

➤ *Tailored pants:* 2 to 2¹/₂ inches.

➤ *Straight skirt:* 2 to 3 inches. You can use any number of finishes for this item, from a hand stitch to a blind hem to a simple turn!

Sew Far, Sew Good

I love to reduce bulk wherever possible so seams and hems lie flat. The simplest way to do this is to trim the seam allowance between ¹/₄ and ¹/₈ inch before turning up any kind of hem.

➤ *A-line skirt:* 1 to 2 inches. The best method for finishing this type of garment is just a double turn with an edge stitch or blindstitch (by hand or machine).

➤ *Extremely full skirt or round tablecloth:* $1/4$-inch narrow-rolled hem. This hem is great on table linens!

➤ *Sleeves:* $1/4$ to 1 inch. You can use a double-turned baby hem or a narrow-rolled hem here.

Tailored Pants

Tailors around the world are cleaning up on this relatively simple sewing fix. Whether you need to shorten men's tailored pants, or pick up a bit of your Capri pants to take advantage of the latest style, follow these simple steps.

Sew You Were Saying ...

A **break** in trousers is exactly that—a break in the center crease or line of the pants leg, a small fold a few inches above the hem.

How Long Will You Go?

Decide on your pants' length. The rule is, the narrower the pant, the shorter they should be. Full pants usually touch the top of your shoe, while narrow pants often hit your ankle, or even slightly above.

Men's business trousers either fall at the top of the shoe or are slightly longer, giving them what's called a *break*. A break is a slight fold of about $1/4$ inch that shows when you're standing straight, but isn't visible when walking. This is, of course, a matter of taste, and what your mirror tells you looks good!

Making It Work

Once you've figured out the length, it's time to mark with tailor's chalk and pin into place. When you're sure about the hem position, trim off the excess fabric and finish the edge. Men's trousers are usually pinked and hand sewn with a blindhem stitch, whereas women's trousers often have a more finished edge.

If you want to trim men's trousers like a pro, add a *tip*—a slight slope—from the front to the back of the hem. After marking the front of your trousers, mark the back $1/4$ inch longer. Draw a straight line between the front and back measurements, and then fold along this sloping line, blind stitching into place. My Italian grandmother the seamstress will be proud of you!

Noteworthy Notions

Next time you're shopping for notions, pick up a Dritz Ezy-Hem. This is a metal gauge that has a curved side and a straight side, each with markings to make the hem turnover easy to see, mark, and sew.

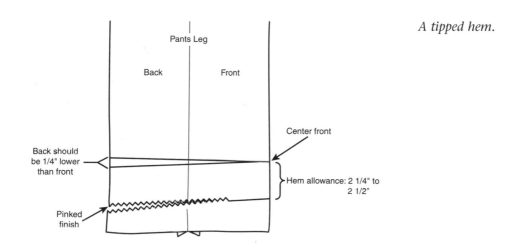

A tipped hem.

Finishing Up

Whew! We made it through hemming, and barely broke a sweat the whole time. These basic skills have the legs to carry you through many a droopy hem, curvy drapery, and overlong pants legs. Whether you're hand sewing or machine motoring, you can apply hemming hints to many aspects of your sewing repertoire. Now you won't be afraid to look down and see what you see!

The Least You Need to Know

➤ One of the most common and easiest ways of hemming is a hand-sewn blind-stitch hem. After turning the hem and pressing into place, stitch by catching just a few threads from the garment fabric and sewing to the hem fold, knotting every eight or so stitches.

➤ One of the most common and easiest ways of machine hemming is the double-turned hem. Simply fold twice and edgestitch. For some extra dash, especially with stretchy fabric, try a double-needle hem.

➤ Here are the most common hem widths: regular skirt or dress—2" to 3"; very wide skirt or tablecloth—$1/4$" narrow-rolled or double-turned hem; tailored pants—2" to $2^1/_2$"; sleeves: $1/4$" to 1" narrow-rolled or baby hem.

➤ Here are the most common hemming errors to look out for: mistaken measuring (keep your arms down and stand up straight!); uneven turning and pressing; wrong hem and edge finish; ease problems.

Chapter 12

Pressing Matters: Ironing Out the Wrinkles

In This Chapter

➤ Pressing as you sew

➤ Getting to the point of pressing: seams, darts, collars, and sleeves

➤ Foolproof fusing

➤ Fusible interfacing foibles and how to fix them

When I first started sewing, my 1940s Singer sewing machine seemed to suit me just fine, so I thought that my iron from about the same era would also suffice. Never mind the black stains, build-up, and cracks on the soleplate—I'd make do. What I made was a mess. There's a time and place for cheap replacements and cutting corners, but ironing is not one of them! Or rather, pressing, as it's called by those in the know.

Pressing as you go is one of the unbendable rules of sewing. Pressing can actually change the shape of what you've sewn for the better (or sometimes worse if you're not careful): It can flatten seamlines, add some curve to a collar, wrap a dart around a buxom shirt, flatten a popping pocket, and make edges and points stand up straight. Pressing has power, and the more powerful your steam iron and the better your tools, the more power you've got at your disposal.

This chapter tells you how to use your iron wisely, on both fabric and fusible interfacing. If you need a refresher course on the different pressing tools and the right iron for your sewing needs, check out Chapter 3, "Power Stitching and Steam Heat."

The Pressing Points

I'm not being highfalutin' when I use the term "pressing"; there really is a difference between pressing and ironing, and pressing is preferable for sewing. The image of a person dragging a heavy iron back and forth over fabric is what ironing is all about—broad strokes sliding across the surface in a laborious, back-breaking way. This kind of motion and weight can distort fabric, stretching it here and there, ruining the time you spent getting it into shape in the first place.

Noteworthy Notions

If you want to either skimp on seam pressing altogether or you want to give it a boost, use a bamboo point turner and seam opener. One side of this notion is for turning points; the other side is flat for running along the seam so that it creases it open. It's not a good replacement for pressing, but it does help in a pinch.

In pressing, you lift the iron and place it down, overlapping it across the fabric until you've covered the whole surface. This way, you won't make waves where you want smooth fabric sailing. When pressing properly, you actually "set" the fabric, storing it just as your computer stores information. This is why it's so important that you press at each stage of the sewing process. Since you know the basic motion, here's how to wield your power on specific areas.

Noteworthy Notions

Got some hard-to-press linen? Valerie Brotman, my favorite vendor of fabulous vintage linens at the tony NYC flea market, gave me this tip: Spritz the linen with water and put it in the freezer. Take it out the next day; the linen will flatten in a flash and crease without a crinkle when you press it.

Steamed Seams

Since we're talking about unbendable rules, another one is that you must press a seam before you cross it with another seam. If you don't, the next seam you sew could come out askew. Here's the best way to press a seam so that it's perfect every time:

1. Press the seam closed to ensure there aren't any sewing puckers or pulls. This "sets" the stitches.

2. Open the seam and press it on the wrong side over a seam roll, using the point of the iron and some steam if the fabric calls for it.

3. Go the extra iron mile: While the seam is warm, press down firmly with a clapper on it. The cool wood of the clapper will draw the heat out of the seam, "setting" it into shape. (On fabrics where a crisp finish isn't as important, you can skip the clapper stage. But if you have hard-to-press fabric or want a tailored look, a clapper can't be beat.)

4. Turn it over, and press on the right side of the fabric. Use a press cloth if necessary.

Darts

Darts are used to make curves that fit your body, so pressing them flat defeats their whole purpose. You need to press darts over a contoured surface that matches the curve of the dart, and take care with the point so that it doesn't pop (that is, stick out), an ugly detail that pressing can cure or create. Here's how:

1. Press the dart flat along the stitching line from the wide end until you're about $1/2$ inch from the point.

2. Place the dart over a tailor's ham, finding a curve that matches that of the dart. Fold the dart to the side that it will face, ideally placing a piece of paper strip under the dart so that its imprint doesn't show on the right side. Use steam and a light touch.

Stitch in Your Side

Don't place the entire surface of the iron down when first pressing open a seam—use the tip; this prevents the seam line from being imprinted on the right side of the fabric. Save using the entire sole of the iron for when you're pressing the right side of the fabric, or when you're pressing broad expanses of fabric with no seam or other details.

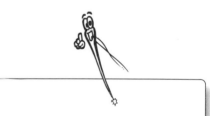

Sew Far, Sew Good

Buy an iron with an iron guard that protects your fabric, often eliminating the need for a press cloth. I swear by my Rowenta Titan soleplate, which distributes heat evenly, prevents pressing shine, and cleans in a breeze.

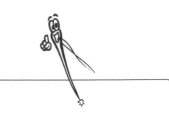

Sew Far, Sew Good

Here's a quick rule of thumb for pressing darts: Vertical darts are pressed toward the center of a garment—front or back—and horizontal darts are pressed down.

3. Turn the dart over to the right side, positioning it over the tailor's ham, and press from the wide part down to the point, easing the point into the garment so that it practically disappears. Use a press cloth if necessary.

Sleeve Arms and Pants Legs

Here's where your big sausage seam roll does the trick. Just place it inside the circular fabric part and press, using the tip to press the seam, and the sole to press the rest. (If you haven't added a seam roll to your supply stash, try a rolled-up magazine covered with a piece of muslin tied at the ends. Just make sure it's packed tight so that you don't press puckers from the roll into the fabric.)

Noteworthy Notions

Because you'll need strips of paper to prevent seam and dart line imprinting, why not prepare a stash ahead of time? Cut strips of about two inches by ten inches from brown paper, paper bags, or envelopes. Or, if you have it around, rolls of adding machine or cash register tape also work well.

Set-In Sleeve

This is a pressing problem only if you don't have the right tools:

1. After setting in a sleeve, press the seam toward the sleeve (away from the garment). A caveat: Don't ever press sleeve seams open!

2. Place the sleeve cap over a tailor's ham, steaming so that the rounded shape of the cap is retained. Nobody wants a sleeve that falls as flat as a pancake, and pressing prevents sloppy sleeves.

Enclosed Seams

Collars, turned edges, cuffs, and other areas all need special care:

1. Always press the seam flat first. If it's a seam on a collar or a tight surface, press over a point presser; if it's a curved surface, use a tailor's ham.

2. Turn and press on the right side of the fabric, making sure that the seam is rolled toward the back so it doesn't show. Use a clapper for a finished look and a crisp crease.

Hot Stuff: Pressing Tips

Here are some things to keep in mind when you've got an iron in your hand:

➤ *The light touch.* Too much pressure can cause shine and overpressing. There's no need to press (despite the term "pressing") at all; just let the weight of the iron do it for you. Not only is it effortless, it's effective. The only exceptions are fusing interfacing or using a clapper, both of which require pressure.

➤ *Cooling.* After cloth is pressed, don't move it until it has cooled. While still warm, movement puts all those crinkles back, and you have to go back to the ironing board. It pays to press ahead and hang your warm garment like you would any other article of clothing.

➤ *Pressing as basting.* Basting, in my opinion, is a drag. Whenever I can, I press hems, edges, and so on in place rather than pinning or basting—pressing power in action.

➤ *Pins.* Never press over pins, which can leave a permanent mark. Also, plastic ballpoint pins can actually melt on to your fabric.

➤ *Markings.* Take care to remove any markings, whether they're made with chalk or markers. Heat has a tendency to cook the marks into the fabric, making them impossible to ever get off. The same applies to stains. Never iron over a stain if you want clean clothes.

➤ *Zippers.* Never press on zipper coils—they melt! Also, stay away from hooks and eyes and other plastic pieces. Who wants plastic goo on a garment?

Sew Far, Sew Good

Always test the heat of the iron on the fabric before pressing it, either with a leftover scrap or with a part of the garment that isn't visible. Use this quick heat guide: low for silk, rayon, nylon, and polyester; medium for blends, light wool, and light cotton; and high for heavier wool, cotton, and linen.

Full Course in Pressing: Fabrics

Certain fabrics need special steam and heat treatment. Don't take a devil-may-care attitude with these fabrics ... or else pressing meltdown may ensue.

➤ *Napped fabrics.* Any fabric with a pile, such as velvet, corduroy, velour, and fake fur is a real pressing challenge. Never press napped fabric on its right side, which crushes the nap. If there are creases in it, dampen them with a little white vinegar. Raise the nap with either a clothes brush or a soft toothbrush. Steam lightly on the wrong side of the fabric.

You can also press over another piece of the fabric. Place the fabric, right side to right side, pressing lightly over the wrong side with a press cloth. This helps preserve the nap. For some serious pressing for velvets and other napped fabrics, try a *needleboard*.

Sew You Were Saying ...

A **needleboard** is not a medieval torture device. It's a bed of nylon bristles that preserves the nap of heavily piled fabrics while pressing. Place the fabric face down on the bed so the fur, velvet, and the like fall in between the "needles," maintaining their fluffy appearance.

➤ *Leather.* Press leather on the wrong side with a warm, dry iron (never hot, never with steam). If there is a crinkle on the front of the fabric that just won't go away, try pressing on the right side using paper as a press cloth. Be careful— if you touch the iron to the right side of the leather, it could leave a lasting impression.

➤ *Wool.* Wool should always be pressed with a press cloth. Period.

➤ *Beaded fabrics.* Never use an iron or steam on sequined or beaded fabric—beads can melt, lose their shine, or curl. Finger press instead, or try the old travel trick—hang in the bathroom while you're taking a long, hot shower.

Noteworthy Notions

Overstressed because you overpressed? Rather than leave that telltale shine, try this: Make a solution of 1 to 2 teaspoons of white vinegar to one cup of water. Dampen a cloth with the solution and carefully wipe the shiny surface. Then press lightly with a press cloth. Don't forget to test first to see if the vinegar causes any discoloration of the fabric.

Pressing Interfacing So It Stays Put

You've proven that when the heat is on, you can tame fabric foibles and fix a wrinkle in no time. But the other major use of steam heat is fusing interfacing. In Chapter 1, "Shear Essentials," I showed you the array of fusibles that are available; now it's time to get out your iron, test the fusible on your fabric, and learn how to make it stick for good.

A common sewing theme is the importance of testing. Nowhere is this more crucial than on interfacing. If you remember to think of fabric as an interactive material, changing with its environment, you'll begin to understand it better. Every fabric and interfacing combination reacts differently with heat, moisture, and pressure, taking on new characteristics. Here's how to find a perfect match.

Testing Tips

I've said it before, and I'll say it many more times before we're through: Always test first! It is crucial to test new techniques and fabrics before applying them to a serious (and seriously costly) project.

1. Cut a strip of the fabric you'll be using, about 6 by 12 inches.

2. Cut 3-inch squares of different interfacing swatches of varying weights, pinking one side. Turn under one edge so that you can using it as a pull tab later.

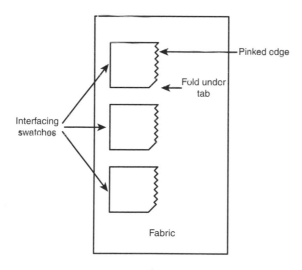

Testing fusible interfacing.

153

Sew Far, Sew Good

Preshrink interfacing as soon as you buy it. Bypass the fridge and stereo, make a beeline to your bathroom, and follow these directions: Soak the interfacing in warm (not hot!) water until thoroughly wet, drain, carefully wring it out, wrap it in a towel to dry further, and hang dry. And remember—don't iron!

3. Fuse interfacing with your iron on the wool setting (skip ahead to the "Foolproof Fusing" section later in this chapter to see the instructions for this).

4. Give the pull tab a good hard yank. Does the interfacing hold? If not, it's a reject right away. Does the interfacing fuse cleanly to the fabric? Are there any bubbles on the surface of the fabric or any shiny dots on the fabric (called "strike through")? If so, it's not the right interfacing choice. If the interfacing holds properly, fold the fabric over, roll it around in your hands, and let it drape. Which interfacing matches your fabric and adds the right amount of oomph? If the line of the interfacing shows, it's too much oomph—the interfacing is too heavy. Once you've made your choice, fuse on.

Musing on Fusings

Almost every sewing book I've ever read says "Follow the manufacturer's instructions for fusing interfacing." I have rarely seen any instructions because interfacing is sold from large bolts with no instructions in sight. Left basically in the dark, you can follow general guidelines and do what I do—stumble around until I find the right heat, pressure, and time so that the fusing holds. If playing with all these variables doesn't produce a solid connection, give your fusible the boot and start over.

Sew Far, Sew Good

Since you cut your fabric and interfacing at the same time, fuse right away! I do it at least a day before I get to my machine, hang it up, and start sewing fresh.

Foolproof Fusing

Here are some tricks and tips to make your fusing experience a faultless one.

1. Press the fabric first. You can't fuse to a flaky surface. The heat of the iron also "primes" the fabric, readying it for fusing.

2. Position the interfacing on the fabric, face down, that is, resin down. (Just so you know, that's the shiny side.) Hold the interfacing up to the light. Don't confuse sides! Also, make sure that there are no foreign objects, such as hairs, scraps of fabric, or loose threads, in between the interfacing and fabric. These will fuse forever into the garment and can show through. Be thorough.

Noteworthy Notions

A lot of commercial patterns and sewing books suggest that you trim about ¹/₄ inch from the edges of the interfacing to prevent bulk around the seams. I've found that fusible interfacing these days is not nearly as chunky as it used to be, so I skip this step with hassle-free results. So can you!

3. With the iron on the wool setting, press lightly in a few areas, starting in the center, just to set the interfacing in the right place. Now you're ready for the serious pressure pressing.

4. Using a dampened press cloth, press firmly in one place for 10 seconds minimum (better yet, 15 seconds). No fast counting allowed. If you're one of *those* types, get a clock with a big fat second hand. Or count sheep very slowly. The point is, don't be impatient.

5. Press with both hands. Pretend that this is your workout and you don't have to go to the gym. This is the only time where pressure is really important when pressing. Do this repeatedly, overlapping until you've covered the entire surface of the interfacing.

6. Let it cool before moving. Even more than fabric, interfacing retains whatever shape it takes when warm.

7. Turn it over and press on the right side, using a press cloth. Don't skip this extra step—it's important for creating a lasting bond.

Stitch in Your Side

Make sure you don't fuse to the wrong side. Just like stepping on gum, the resin goo sticks to your iron and is a pain in the soleplate to get off.

Fusing Foibles

No matter how careful you are, there always seems to be some fusion confusion. Here's the hit list of horrors:

➤ *Fabric bubbling.* This is the most common and troubling fusing problem. Sometimes the reason for fabric bubbling is because the interfacing shrunk. The solution is preshrinking. The other more likely reason is that not enough pressure was applied when fusing, so some areas stuck and others didn't, creating the bubbling effect. Time to break a sweat and apply a firmer hand.

➤ *Interfacing bubbling.* This is often caused by a too-hot iron. Take the temperature down a few notches and try again. It could also be that the fabric has shrunk, so you need to preshrink the interfacing.

Stitch in Your Side

This *is* the bubbling rule: If the fabric bubbles, the interfacing has probably shrunk; if the interfacing bubbles, the fabric has probably shrunk. Either way, you will need to preshrink both the fabric and interfacing to get the right permanent bond.

➤ *Strike through.* This is the appearance of unsightly dots that show on the fabric. Its cause may be an iron that's cranked up too high or interfacing that's too heavy for the fabric. Take the weight and heat down a few notches and test again. When all else fails, try another interfacing.

➤ *Position problems.* If you position the interfacing incorrectly or just plain make a mistake and want to remove it, go right ahead. You should press the interfacing again to warm the resin and then remove it. You can never reuse interfacing, so don't even try. You can remove it, however, so get a new piece and do it again.

I hope that this chapter has impressed upon you all the pressing tricks that can make your sewing so much simpler, faster, and more accurate. Pressing is no side note—it's a before, during, and after activity that is integral to the sewing results.

The Least You Need to Know

➤ Pressing seams and other sewn areas "sets" them; it "saves" them in that position, just like your computer stores information. This is why it's so important to set each sewn area with heat and steam before moving on to the rest of the garment.

➤ Always press a seam before you cross another one. Press the seam closed first to set the stitches. If appropriate, press the seam open. Then press with a press cloth on the right side of the fabric.

➤ Fusible interfacing requires the right combination of the following to hold for the long haul: the right weight and type of interfacing, and the right pressure, steam, moisture, and heat.

➤ With all these variables, you must always test before using fusible interfacing. Test different types of interfacing and see what works best. Fusing problems are usually caused by the fabric or the interfacing shrinking during steaming; the iron being too hot or cold; or the interfacing not reacting well with the fabric. If fixing these variables doesn't cure what ails your interfacing, pick a new one.

Part 4

Fashion in a Flash

Now that the ABCs of seams are under your home-sewn belt, it's time to conquer the commercial pattern and enter the world of fashion creation. Patterns speak a foreign language; we're going on a quick Berlitz course to patterns so that you can translate the tissue into fabric and the fabric into real, live, three-dimensional garments that dip with your hip and glide with your stride.

Rather than taking you through the whole process of making a garment, the rest of this section gives you the lowdown on the special skills and details needed to make a few of the quickest, easiest, and most simple styles. These details have universal applications—learn how to sew a dart that's right on, and you've learned how to make a flat piece of fabric fit your form. Tackle a fitted waistband and you can insert a cuff and a collar with ease. And finally, we'll take a quick course in fitting as you sew, the right way to make a garment that fits like a glove instead of a gunnysack!

Chapter 13

Tissue Issues: Understanding Commercial Patterns

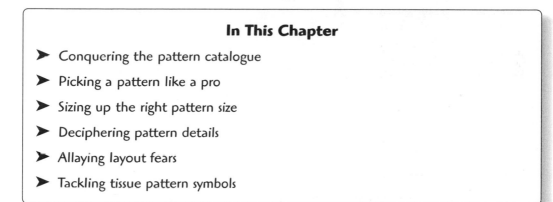

In This Chapter

➤ Conquering the pattern catalogue

➤ Picking a pattern like a pro

➤ Sizing up the right pattern size

➤ Deciphering pattern details

➤ Allaying layout fears

➤ Tackling tissue pattern symbols

Commercial patterns speak a foreign language, one that you have to decipher and understand before you can take advantage of everything they have to offer, which is a lot. You enter that world through the pattern catalogues; flip through them to find fashions and home-sewing projects that you want to make. You have to know what their secret code is telling you, and how to read it before moving on to the pattern envelope and its contents, the pattern instructions, and actual tissue pattern pieces …. Oy—so much new info! But we'll cover it all.

Flipping Through Catalogues at a Fast Clip

The catalogue—a book listing the currently available patterns—is your first key to what's going on when it comes to patterns. The big names—Vogue, McCall's, Simplicity, Burda, and so on—all have their own catalogues that are divided into sections by clothing and project category.

You can find pattern catalogues at stores that sell notions or, more often, at fabric stores, but check ahead to see which brands are available. Each brand uses what's called a *sloper*, or the master pattern for each garment. This means that there is a basic bodice sloper, a basic skirt sloper, etc., that is altered to form different designs. The sloper contributes to the slight differences in the brands and how they fit. These differences are further complicated by different sizing, markings, and instructions. I'm used to one brand and try to avoid using others; and it's not just because I'm a creature of habit. I know what fits and what works, and stick with it. With a little practice, you'll figure out your favorites, too.

Sew You Were Saying ...

A **sloper** is the master pattern that a company uses for each garment part—bodice, pant, skirt, etc. While each company uses their own sloper, the basic design is almost the same. Each unique sloper does contribute to differences in sizing and fitting, so it pays to become acquainted with each company's quirks.

It's So You!

The first thing you need to look at are the pictures of the garment, all gussied up and on models. Many times, there's a photo and a drawing; sometimes, there's just a drawing of the finished garment. This shows the entire "look" of the garment: the design (back and front views), fit, and drape.

When deciding on a pattern, pick a style that flatters you, that you know will look good because it's tried and true. It's a drag spending hours making something that you know will never look good on you, no matter how carefully crafted it is. If you look better in a V-neck rather than a scoop neck; if an A-line skirt just doesn't suit you; if you know that a three-button jacket is more flattering, make sure you base your pattern decision on these criteria.

Noteworthy Notions

Most companies have a basic fitting pattern that you can construct out of muslin, helping you determine how to alter their patterns to fit you exactly. The muslin is marked up and fitted properly, and then the alterations and markings are transferred to each individual pattern. This is worth the minimal time and cash investment to gain a pattern fit on future projects.

Keep a Level Head

Always choose something within your skill level, which is indicated in the catalogue and on the envelope. Beginners should start easy, building on their skills. It's no fun being frustrated when you simply can't conquer a detail that's above your nimble thimble level. Patterns are often ranked from "very easy" to "advanced." Pay attention so that you actually move up the skill level rather than getting a pattern that's too complicated, and then end up giving up.

Sizing Up

After choosing a style, you need to pick the proper size. The pattern envelope contains a wealth of information on sizing and body measurements. The common measurements included are bust, hips, waist, width at lower edge (across the hem of the jacket, shirt, dress, skirt, etc.), the finished back length or side lengths, and the pants width.

Always choose the pattern based on the measurements, not the sizing. Patterns are not sized the way ready-to-wear clothes are. The sizes are almost always smaller because they haven't been changed to reflect the way American bodies have changed over the years—they are still based on the measurements. Don't worry if you're a size 14 according to the pattern when you're normally a size 10. Measurements don't lie, and it doesn't matter what size the pattern is labeled.

Keep in mind these guidelines when choosing a size:

➤ *Top or jacket.* For a top, select the size according to the bust or chest measurement. You can make adjustments to the waist much easier than to the bustline, especially on a jacket.

➤ *Pants or skirt.* The hipline, rather than the waistline, is the key measurement. Again, it's much easier to alter the waist by taking it in or letting it out instead of changing the hip construction.

➤ *Between sizes.* If you fall between sizes on these measurements, you should usually choose the larger size rather than the smaller.

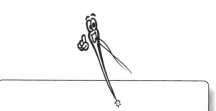

Sew Far, Sew Good

Keep a chart with all your measurements handy at all times. Update them as your body shifts; remember, just because one measurement changes doesn't mean they all change equally.

Stitch in Your Side

If you buy the wrong size and need to alter it, remember that you can't simply add or subtract the same amount all around the pattern. For example, if you need to go up one size, the shoulder measurement simply will not change as much as the waist size. Rather than run pell–mell into alteration, try it in muslin first and mark up the changes that you'll need to make. You'll figure out your figure's unique characteristics.

Figuring Fabric

When you've chosen a size, you can select the amount of fabric needed. The fabric chart is multisized for different fabric widths (35", 45", 54", 60", for example), so take note before you ask for a piece to be cut for you. If in doubt, see the yardage chart in Chapter 4, "Going with the Grain: Fabric Facts."

Some fabric must be laid out in one direction because it has a raised surface called a "nap" that lays in that direction. Fabrics with a nap include velvet, pane velvet, some corduroy, and fake fur. You must take this into account when deciding on the yardage. Napped fabrics almost always use more fabric because the pieces must be laid out in one direction. This is indicated on the pattern envelope as the "with nap" yardage. If you have any doubt, buy the "with nap" yardage so you're not caught with too little fabric.

Ditto for plaids and stripes—since the layout of these fabrics takes into account a repeating design, you'll often need more fabric. First, make sure your pattern envelope doesn't say that the pattern is unsuitable for stripes or plaids. This is not just a cautionary device—it really means that the pattern simply will not work with a repeating design. If you can use a plaid or stripe, allow for matching the pieces with an extra half-yard or yard, depending on how wide the repeat is. For a very wide repeat, buy at least an extra yard.

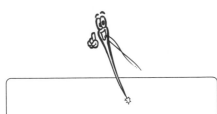

Sew Far, Sew Good

A lot of patterns provide a range of sizes in one pattern envelope, which is really helpful if you're a different top and bottom size; you can mix and match. If you're using a pattern with only one size and your top and bottom are lopsided, use this rule when choosing the pattern size: Follow your top (shoulder, bust, chest) measurements, rather than the bottom (waist, hips). This is because it's much easier to alter the bottom garment than the top—trust me.

Don't Sway from What They Say

Pay attention to the fabric recommendations, which are always listed in the pattern instructions. If the catalogue says the pattern only works with double-knit or two-way stretch, believe it. Don't try to dress up a stiff linen in a garment made for a drapy silk—it won't work. If the catalogue says avoid stripes or prints, do it. If it suggests a crepe or chambray, and you're lost about which is which, ask for some help from the fabric sales staff. They're usually amazingly helpful and knowledgeable, and well worth consulting.

Pushing the Envelope

All the patterns in a catalogue are numbered to help you locate the pattern envelope. The contents of the envelope are the sewing instructions and the actual tissue pattern pieces. The front of the envelope displays the drawings or photos of the finished project. The back of the envelope has more information about the project and what you need to complete it. Among the details included are …

➤ Description of the garment, including any design details, such as welt pockets, princess seams, set-in sleeve, etc., that help you decide on the time investment and skill level needed.

➤ Drawing of the front and back view of the garment, showing seam lines, particular details, and construction lines.

➤ Notions needed: This is a quick list of all the notions that are required, such as buttons, snaps, elastic, seam binding, cording, zippers, etc.

➤ Finished garment measurements.

➤ Fabric recommendations.

➤ Fabric yardages.

➤ Interfacing yardages.

➤ Lining yardages.

Piecing Together Patterns

Decisions have been made, fabric has been purchased. Now's the time to open the envelope, hunker down, and get cracking. You're faced with two elements: the instruction sheet and the actual pattern pieces.

Deconstructing Instructions

What do all these symbols mean? An entire page of the instructions can be devoted to line drawings of the pattern pieces and the pattern, interfacing, and lining layouts. If you've never worked with them before, at first glance they can look like an engineering manual.

Don't be cowed. Start with the pattern pieces. Every pattern piece is numbered. Since most patterns have multiple garments, pay attention to the labeling on each actual piece and the list of which pieces are needed for each garment.

Cut out your project's pieces, leaving the others still attached to the tissue so that you can fold them back up and return them to your pattern envelope (or better yet, a larger bag). Cut loosely, without precision; the time to be precise is when you're cutting the fabric, so there's no need to waste time on pattern perfection.

Before laying out the pattern pieces and cutting your fabric, read through the step-by-step instructions carefully. Remember, there isn't just one way of skinning a fake-fur jacket. There are other ways of attacking a garment, and soon, you'll rely less and less on the instructions and more and more on your instincts and skills.

Following are the usual symbols and markings that point you in the right pattern direction:

➤ *Fabric key.* This helps you identify the fabric, both in the layout chart and the actual instructions, so you can determine the right side, wrong side, lining, and interfacing by their shading. For example, on the layout chart, the right side of the pattern is often white, the wrong side is dotted, and the fabric is black. But this changes with each company, so check your charts.

➤ *Layout charts.* These are maps that guide you on how to lay out your pattern on the fabric for cutting. You need to take care of where the selvage line, grainline, and folds are. In addition to the fabric layout, interfacing and lining layouts are provided.

Sew Far, Sew Good

Don't forget to press (that is, iron) the tissue pattern pieces before laying them out on the fabric. Crinkly pattern pieces create inaccurate garments. Also, the static electricity created when ironing will actually help the tissue stick to the fabric, giving you a hand during the cutting process.

A sample fabric key.

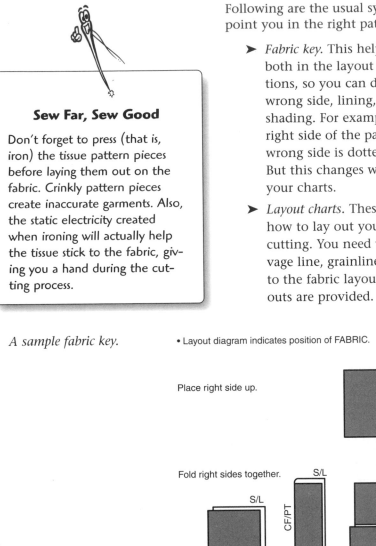

• Layout diagram indicates position of FABRIC.

S/L = Selvage

CF/PT = Crosswide Fold

F/P = Fold

Place right side up.

Fold right sides together.

Sample layout chart.

JACKET A PIECES: 1,2,3,4,5,6,8 & 10

45" (115cm) * S/T 8-10-12

45" (115cm) * S/T 14-16-18

➤ *Folding instructions.* Most fabric is folded sel-vage to selvage when cutting it out. Some layouts, however, suggest different folds for optimal use of the fabric. If a pattern piece is positioned on the fold, extending past it, it means that it should be cut on a single layer of fabric rather than a folded double layer.

➤ *Star symbol.* This indicates special instructions involving the layout that can be found in the opening charts.

➤ *Term definitions.* If a special stitch is used, such as an easestitch or staystitch, the pattern will define it for you (but not very well, so don't rely too heavily on these definitions).

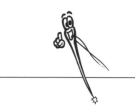

Sew Far, Sew Good

Many companies swear they give you the best way of laying out your pattern so you don't waste money on extra fabric. But this isn't always the case; you can certainly play around with the layout to find what suits you and your fabric best.

Getting the Pattern Pieces to Fall into Place

The tissue pieces have their own markings and symbols that are crucial when speaking pattern dialect. Take the time to learn them once, and just like riding a bike, you'll remember them forever.

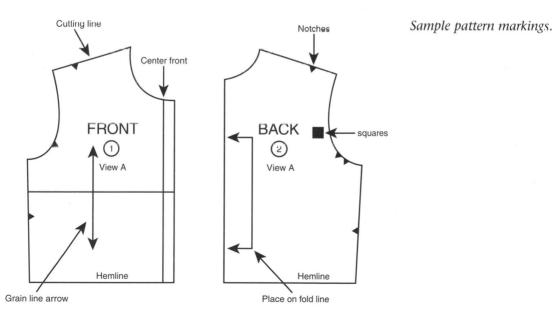

Sample pattern markings.

Stitch in Your Side

When you see a pattern piece with a grainline running diagonally (rather than straight up and down) through it, don't be distressed. This is a piece that should be cut on the bias. Just position the piece so that the straight line on the tissue piece aligns with the grainline, and you're set.

➤ *Cutting line.* This is the outside border of the pattern piece. On a single-size garment, it's a solid line. On a multisize garment, it'll be different for each size (for example, a broken line for size medium).

➤ *Grainline arrow.* Each piece has a grainline arrow that indicates how the pattern piece should be placed on the fabric. This is indicated with a solid line with directional arrows on it. *This is crucial!* If you don't place the grainline on the straight and narrow, your garment will never hang properly. The way to find the exact grainline placement is to measure the distance from one end of the grainline arrow to the selvage. Match the other end to the exact same measurement, and you're golden.

Aligning the grainline with the selvage.

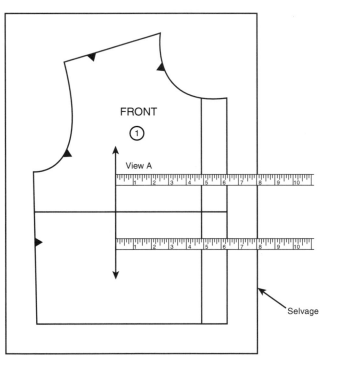

➤ *Notches.* These are indicated with small triangles that point out from the garment cutting line. They indicate where pieces of fabric are joined. It is the industry standard to place one notch in the front piece of a garment, two in the back, and three at other places. Never cut the triangles out as indicated—it's a total waste of time. Instead, make small snips with your scissors about $\frac{1}{4}$ inch into the garment's seam allowance. Never cut any deeper—you'll snip into the seam allowance or weaken it with a too-wide snip.

➤ *Position indicators.* The bust apex, the center front, the waistline, and more are all indicated on the pattern for your convenience.

➤ *Fold line.* If a piece of fabric is to be placed on a fold (making it twice the size of the pattern piece, an exact double on the other side), it's marked with a double-ended arrow that points to the fold and says "place on fold." It may take a few cutting disasters before you figure out how to prevent fold foibles. The standard fold pieces are the backs of shirts, jackets, or dresses, collars, and interfacing.

➤ *Circles, squares, and triangles.* There are a variety of placement symbols that are marked on the pattern, not all of which are completely necessary. Reading through the instructions ahead of time will help you decide which ones you need to transfer.

➤ *Zipper placement.* Zippers are indicated with a zigzag line and a circle at the end.

➤ *Hemline.* This is a line that shows the finished length of the garment. You can use this to lengthen or shorten the hem.

➤ *Adjustment lines.* This is where you may lengthen or shorten a garment without affecting its overall shape and fit. This is especially important on an arm or skirt where the shape and drape will be changed by simply raising or lowering the hemline.

➤ *Darts.* These are triangular broken lines that meet at a circle.

➤ *Buttonhole markings.* These are indicated either on the pattern pieces or on a separate buttonhole guide.

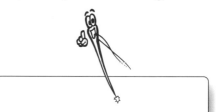

Sew Far, Sew Good

While the pattern always indicates the button placement, I like to wait until my garment is completely constructed before deciding on button placement. Buttons need to close a garment around you and your unique body. Wait until you're done and position the buttons where they should be on your body. Use this guideline: If it's a blouse or jacket that needs some real closure, always put one button exactly on the bust apex, building the other buttons around it.

Layout Lowdown

Here are a few more tips that'll help you with the layout:

➤ *Never use pins when laying out the pattern and fabric.* Always use weights. They work just as well and save an enormous amount of time. In fact, they work better because pins distort the fabric and cause puckers—deadly!

➤ *Always find the grainline of your fabric before laying it out.* I used to think it was good enough to match the selvage lines. Little did I know about fabric distortion, which occurs when it's bolted, stored for a long time, or woven a little off-kilter. You need to straighten the grain before you lay out and cut your fabric. It's a simple solution to an often vexing problem.

➤ *Iron.* Need I say more?

You now know enough to crack the pattern code. Commercial patterns open up a whole new world of fashion for you and your home, making it all the easier for you to pick projects that match your taste, skill level, and style.

Noteworthy Notions

When you've learned the basics of putting together a home-sewn garment, get rid of your pattern instructions. Follow these simple steps and your garment will fall into place in the proper order, making it easy to fit as you sew:

1. Prepare darts, tucks, and pleats.
2. Sew style lines, except for side and shoulder seams.
3. Interface.
4. Prepare pockets.
5. Insert zippers.
6. Sew shoulder seams.
7. Close up side seams and inseams.
8. Prepare collar.
9. Prepare sleeves.
10. Attach collar.
11. Attach facings.
12. Set in sleeves.
13. For dresses, attach skirt to bodice.
14. For skirts or pants, attach waistband.
15. Hem.
16. Sew on buttons.
17. Sew any finishings.

The Least You Need to Know

➤ Don't ignore your own body type in favor of a trendy fashion when choosing a pattern. Just because it's home sewn doesn't mean it will look any better than a store-bought fashion that never suited you. (Bell bottoms will never work on me, no matter how much stitching care I devote to them.)

➤ Don't push the envelope—the pattern envelope, that is. Follow the fabric suggestions, the notion needs, yardage, and size measurements that are listed on the pattern envelope.

➤ Don't forget these rules when laying out the pattern pieces: Press both your fabric and tissue pieces; locate the grainline of the fabric and lay it out accordingly; follow the "with nap" layout for piled fabrics; and pay attention to any special instructions, such as cutting on the fold.

➤ Don't forget to transfer all the key marking, clips, notches, and doohickeys (well, maybe not the doohickeys) from the pattern pieces to the garment fabric.

Chapter 14

Skirting the Issue: Painless Pants and Skirt Details

In This Chapter

➤ Stretchy stuff: elastic waistbands

➤ Waistband witchery: attaching the waistband

➤ Stitch in the ditch: an all–around sewing boon

➤ Dart details: deepening your wardrobe

I actually first started sewing when I couldn't find any pants that fit. From top-of-the-line designer boutiques to cookie-cutter chains, I scoured stores for close-fitting pants that flattered my figure. After a grueling and demoralizing weekend of pants-hunting, I finally made do with two pairs of the same kind of pants that weren't exactly right, but that I thought I could get away with.

I never wore either pair and wound up donating them to my local charity. I really hope they fit someone else. Now I make all my pants, and can concoct a pair of perfectly fitted slim black pants with a side zipper in less than an hour.

I said black, but I also own them in 10 other colors, some of which match my jackets so they look like store-bought suits. This is the greatest satisfaction of sewing—getting exactly what you want in the perfect fit, whether it's a pair of pants or kitchen shades that are made to measure.

Getting Started on the Right Foot

Rather than take you through the whole process of making a pair of pants or a skirt, I'm going to show you the special details and skills needed to make a few of the quickest, easiest, and most simple styles. We'll avoid tailoring details, like fly fronts, men's waistband collars, and cuffs.

We'll stick to the parts that have so many other applications in completely different sewing projects, the basic building blocks of a lot of garments. Since the techniques I'm going to illustrate are universal, I'll use the term "pants" throughout, but the skills apply equally to skirts and other clothing.

My teacher instilled in me the tenet of a technique library that you can draw on; for example, if you know how to insert a waistband, you can apply the same method to a cuff or a collar. Once certain skills are part of your sewing toolkit, you'll be throwing together all sorts of clothes without even peeking at the pattern instruction sheet.

Noteworthy Notions

If you can get a grip on elastic waistbands, you can make pants, skirts, pajamas, boxers, baby clothes, lingerie, exercise wear—the list goes on and on. So hang on for a mind-(and waistband-) expanding experience.

Stretch Your Repertoire with Elastic Waistbands

If you want to whip up a pair of pants in no time, elastic is the way to go. There's no messing with zippers, hooks and eyes, or any other closing details. The prep work, sewing time, and fitting issues are kept to a bare minimum. After cutting the material, the only sewing involved are the side seams, waistband, and hem. Since you've already tackled seams and hems, all you need is to wrap your mind around stretch waistbands.

Noteworthy Notions

You can alter any pant or skirt pattern so that they have an elastic waistband. There are two things you need to keep in mind and change accordingly:

1. The clothing has to slip over your largest part. To ensure this, draw a straight line up from that point on your pattern, rather than tapering, as you would for a zipper or hook-and-eye closure pant.

2. Extend the pattern straight up from the waistline to create the casing. Add twice the width of the elastic and ¼-inch seam allowance. Now all you need is the elastic and you're minutes away from wearable pants.

Stretchy Stuff

Elastic comes in lots of different sizes and varieties. The best kind for a waistband is nonroll woven elastic for the obvious reason that it doesn't get all bunched up, twisted, and rolled over in the casing that keeps it in place. There's nothing worse than an elastic waistband that is a curvy, crumpled mess and can never be straightened out, no matter how hard you try.

What's the difference between nonroll and other elastics? Nonroll is knitted together, rather than braided, with a durable lateral rib that retains its shape. The knitting process keeps the elastic from changing shape dramatically, turning into a pretzel when you least expect it. It's available in widths ranging from ½ inch to 2 inches. The brand Ban-Rol is a reliable and widely available nonroll elastic, so look for it.

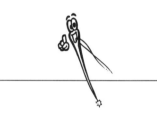

Sew Far, Sew Good

To figure out the exact amount of elastic you need, don't follow the pattern instructions. Wrap the elastic comfortably around your waist while you're sitting down (even the best body tends to "relax" when sitting), and try different amounts of stretch. Remember that it can't be too tight, not only because it'll painfully dig into your waist, cutting your figure line, but it also needs to stretch enough to go over your hips and caboose.

175

Stitch in Your Side

Most patterns say that waistband elastic should be joined into a circle by overlapping the edges and sewing them together. However, this method creates bulk and sometimes frayed elastic pieces that stick out from your clothes. Yuk. Instead, try trimming a small piece of sturdy (but not bulky) fabric or a piece of seam tape. Line up the elastic so that the edges touch each other (not overlap), place the swatch under the butted ends, and zigzag stitch each side in place. Trim the fabric swatch close to the elastic and you're ready to roll—waistband roll, that is.

Casing the Joints: Waistband Casings

The most common elastic waistband uses a casing, or a flap of material that's folded over, completely encasing the elastic. It's not a separate waistband (which we'll get to later in this chapter), but an extension of the fabric that simply folds down. According to Nancy Zieman, this is the simplest way to wrap up your elastic and stitch a waistband:

➤ Use a commercial pattern that calls for elastic sewn into a casing. The most common elastic width is 1 inch.

➤ For pants or skirts, sew the side seams and press.

➤ The casing for a 1-inch elastic band is usually 3 inches (1½ inches folded over). Mark, fold, and press.

➤ I like to fold the raw edge of the casing fabric a scant ¼ inch and press it in place. You will be stitching the bottom edge later, so there's no need to finish it now.

➤ Edgestitch the fold of the casing ⅛ inch from the top edge.

➤ Cut the elastic and sew the edges together (or sew them to a piece of fabric as suggested in the sidebar on the left).

Stitching elastic ends together.

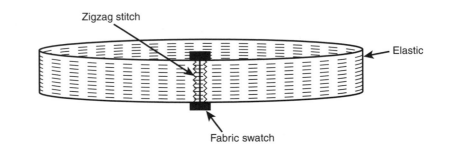

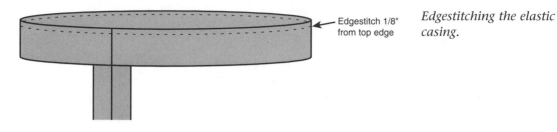

*Edgestitch 1/8"
from top edge*

*Edgestitching the elastic
casing.*

➤ Position the elastic in the open casing. Since it's shorter than the fabric casing, you need to stretch the elastic so that it's distributed evenly in the casing. Pin at least at the center back and front, and two side seams. Add any additional pins that will ease your sewing anxiety.

Noteworthy Notions

If you're feeling unsure about the simple stretch test for figuring out the length of elastic you'll need, use this equation: Take your waist measurement (no cheating allowed), and subtract four inches to allow for the stretch and a snug fit.

➤ Here's the smart part: Switch to your zipper foot with the needle. Stretching the elastic so that the fabric smoothes when sewing, stitch with the edge of the zipper foot right next to the bottom edge of the elastic. The elastic is neatly encased between the stitching, giving it very little room for any give or any of the usual fabric bunching associated with elastic waistbands.

*Finishing the waistband
casing.*

Zipper
foot

Elastic in
casing

Noteworthy Notions

The reason this casing works so much better than others is that you sew the garment fabric around the elastic, rather than the old-fashioned way of sewing the casing, and then pulling the elastic through a hole you've left on a seam with either a safety pin or a special notion called a bodkin. Who needs the extra hassle of working the elastic through, and then sewing up the loose ends?

A More Stable Elastic Alternative

You just learned the truly painless way to insert an elastic waistband. But if you're making something that's going to get a lot of wear and tear, or if you want a more finished look, there's another, almost as easy way to stretch and sew.

In this method, you sew the elastic into the garment, stitching right on the elastic. It's sure to stay put that way.

Sew Far, Sew Good

Are you a fan of beautiful cotton shirting? I am, and make men's boxers (for both men and women) using this elastic technique. Once you get it down, it only takes 20 minutes and a yard of fabric. Brooks Brothers, look out.

➤ Again, use a commercial pattern that calls for elastic casing.

➤ If you're using a 1-inch elastic band, trim the casing material amount to 2½ inches.

➤ Cut the elastic and sew the ends together, using the technique described above or just overlapping and zigzagging into place.

➤ Since the elastic is shorter than the fabric, it needs to be stretched while sewing. You need to keep track of how much and where the elastic goes so that it stretches evenly. The easiest way to do this is to divide both your fabric and elastic into quarters and mark; to do this, I use pins on the fabric and pencil on the elastic (who'll see it?). Line up the markings. Insert the elastic into the casing, repinning together at the quarter marks.

➤ Here's the real difference: Place the elastic at the top of the raw edge of the right side of the fabric. Overlap it $1/4$ inch, pinning it into place at the quarter marks and where necessary to maintain the $1/4$ inch seam allowance.

➤ Zigzag stitch through the elastic and the fabric at the $1/4$ inch mark, stretching so that the elastic fits the fabric. This is the seam allowance, and will be folded under.

➤ Turn over the elastic twice.

➤ Pin the elastic into place at the quarter marks. Sew a zigzag stitch right through the fabric and the elastic $3/8$ inch on the right side from the top edge and $3/8$ inch from the turned bottom edge. The waistband should lay flat and be perfectly stitched into place.

Stitch in Your Side

Want to avoid wilted waistbands? Keep your iron away from them, especially when the heat is cranked up. Try pressing right up to the edge of the elastic, and then apply a blast of steam a few inches away if you must iron out any kinks around a waistband.

Stretching the Limits: Different Elastics

While nonroll elastic is the easiest, simplest, and most common elastic for pants, sleeves, and other projects, there are other elastics available to the home sewer. Here are a few of the most common types for you to experiment with:

➤ *Clear.* This is a very cool kind of almost see-through 100-percent polyurethane elastic that stretches an enormous amount (three times its resting length). You must stitch directly through this elastic to stitch it in place (that is, it can't be used in a casing). The great thing about clear elastic is that its stretch and retention aren't damaged by the needle. Clear elastic is often thinner than other elastic bands and is usually available in $1/4$- to 1-inch widths. Clear elastic is perfect for swimwear because it's chlorine-resistant. Other uses include lingerie and shaping in sheer fabric where a thick white strip is too visible.

➤ *Stitch & Stretch.* This is a woven polyester elastic with several rows of elastic cording. Secure the cording at one end, stitch the elastic in place, and pull the cording from one end to gather the band the desired amount. Usually available in $1^1/2$- and $2^1/4$-inch widths.

Sew Far, Sew Good

If you're using a thicker waistband for workout wear or just for comfort, you can add an extra stitch through the center of the waistband for extra hold. It also looks extra-cool.

➤ *Drawcord.* A wide (usually 1¼ inch) elastic band with a ready-to-use centered drawcord that is used as a waistband tie. Very useful for sportswear.

➤ *Lingerie.* This is a thin (¼ to ½ inch) elastic with a decorative edge for use on underwear.

➤ *Round cording.* This is thin (1/16 to 1/8) cording. Use it for the hair scrunchy described in Chapter 19, "Crafty Gift Giving," and for other crafts and projects.

Sew Far, Sew Good

We sewers are always looking for ways to save time finishing edges. For waistbands, the best way to get around finishing the raw edge is to cut the waistband fabric along the selvage. No need to do any stitching for finishing; the manufacturer has already fused the edge for you.

Facing Down Faced Waistbands

While elastic is the easiest waistband, faced waistbands—where a separate interfaced band is attached to pants or a skirt—are the most common. But they're also commonly avoided because the steps aren't clear in the pattern instructions and the real time-savers and tips are left out. There's no more need to waste energy worrying about waistbands; this kind of waistband and its easy insertion is the key to learning how to insert collars and cuffs as well, so any practice time is well-spent.

Noteworthy Notions

Need interfacing for your waistband? Why not use one that's made-to-measure specifically for waistbands? Try these products: The Dritz slotted nonwoven fusible comes in widths of 1¼- and 2-inch—the slots are terrific fold and stitching lines—or Ban-Rol, available in widths of 1, 1½, and 2 inches.

This type of waistband is fitted, so it always goes hand in hand with a closing of some kind—a zipper, a pocket flap, or a hook and eye. No matter what the opening, the basics are the same. Here's how:

➤ Follow the pattern instructions for cutting out the waistband and interfacing, making sure you notch the garment fabric and waistband for proper placement.

➤ Fuse the interfacing to the wrong side of the waistband.

➤ Finish the long, unnotched edge by zigzag stitching, serging, or turning over the edge and edgestitching (or use the selvage trick described in the sidebar).

> **Stitch in Your Side**
>
> Interfacing your waistband? Make sure it's the right weight for your fabric. Too light and it'll scrunch up; too heavy and you'll get a gut full of what feels like cardboard. In doubt? Then test!

➤ Align the placement notches, center lines, or other markings, placing the right side of the waistband against the right side of the pants fabric.

➤ Stitch in place, allowing for a $5/8$-inch seam allowance. Trim to $1/8$ to $1/4$ inch, pressing the seam allowance up toward the waistband. If you have thick fabric, made even bulkier by interfacing, grade the fabric and interfacing; that is, cut one $1/8$ inch shorter than the other.

➤ Depending on the waistband closure, finish the edges of the closure (for a zipper, hook and eye, etc.).

➤ Turn over the waistband, wrong side to wrong side, pinning along the seam line so that the edge that is inside the garment extends $1/8$ inch below the outside stitching line.

> **Noteworthy Notions**
>
> Commercial patterns always call for trimming the interfacing edges before fusing to the waistband. If you trim carefully after the waistband is sewn to reduce bulk, you can skip this step entirely. Try it, you'll see.

➤ Here's the crucial step: "stitch in the ditch." This is a technique that allows you to stitch in the seam well where the waistband joins the garment. In practical terms, this means that the stitching doesn't show on the front of the garment. You can accomplish this by spreading the front seam apart slightly with your fingers, stitching exactly in the seamline. The back of the waistband extends below this point about ¹/₈ inch, meaning that you will stitch the waistband closed.

Stitch in the ditch.

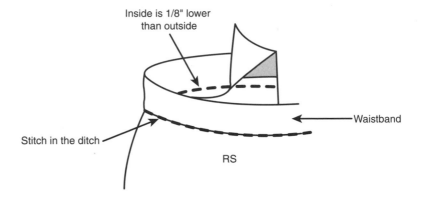

Inside is 1/8" lower
than outside

Waistband

Stitch in the ditch

RS

Stitch in Your Side

When you're "stitching in the ditch," you get perfect results when you press. Always press open the seam where the waistband (or cuff or collar) joins the garment. Pull gently at the seam with your fingers while stitching to allow the stitches to fall in the ditch. Set yourself up to stitch rather than ditch your efforts.

If this is your first stitch in the ditch effort, go slow. Learn how to regulate the speed of the machine and manipulate the fabric so the stitching exactly overlays the previous stitching. This stitching has so many other applications—collars, cuffs, neckline facings, tacking on facings—wherever you want to hide the stitching on the front of the garment, leaving it clean and simple. And all without hand stitching!

Darts Mark the Spot

The greatest thing about fabric is that you can turn it from a flat-as-a-pancake piece into a three-dimensional object that has a life of its own. How do you do that? One of the easiest ways is with darts, which are placed anywhere a body dips and rises. If you're a double DD, you're in luck with a well-placed deep dart that hugs your bodacious body (see Chapter 16, "A Fitting Finale: The Perfect Fit"). Ditto for waistlines, hips, and some shoulder areas, where darts hit the contouring mark. They're especially useful on the front and back of fitted pants and skirts so that they lay flat across your curves. And you get all this fit payoff for something that's so easy to sew.

➤ Mark your darts carefully (for advice, see Chapter 7, "Ready, Set, Prep!").

➤ Stitch the dart, slowing down and shortening the stitches to 1.5 mm at the last inch of the dart, sewing right on the dart edge fold a few stitches.

➤ Never cut and tie the strings as it says in so many books. Instead, stitch off the dart a few stitches, letting the threads unroll a bit. Backtrack so that you stitch at 0 stitch length a couple of times in the dart seam allowance. Now clip the threads.

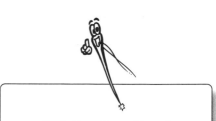

Sew Far, Sew Good

Remember this easy rule: The deeper your curves, the deeper the dart. And the converse: If you've got a washboard everything, make your darts smaller.

You can stretch the skills you've learned in this chapter—elastic applications, waistband insertion, and dart detailing—to so many other types of garments besides pants and skirts. These are important building blocks to your sewing toolkit: Now you're ready to tackle cuffs and collars!

Noteworthy Notions

Got a deep dart? You need to reduce the bulk by slashing the seam allowance down the center until you're three-quarters of the way down. Press both sides open and the remaining, unslashed part at the bottom to one side. No more looking like your wallet is hidden in your skirt front!

> ### The Least You Need to Know
>
> ➤ Confused about waistband size? Do this simple equation: Take the relaxed (not tight!) waist measurement and subtract 4 inches.
>
> ➤ Adding a fixed waistband? Try the most useful way of attaching: the stitch in the ditch. It'll produce a perfect front and a secure wrong side of the garment.
>
> ➤ Sewing a dart? Never stop to tie the ends! Instead, sew straight off the tip, pull the material back, stitch a couple of stitches up and down in the dart seam allowance to secure the stitching, and trim your threads.
>
> ➤ Need a dart? Remember this rule: the wider the curve, the deeper the dart.

Chapter 15

Off the Cuff: Simple Sleeves and Collars

In This Chapter

➤ Easy sleeve easing

➤ Set-in sleeves, if you please

➤ Placket alternatives

➤ Perfect collar and cuff points

It's every home sewer's nightmare. You've constructed a beautiful jacket, complete with welt pockets, princess seams, and fancy dart action. Now comes the time for setting the sleeve.

You're sweating the first time you baste the sleeve in place. You're tensing after you've ripped out the puckered mess and try the second time. The third time evokes swear words. The fourth time results in ripping the sleeve to shreds and throwing it into the compactor. Does this describe your set-in sleeve efforts?

There's help in store. Every home sewer can set a sleeve without sweating, swearing, or tearing. You just have to know where to take it slow and where to bend the rules.

Sew You Were Saying ...

When sewing together two pieces of a garment in which one is longer than the other, you must **ease** the longer piece, or gather it gently so that it fits into the shorter piece. This happens anytime you sew a set-in-sleeve. You need to ease the sleeve cap, or the area at the top of the sleeve, so that it becomes shorter and curved, fitting neatly into the armhole of the garment.

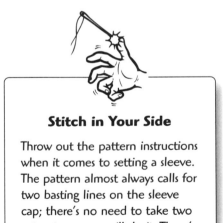

Stitch in Your Side

Throw out the pattern instructions when it comes to setting a sleeve. The pattern almost always calls for two basting lines on the sleeve cap; there's no need to take two extra steps—one will do it. There's also no need to pin everything in sight; pinning actually creates puckers, the very thing you're trying to erase. Chalk it up to sewing overkill, and simplify.

The same applies to the rest of the sleeve; cuffs and plackets can be your friend rather than an unnecessary foe. I know—the pattern directions are so obtuse, the drawings illogical, and the methods out of date. But once you learn how to create a cuff, you're ready to conquer collars. This chapter will show you how to make every sewer's *bête noire* a better way.

Stress-Free Sleeves

The seemingly illogical thing about sleeves is that you have to take a flat sleeve and set it into a smaller armhole opening that also happens to be round; just like trying to fit two mismatched jigsaw puzzle pieces, it won't work if you force it. In fact, force has nothing to do with it. It's finesse that counts.

My finesse has often failed me when I'm working on sleeves, especially silky sleeves that slide every which way including loose. So, practice sleeve-setting on easy-to-handle cottons, muslins, or stable lightweight wool. Then you can get a grip on the gathering and easing before you work with stretchy or slippery—and expensive—material.

Easy Easing

The way to get around the flat-sleeve-in-the-round-hole problem is by *easing* the sleeve before you set it. Easing gathers the sleeve with a basting stitch, giving it a rounded and curved shape before you even attach it to the armhole of the garment.

The sleeve cap's circumference is usually one inch or so longer than the armhole, so it clearly needs to be crimped. It's great to see a sleeve take shape right under your hands, curling gently so that it fits the slope of your shoulder. The way to create a curved shape without any nasty puckering is to do a little work before attaching it, and then a little insurance after setting it so that you cover all the bases.

➤ Here's where the notches and markings really get the job done right. Always notch the front and back of the sleeve (one in front, two in back). Instead of marking a dot or circle at the center of the sleeve and sleeve cap (as it often indicates on the pattern pieces), I like to snip the center just a bit into the seam allowance as an easy placement guide for matching the center of the sleeve cap to the center of the armhole.

➤ If you're all notched up, you're ready to sew. Stitch a basting stitch about $^3/_8$ inch from the edge right inside of the stitching line (if you're using a $^5/_8$-inch seam allowance). This isn't a final stitching guideline, so it doesn't have to be exact. It *does* have to be loose enough so that you can pull on the thread, gathering together the fabric. The basting stitch length varies with the fabric. Heavy to medium fabrics need the longest stitch length (4 mm), and lightweights like silk need a slightly shorter stitch.

Stitch in Your Side

Never neglect sleeve markings and notches. I used to have so much trouble setting a sleeve; no matter how carefully I eased and stitched, it always came out wrong. This was before my teacher showed me the importance of matching up markings. This is another rule that I learned the hard way, but you don't have to!

Noteworthy Notions

Here's an example of where ironing not only gets the kinks out, but actually helps form the garment. After you've finished easing the sleeve, put it around the edge of a tailor's ham and steam the eased area. Pressing and steaming help shrink the cap slightly, making it easier to insert.

➤ Take the sleeve out from under the needle and pull gently on the thread tails, gathering the fabric slightly. Use your fingers to distribute the gathering evenly around the sleeve. One of my big problems in the past was that I thought I had to bunch the whole sleeve up, and went way overboard on the gathering. No wonder my sleeves always puckered. Take it easy on the ease and you should see a slight roundness forming, a gentle curl to the sleeve edge that will make it a snap to set.

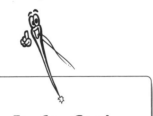

Sew Far, Sew Good

Make sure when you sew the basting line that you leave a "tail" behind you—the thread should hang out several inches at the start and finish of the stitching line so that you can pull on it easily.

➤ After steaming, get ready to sew. Put the sleeve into the armhole, right side to right side, matching the notches on the sleeve and on the armhole. Put four (count 'em, four) pins to hold the sleeve in place: one at each notch, at the side seam, and the center top. This is something you're never read, but my teacher tipped me off: Place the pins *inside* the seam allowance, not right on the edge. This way, you can adjust the ease without pinning and repinning, making the ease more accurate and cutting down on presewing time.

➤ Using your fingers, carefully distribute the ease, making sure that the center top is especially smooth and without any visible gathering outside of the $5/8$-inch seam line.

Noteworthy Notions

Want a new use for your kids' standard No. 2 pencil? Try this tip that a lot of home sewers swear by: Use the tip of a pencil eraser to ease the sleeve cap. The eraser has the gift of grip.

➤ Baste the sleeve in place. Take a good hard look at it. Is it smooth? Are there any telltale puckers or gathers? If the answer is a resounding yes, take out the basting and try again. If there's just a hint of a wrinkle, take out the basting about $1^1/2$ inches before and $1^1/2$ inches after the offending pucker and restitch, distributing the ease more evenly, smoothing with your fingers.

➤ If the basting is on the mark, zip ahead and stitch in place.

➤ Trim the seam allowance to $^1/4$ inch, and zigzag stitch the edge to prevent ravelling.

➤ Press the seam flat making sure that it's pressed toward the sleeve not the body of the garment. Steam the wrong side of the sleeve over a tailor's ham. Now you're set and so is your sleeve.

How to Avoid the Placket Racket

Sleeves are true staples of sewing; plackets definitely are not and should be avoided like the plague. But even the hardiest sewer sometimes wants to whip up a tailored shirt and has to face down the evil placket.

Plackets are reinforced openings that are often fastened with a closure of some kind on sleeves and shirts that allow hands and heads to slip into the garment. Sounds simple, doesn't it? Little do you know how much sewing heartache plackets can bring to the most experienced sewer.

I'm going to offer you an alternative to plackets and cuffs so that you can eliminate the placket racket. My teacher used to be a men's shirtmaker, and she said that when you're sewing a few hundred shirts a day, you learn to cut corners.

Stitch in Your Side

I used to bunch up sleeve ease at the top center of the sleeve, pushing all the extra fabric into one big pucker at the most visible part of my sleeve. Don't do it! Try to distribute the ease equally on each side of the sleeve cap, smoothing the gathers out toward the sides.

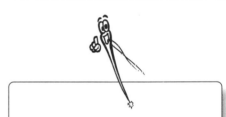

Sew Far, Sew Good

If your basting line is getting the best of you, try this quick fix: Readjust the sleeve so that the new stitching line is a few eighths of any inch inside the previous line. This will push the puckers further into the seam allowance, making it easier to sew smoothly.

Noteworthy Notions

Remember that you're the master of your sewing destiny. If the pattern calls for compli-cated pockets and plackets, you can simply eliminate them. I'm a fan of the streamlined look (which also happens to be in style now), so dump some fussy details and you'll shave hours from your project.

The No-Placket Solution

This is the ultra-easy way to finish a tailored shirt without any of the time-consuming techniques. Sandra Betzina, a master of squeezing the most sewing into the least amount of time, turned me on to this trick in her book *No Time to Sew*, and it has served me well. Rather than make a complicated finish, you can widen the armhole opening and place a button and buttonhole on the sleeve hem, creating a closing that's as simple to sew as a buttonhole. Here's how:

➤ Alter the sleeve pattern you're using so that the opening at the wrist is wide enough to accommodate an overlap that buttons into place. Test this first on the tissue pattern piece; if you need more space, widen gradually from the elbow to the end of the sleeve.

➤ Finish the sleeve edge by double-turning and topstitching.

➤ Press the sleeve over a sleeve roll. At about six inches up from the hem on the opposite side of the seam, press a crease. This crease will form the fold that'll close up your sleeve opening.

➤ Create a buttonhole $1/2$ inch away from the crease, parallel to the topstitching.

➤ Try on the sleeve to determine where you need to position the button; sew into place. You're placket-free and buttoned up.

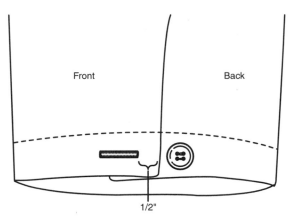

The no-placket solution.

Fooling the Placket Police

Rather than making a time-consuming and potentially perilous placket, why not try a couple of placket cheats? Here are a few suggestions for skipping over the complicated placket:

1. If you're fortunate to have a side seam in your sleeve, you can create an opening at the bottom of the sleeve that replaces the placket. Simply end the seam stitching about 3 inches above the sleeve edge. Turn and finish the edges of the opening (use a baby hem for optimal results).

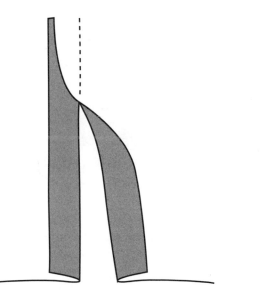

Sleeve seam opening.

2. Create a dart opening over the placket position. Stitch a dart in the sleeve that is about 2 to 3 inches long. Slash the fabric up to the dart tip, taking care not to cut too close to the stitching. Baby hem the opening edges. Edgestitch around the opening.

Sleeve dart opening.

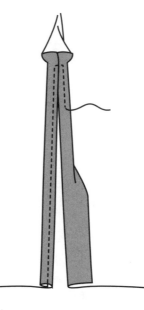

3. Cut out the placket entirely by cutting a facing strip out of the sleeve and turning and stitching in place. Cut into the sleeve at the placket location; the opening should be one inch by one inch. Turn up the clipped square, fold, and stitch into place. Okay, it's not really an opening, but you can attach the cuff to the edge of the sleeve and no one will be the wiser.

Easy faced sleeve opening.

Now you've worked down the sleeve, from the armhole to the placket—time to move to the cuff. The great news is that cuffs and collars use the same technique; once you've mastered one, you've got both under control.

Crafty Cuff and Collar Tips

One of the true sewing tenets that you never learn when you follow the pattern instructions is the importance of assembling each part of a garment before attaching it to the whole. Imagine you're on a car assembly line, and need to finish an entire section before installing it. Would you put half a seat in to half a chassis? It's so simple, and it makes so much sense, but I had to hear it from a garment industry pro before I learned. Practically speaking, this means that you should put together the whole sleeve (if it's a two-part sleeve) before attaching it to the garment, even if the instructions tell you to construct the sleeve piecemeal.

Ditto for cuffs and collars: Sew the two sides together, trim the seam allowances carefully, turn them right side out, and attach them as a whole. It's a very rare occasion that you would put one part of the cuff or collar on first, and then add the second part. Piecemeal work leaves way too much room for error.

I can't tell you how many collars conked out on me, ruining the whole shebang, all because I attached the upper and lower pieces to the garment separately. Here are more tips on how to create cuffs and collars the easy way:

> **Sew Far, Sew Good**
>
> To stand at attention, cuffs and collars need interfacing. Remember, these details often need a stiffer interfacing than you used on the garment bodice. If you're making fancy French cuffs, by all means, pull out the stern stuff for a crisp, tailored look. Try Fuse Shirtmaker or Pellon ShirTailor.

➤ Interface first. When it comes to interfacing cuffs and collars, throw out your pattern instructions. I use this rule: Interface the top side of the cuff and the bottom side of the collar for the best results.

➤ Sew together the two sides of either cuffs or collars, paying special attention to the point (which has to match up exactly, especially on a collar). Here's the big lesson on how to sew a perfect point every time: Shorten your stitches as you get close to the point (about one inch away). When you reach the point, stop. Put your needle down, pivot the fabric so that it is at a 45° angle to the point, stitch *exactly one stitch*, put your needle down again, pivoting again so that you stitch down the other side of the point. Continue stitching the cuff/collar according to the directions.

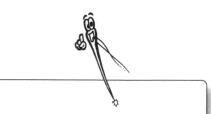

> **Sew Far, Sew Good**
>
> If you're pressing a collar, you need to take sides. The upper collar should have the advantage over the under collar; that is, press so that the seam falls more towards the underside than the topside of the collar. The seam should always be hidden on the under collar.

Stitching the under collar to the garment.

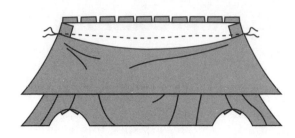

➤ Turn right side out, using your point turner (or the end of your shears for a quick fix). Press.

➤ Take care that the collar (or cuff) is exactly symmetrical. This means that both sides of the collar have to match perfectly—you don't want one side to droop and one to stand at attention. Fold the collar in half before attaching, ensuring that both halves match up. Make any necessary corrections.

➤ To attach the cuff/collar, you need to sandwich the seams within the two layers of the cuff/collar. Pin on only one side of the cuff or the underside of the collar, matching the center of the collar and any notches. Following the pattern instructions, stitch one side only of the collar/cuff to the garment. Trim the seam allowance.

Sew Far, Sew Good

When sewing a collar, cuff, or any other fine point, take care to trim the point carefully. Any extra fabric caught in the turned point may produce bulk or bulbs—ugh. The best way to trim close to the point without mistakenly catching any stitches is to hold the point with your thumb and index fingers; trim around your fingers, as close as you can without snipping your epidermis.

Noteworthy Notions

A perfect point is a necessity for a pointed collar or a well-turned cuff. This is where a handy point turner really does the job. This is a notion that you use to push out the last little bit of fabric that gets stuck in the point, turning it completely inside out. A bamboo point turner is the cheapest and the best way to push the point.

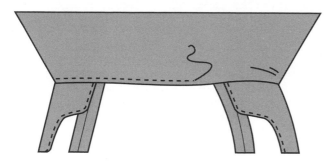

Finishing the collar stitching.

➤ Fold the other edge of the cuff/collar over the seam allowances, folding under the seam of this edge. Using the stitch-in-the-ditch method, topstitch in place, enclosing the seams entirely.

After making a beautiful bodice, you can face sleeve details and collars with courage. With a little patience, practice, and a few professional pointers, set-in sleeves, cuffs, and collars will become second nature. Soon, you won't need to look at sewing instructions to handle these necessary elements.

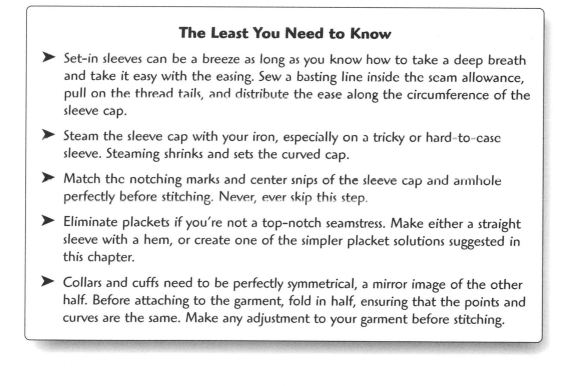

The Least You Need to Know

➤ Set-in sleeves can be a breeze as long as you know how to take a deep breath and take it easy with the easing. Sew a basting line inside the seam allowance, pull on the thread tails, and distribute the ease along the circumference of the sleeve cap.

➤ Steam the sleeve cap with your iron, especially on a tricky or hard-to-ease sleeve. Steaming shrinks and sets the curved cap.

➤ Match the notching marks and center snips of the sleeve cap and armhole perfectly before stitching. Never, ever skip this step.

➤ Eliminate plackets if you're not a top-notch seamstress. Make either a straight sleeve with a hem, or create one of the simpler placket solutions suggested in this chapter.

➤ Collars and cuffs need to be perfectly symmetrical, a mirror image of the other half. Before attaching to the garment, fold in half, ensuring that the points and curves are the same. Make any adjustment to your garment before stitching.

Chapter 16

A Fitting Finale: The Perfect Fit

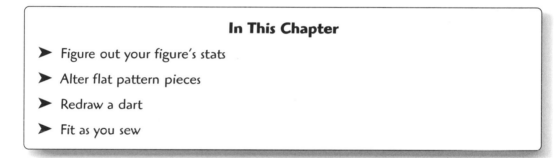

In This Chapter

➤ Figure out your figure's stats

➤ Alter flat pattern pieces

➤ Redraw a dart

➤ Fit as you sew

My grandmother is a seamstress, and I used to love it when she would come over and whip me up a new suit in an afternoon. She never used a pattern; she just used me as a real, live mannequin, making me try on every piece as she worked. She knew, and I learned firsthand, the beauty of fitting as you sew, rather than wasting a lot of energy on time-consuming alterations.

A perfect fit is one of the many benefits of sewing, especially if you're not a perfect size. Most of us have what I would call "challenging" figures; my particular challenge is that I'm a former gymnast, and my upper body and shoulders are a larger size than my lower body. I can compensate for this when I make my own clothes, but ready-to-wear must be painstakingly altered, something I'm not always willing to commit to. With a few lessons on quick pattern alteration and fitting as you sew, you'll solve many fit disasters and make your home-sewn garments fit like a glove.

Measuring Up: Body Parts

Before you can learn how to fit your body, you have to learn about your body. Take a frank assessment; you're not doing yourself any favors by cheating. This is where your tape measure is essential. Make sure you take your measurements over your underwear-clad bod (for both men and women), measuring snugly each of these parts:

➤ *High bust (women only):* This is right under your arms.

➤ *Bust/Chest:* Measure around the biggest part.

➤ *Waist:* Bend over; your waistline is right at the crease. Put your finger there, wrap your tape measure around and see where the inches fall.

➤ *Hips:* Use the largest measurement.

➤ *Upper arm:* Again, measure the largest part.

➤ *Back width:* Measure across the midback, which is usually three inches down from the shoulder.

➤ *Shoulder width:* Measure from tip of one shoulder straight across the back of the neck to the tip of the other shoulder.

Sew Far, Sew Good

Got a friend who wants your shopping advice for that special occasion? Ask for some *quid pro quo*—have them meet you before hitting the mall and give you a hand with your arm, back, skirt, and pants length measurements. You need the help unless you moonlight as a contortionist.

➤ *Arm length:* Measure from the base of the neck (where it bends) to the middle of the wristbone over a slightly bent elbow.

➤ *Torso and dress length:* Center back to waist, and center back to the hem of your usual-length skirt.

➤ *Skirt length:* From waist to usual hem.

➤ *Crotch depth:* While sitting straight like a good student in a hard chair, from the side waist to the chair.

➤ *Crotch length:* From back center waist to front center waist, through your legs.

➤ *Thigh:* I hate to say it, but one more time— measure the widest part.

➤ *Pants side length:* From waist to hem along side.

Noteworthy Notions

Wanna make your life easier? Update your size chart occasionally as your body parts shift (you have been working out a lot lately, haven't you?). Keep the chart handy and refer to it often (but don't post in on the fridge unless you're a glutton for punishment!).

Commercial Patterns

Now that you've got a handle on your hips (and other body parts), you have a template to measure against the commercial patterns. Before you even get to the fitting stage, you need to purchase the right pattern size and assess its measurements against yours. The first rule of commercial patterns is that you should never follow the sizes (such as 6, 8, 10, etc.). Instead, always follow the body measurements that are listed either on the pattern envelope or inside, on the instructions. Patterns don't follow the sizes that you and I normally buy; instead, they run much smaller. I think this is because ready-to-wear is sized much larger than it used to be (making us all feel svelte when shopping, and more likely to buy something), whereas patterns have followed the commercial sloper (or master pattern) of times gone by. This is why I wear a size 8 when I'm shopping, but almost always buy a 12 when I'm picking up a pattern.

Here are a few things to bear in mind when choosing a pattern size:

➤ Remember that your measurement and the finished measurement of the garment should not match exactly; if they did, your clothes would be skin-tight and you would need some canola oil to get them on. Add some *ease*, especially in the chest, hips, upper arm, and waist, ranging from one to three inches, depending on how form-fitting you like your look.

Stitch in Your Side

Patterns are almost never returnable unless you haven't opened them. That's why you need to check the measurements carefully in the store, double-checking against your figure cheat sheet. Remember, you're usually stuck with the pattern you purchased.

Sew You Were Saying ...

Ease is that extra amount of fabric added to a pattern beyond the body's measurements that allows for movement. If the garment was made exactly to your measurements, you would never be able to walk in it. The amount of ease added depends on the garment—a stretchy pair of pants needs less ease than cotton poplin. A bustier needs less than a blouse. In addition to the wearing ease, there's also design ease, the amount of ease that the fashion or style of the garment dictates. A swing coat has plenty of design ease, which you will want to retain when altering.

Stitch in Your Side

Don't cheat and buy according to your ideal size, not your real size. Just like those thin pants you've got in the closet, your new garment won't see the light of day.

➤ If you're like me and your top and bottom sizes are different, pick your pattern based on the top, which is harder to alter. Pants and skirts can be adapted without too much hassle. Or you can buy multi-sized patterns that come in one package, cutting one size on top, another on the bottom.

➤ If your hip measurement doesn't fall into the hip/waist range offered on most commercial patterns, go by your hip size rather than your waist for pants or skirts. You can always take in or let out the waist with ease.

➤ Why take bust and high bust measurements? Patterns are made for a B-cup bra size, meaning that the difference between the bust and high bust size is usually 2 inches. If it's more, you've got a bigger cup size and need to buy a pattern according to your high bust size. If you buy according to your bigger bust size, the top will be oversized in the shoulder and neck.

➤ If you're between sizes, buy the larger size. You can always downsize a garment, but it's much harder to size up. Books always say the opposite, but I've made too many things that just don't bridge the gap—the size gap, that is.

Playing with Paper: Altering Flat Patterns

You've now got all the tools at your disposal—your body's and your pattern's measurements. It's time to take a realistic assessment of the flat pattern sizes and see where they hit and where they miss, your first indication of where you need to alter.

Before cutting out the fabric, you should always alter the flat pattern pieces, checking on key areas of fit and length. Other alterations will follow when you're sewing, but you need to cover your major bases in the pattern stage. Luckily, many patterns have handy measurement "cheats" printed on them—the apex of the bust, the center front, the center back, the finished lengths and widths at certain points. Use as many of these measurements as are printed on the pattern to compare, noting where there's a difference and marking it down.

Sometimes, you need to do the calculation, measuring the pattern yourself. Lay out the pattern, press it for accuracy, and get out your tape measure. Follow these measuring guidelines:

➤ Since almost all patterns include seam allowances, don't add them to your calculations.

➤ Remember that the pattern pieces are almost always one half of one side. A back piece of a shirt is a mirror image on the other side. To measure the full amount across your body, measure the pieces and then double where appropriate.

➤ If you're making adjustments on one piece, make sure you make adjustments on any corresponding parts. If a top lines up with a matching skirt, make the appropriate changes on both pieces.

➤ Always keep grainline, center lines, and fold lines straight.

➤ Place the tape measure along the same line as your body measurement. For example, measure the hipline of a skirt pattern, subtract the seam allowance ($^5/_8$ inch for each side), and then double it for the finished measurement. How does it compare to your hipline? If it's off, make a note.

➤ If there are darts, simply skip them. Measure from side seam to the start of the dart. Skip over the dart and measure to the next seam.

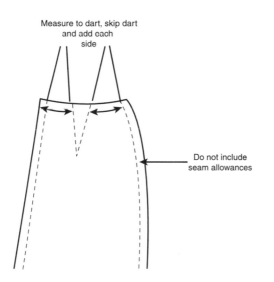

Measure to dart, skip dart and add each side

Do not include seam allowances

Flat pattern measurement.

➤ The horizontal measurements are by far the more crucial fit points. If a shirt isn't wide enough across the chest or a skirt can't make it over your derrière, you're in trouble. Always measure the wide stress points of a pattern. Length can always be altered at the very end.

➤ Shoulder measurements always need to match exactly. Remember that a top (dress, jacket, shirt) hangs from the shoulders, so they are crucial.

Noteworthy Notions

When flat-pattern measuring, always focus on your out-of-the-ordinary areas. Popeye arms? Get to them first and foremost. Flat-as-a-pancake behind? Get the lowdown on that low area. Short-waisted? Don't give that place the short shrift. This is where knowing your body and the particularities of patterns really helps shorten tailoring time.

Pivot and Slide: Not a Dance Step, But a Fit Technique

You may be a perfect tissue-pattern person, but I know I'm not. My patterns usually need a nip and tuck here and there before I begin cutting. No need to despair—you can alter and adapt your tissue without too much trouble. Patterns always recommend cutting and pasting (cutting the pattern and taping for shortening, and lengthening by cutting and adding extra tissue) or laboriously folding. But there is an easier, faster way, which both Mother Pletsch and Nancy Zieman espouse: the slide and pivot method, where you keep your pattern intact in most cases, moving it on the fabric before cutting. Check out their books and tapes for complete top-to-bottom fit guides, but here are some basics to get you started on the road to fit recovery with the slide and pivot method:

➤ Sliding is moving the pattern up or down, or to each side. It simply adds or subtracts an equal amount from each piece of the garment. Pivoting is a different technique where you need to add or subtract from one specific area, such as a waistline.

➤ Rather than cutting the pattern when lengthening or shortening, try sliding. For example, you may need to lengthen an A-line skirt, and want to maintain the original line instead of just adding length. Place the pattern on the fabric. Mark the pattern all the way around until you reach the point where the pattern suggests lengthening or shortening. Slide the pattern down the appropriate amount and mark. Often, when you do this, the old and new lines do not match exactly. Simply connect the old and new lines.

➤ You can also slide when adding width. If you have a skirt in which you need to add four inches to the total hip measurement, slide two inches to each side if there are two skirt panels and one inch if there are four panels. Measure and mark on your fabric all around.

➤ If there are darts in the garment, make sure to maintain their original placement. Mark them first before sliding the pattern. Remember, darts are placed a fixed distance from center front, not from the sides, so use that as your guide.

➤ If you've widened your skirt and find that the waist is too large, you can take in on the seams starting a few inches down, gradually curving inward, or you can deepen the darts. But this kind of alteration is best left for later, when you're fitting as you sew.

➤ To slide to change the length, just move up or down the right amount. You can do this on your sleeves and waistlines as well.

➤ Pivoting is best when you need to add or subtract from one part of a garment, but not the other. For example, if you need to add 4 inches to the waistline of a skirt, and retain the rest of the shape, place the skirt pattern on the fabric. Mark the skirt all the way around up to the hipline. Pin on the hipline. Pivot out so that the waistline is 2 inches wider.

Sew Far, Sew Good

The pivot technique can be used on all your garments, from the armhole, to the bodice waist, to the sides of jackets and shirts. As long as you retain the integrity of the shape of the pattern (for example, the curve of the armhole), you should be in good shape.

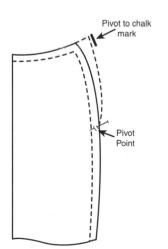

Pivoting to alter the top of a skirt.

Pivot to chalk mark

Pivot Point

Bull's-Eye: Taking Aim at Darts

One of those details that often needs some manipulation is bust darts. Darts need to be aimed straight at the apex, or the widest point of the bust, but stop just about one-half to one inch shy of that point. The problem is that they're aimed all over the place, need to be deepened or shortened, or even worse, don't exist at all. The easiest thing to do is move a dart: Raise it, lower it, shorten it, or lengthen it, as shown in the following figure.

Dart manipulations: lengthening and shortening.

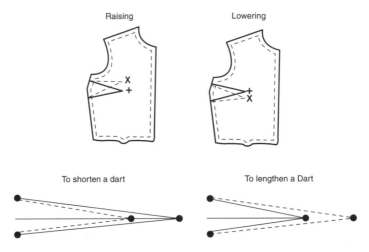

Raising   Lowering

To shorten a dart   To lengthen a Dart

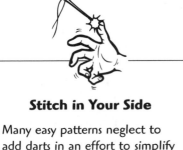

Stitch in Your Side

Many easy patterns neglect to add darts in an effort to simplify and cut down on steps. If you know you need darts, add them. I always add darts; my C cup runneth over in a no-dart dress. Who wants those telltale pulls over a big bust?)

Many garments will fit and look much better if you add a dart. Following are some easy steps for creating a dart on your pattern. (For more information on creating darts, refer to *Mother Pletsch's Painless Sewing: With Pretty Pati's Perfect Pattern Primer and Ample Annie's Awful but Adequate Artwork,* by Pati Palmer and Susan Pletsch [Palmer Pletsch, 1996]) The easiest dart to add is a bust dart, which often starts about 1 inch down from the armscye (armhole). First, you'll need to mark, cut, and then transfer the pattern to large brown paper, tissue paper, or special pattern paper. Then, follow these steps:

1. Mark on your pattern where you want the dart to start.

2. Mark the apex on the pattern.

3. Draw a line from the start of the bust start to the apex. Next, draw a line straight down from the apex to the bottom of the garment. Make sure it's at a right angle.

4. Get out your scissors and, with a steady hand, slash the line from the bottom of the garment, up through the apex, and through the line going to the armhole. Stop just shy of cutting through it entirely, leaving about $1/4$ inch attached so that you can pivot the pattern.

5. Cut through the bust start, stopping $1^1/2$ inches short of the apex.

6. It's now time to transfer your cut pattern to the new pattern paper. Lay out the cut pattern, spreading out the bust start. Because the bust start takes up more fabric, you need to provide for it by spreading out the line you slashed from the bottom through the apex and armhole.

7. The larger the cup size, the larger the dart. The amount of spacing you create should correspond to your cup size. Move the pattern about $1/4$ inch wider per cup size, starting at $1/4$ inch for a B cup and moving up.

Fit As You Sew

No matter how many measurements, alterations, and precautions you take, nothing beats putting that baby on while you're working and tailoring it exactly to your body. Just like you would drape a mannequin, you can shape each piece to fit your own body. It's a little harder to shape a garment to your own body than to a model, but there's no limit to how many times you can try on, retool, and try again.

➤ Start with your tissue pattern. After you've pressed and altered it, pin it in place along seam allowances and try it on. For the top, fit the shoulder and then add the sleeve. See if it sits right; if not, make the necessary adjustments.

➤ Cut the fabric. Pin in place with the wrong sides together.

➤ Make new markings and adjustments right on the fabric while it's on your body, using an air- or water-soluble marker.

Sew Far, Sew Good

Tissue doesn't lie. Although it may not drape as well as fantastic faille, it still shows the flaws, so take some time to try it on. See how you look swathed in tissue.

Noteworthy Notions

Squint a bit when you're looking in your full-length mirror when your jacket and skirt are pinned, wrong side out. Remember, you're looking for fit rather than finish. Wear your best shoes, a pair of hose (if it's a dress), and try to dress it up right so that you see it in its best light. This way you won't get discouraged by all the pins! We're talking creative visualization here!

➤ Be on the lookout for an even hang. The garment should hang straight, not pull up in one place or the other. If there's a dip in your hip, it means it's too low, so you'll need to adjust the hipline.

➤ After pinning in place and marking, always baste at the longest stitch length and then try the garment on again, this time trying on right side out. I always use this method for pants or skirts, never altering until I've got them on me, when I can taper to my heart's delight.

➤ Check closings carefully. Buttons, zippers, snaps all need to be in their proper place for a garment to hug your figure rather than flop around. Gaposis is never allowed, and can be easily corrected at this stage.

Stitch in Your Side

The fabric lines are a dead give-away of fit problems. Up-and-down lines mean clothing is too loose. Sideways lines (especially across hips or bust) mean too tight. Time to alter.

➤ Never, ever cut seam allowances and fabric when altering until you're sure that you've got the right fit.

➤ Do all your fitting and altering before adding the final touches that are difficult to alter—waistbands, facings, collars, and cuffs are best left to the later stages.

➤ Check all your lines—vertical lines, center lines, and hemlines all need to fall into place. An askew apex or off kilter hem is an indication that the garment needs alteration. Take apart and re-pin or baste in place and try again. For extra insurance, mark the grainlines on the garment with chalk or a marker. Do they point at the ceiling and floor?

➤ Check the neckline. If it's too loose, you can take it in at the shoulder seam or center back. If you're altering before adding the facing, make sure you account for the seam allowance, which will tighten the neckline. If it's too tight, add an even amount throughout the neckline.

The phrase "one step at a time" is tailor made for fitting. Fitting doesn't start when you've pieced together your garment; it begins with your buff body and your friendly tape measure. Take time to learn about your body and take down the stats. Then you can proceed to the pattern stage; your tissue facts need to be determined when the pattern is flat. Alter the pattern before you start cutting fabric. Any final alterations can be made as you sew. As long as you follow these tailoring truisms, you'll be able to create flawless fit. What better finale to any sewing project?

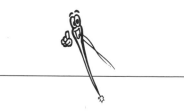

Sew Far, Sew Good

There are many times when I've made a dress or top, only to find that the armhole or neckline droops, making my great garment look home sewn. The quick fix for this problem is clear elastic tape. Simply sewing the $1/4$-inch tape into the seam allowance of the droopy part adds snap and shape. Try it.

The Least You Need to Know

➤ Before you even pick up a pattern, grab your tape measure and make a measurement chart. Record all your figure's key areas, keeping them up to date.

➤ Before you cut out the fabric, alter the tissue pattern pieces so that they conform more closely to your contours. Match the key measurements with sliding, pivoting, or even cutting and pasting. It will be too late for any major changes after you cut the fabric.

➤ Before you start sewing, try on the tissue pieces that have been pinned into place, and then try on the fabric pieces that have been basted.

➤ Before your final stitching, give your lines a good look: Grainlines, sleeve lines, hemlines, necklines, and darts all need to be pointing in the right direction.

Part 5

Home Sewn: Home Accents and Gifts

The true beauty of working with fabric in your home and learning how to throw together a set of throw pillows is that you can create exactly the world you want to inhabit. A well-placed pillow, a swag of silk, a sheath of charmeuse, and a set of stunning Roman shades can make the difference between a hum-drum home and one with warmth, style, and panache. Since you've already covered the basics of plain old hemming and straight stitching, curtain creations are simply a matter of mastering measuring and hanging.

From curtains we'll spread out to the rest of the room, covering tables, cushioning seats, and creating designer bed dressing. Do-it-yourself decorating with fabric is the simplest and most cost-effective of sewing tasks, putting your personal stamp on your most personal place—your home.

And while you're busy putting the personal touch on your home, why not extend it to gift-giving? Nothing says you care more than a home-sewn, completely personalized gift. Sure, anyone can go out and spend a bundle on a crystal decanter, but an invest-ment of time, energy, and creativity will mean so much more. I'll give you some gift suggestions that will be much more than a token of your esteem for your friends and family.

Chapter 17

How Much Is That Dressing in the Window: Curtains and Shades

In This Chapter

➤ Widen your window style horizons

➤ Measure up curtain fabric

➤ Cook up some café curtains

➤ Hold your heading tape high

➤ Batten down Roman shades

Some of my earliest sewing forays were into window dressing. As a New Yorker, I'm surrounded by the Manhattan skyline—stunning views of high-rises and skyscrapers. While I love seeing out, I certainly don't want anyone to see in.

I've watched *Rear Window* a few too many times, so curtains are a necessity. I made a simple set for my first out-of-college apartment—just plain old fashioned cotton panels hanging from a fabric casing—and have graduated to a fantastic set of lined, wraparound vintage cotton curtains with a triple-pleat gather. They really set the tone for my whole bedroom, and so should your window treatments.

This is the true beauty of working with fabric while decorating your home. A well-placed pillow, a swag of silk, a room-dividing sheath of charmeuse, and, of course, a set of stunning curtains can make the difference between a hum-drum home and one that has warmth, style, and panache.

One Step at a Time: Getting Started

All of this can come to you at a minimal cost, both of time and money. I figured this out when I went to Manhattan's Lower East Side, famous for its fabric bargains and low-cost custom-made curtains. After finding a not-so-bargain-basement fabric that I thought I could live with, the estimates for making curtains for my bay window actually ran into the thousands of dollars!

This is when and where I took control; since I'd already covered the basics of plain old hemming and straight stitching, curtain creations were simply a matter of mastering measuring and hanging. We're going to learn the easy way to window dressing, starting with choosing the right look, measuring for fit, and hanging techniques. Before you actually buy the fabric, you need to measure properly. This is a three-step process: decide on the position of the curtain; decide on the hanging method (tracks or poles); decide whether there will be a heading tape. Then, and only then, can you determine the fabric amount. After calculating fabric amounts, we'll glide through some of the most versatile, simple, and elegant window treatments, from breezy sheer sheaths to the Roman shade.

Noteworthy Notions

In the market for some fabric accents for your home? Shop regularly with no particular goal in mind. Pop into fabric stores, scout the sales, clip announcements of vintage auctions. You never know when the fabric that's the perfect companion to your unique nubby knit couch will show up. Just like good flea-marketers, fabric-foragers need to show some resourceful research and just plain scavenger hunting.

Homespun Fabric Choices

What kind of fabric you choose to decorate your windows is just as important as the style of window decoration. Flip through some decorating magazines and you'll see how a pair of heavy velvet curtains add weight, gravity, and richness to a room; a gauzy, free-flowing sheath can connote an airy, light, fantasy world; a tailored crisp cotton duck can mean clean lines and clarity; a heavy raw silk swag in a rich burgundy can carry you away to the Far East.

What kind of fantasy world do you want to create? Because that's exactly what fabric can do; it sets a mood, expresses itself, and makes a statement about how and where you live. Here are some important cues that will help guide your choice:

➤ *Weight.* The weight of the fabric should complement your home furnishings. If you have a house full of playful and colorful Ikea stuff, choose accordingly. If you favor Biedermeier and bulky antiques, your fabric needs to be made of sterner stuff. My apartment has streamlined 1950's furniture, so I chose a vintage cotton with a subtle print for my curtains.

➤ *Fabric color/print.* A splashy print can make a statement; a subdued solid hue can accent the furnishings rather than the window. Where's the focal point and where do you want your eye to be drawn? You can decide if you want the color of the curtains to either match, complement, or contrast with the walls and furnishings. Put together a set of paint chips and fabric swatches from your room, tuck them in your backpack, and you'll always be ready to mix or match possible fabric choices.

➤ *Light.* How much light do you want to let into your life? Light worshippers need to keep the coverage to a minimum, relying on lightweight sheers—cotton, linen, batiste, voile, organdy, and so on. If the song "Here Comes the Sun" makes you cringe, you want heavier, darker fabrics.

> **Sew Far, Sew Good**
>
> If you're making window dressing decisions, buy a bunch of home decorating magazines. Clip anything that you think is interesting, eye-catching, appealing. Pretend your window treatment is as important as your haircut (it is!); didn't you ever show your hairdresser a style you like and say "I want that!" (and if you did with a Dorothy Hammill bob or a Jennifer Aniston shag, you know exactly what I'm talking about). Do the same for your home.

Noteworthy Notions

I love light, but not when I'm sleeping. Even if I'm catching 40 winks in the middle of the day, total darkness is required for some real shut-eye. This is easy to accomplish with some black-out lining, which is what is used on hotel room curtains. It's cheap (about $4 a yard), hangs well, protects your curtain fabric from dirt, and certainly keeps light from creeping into any bedroom. Buy it at any drapery store.

Stitch in Your Side

Remember those loud plaid pants that your Uncle Al wore? The ones that gave you a headache? Remember them when using a print on your windows. If you're using a large repeating pattern, is the window large enough to display the entire repeat (repeatedly!)? Is the print so loud it shouts down everything else in the room, including you and your Pucci print dress? Prints should go with your décor, not compete with it.

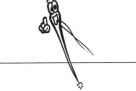

Sew Far, Sew Good

You accentuate the positive and eliminate the negative when you dress your body; your windows should be clothed as carefully. If your window is over a hideous old radiator that no longer works, cover it with long, lustrous curtains. If your view is a water tower atop an all-night garage with a flashing red neon sign, by all means, use drapes to create an all-new view.

➤ *Window size and shape.* Got a tiny window? Hang the curtain outside of its border to make it look bigger. A shortie? Hang the curtains to the floor to lengthen the look. Wrap-around or bay windows need no size enhancement, so curtains can fit inside. Size is often an illusion; think about how tall Tom Cruise really is.

➤ *Use.* Are you the type who likes to get up in the morning and fling the curtains wide open? Or do you like stationary embellishments, elegantly draped swags that only serve a decorative purpose? Or, since you occasionally vacuum while wearing your favorite teddy, do you favor shades that go up or down with a quick pull? Decide what your needs are, and the curtain design will fall into place.

➤ *Practicality.* If the exhaust of your local Chinese restaurant is aimed straight at your window, your curtains will be covered with chop suey slime and fried dumpling detritus—use washable fabrics only. Does the window face a cold front coming off of Lake Michigan? Use heavy, warm fabrics to keep the warmth in and the cold air out.

Hangin' in There: Poles and Tracks

After hunting and hoping and trying and tossing out the rejects, you've finally found the perfect fabric for your windows. Now comes more drape decisions: what to hang your curtains on. The possibilities are endless, and you can let your creativity run rampant, but there are two traditional choices: poles and tracks.

➤ Poles are ideal for curtains that won't move much—café curtains, swags, tunnel pocket curtains—all of which are meant to stay put or just be pulled back with a tie. Poles have become pretty sophisticated affairs over the years, a decorative element in their own right. A warm wood, a steely chrome, a sleek copper with fancy fillips— all make a room with a specific view, so decide on the right role for your pole.

➤ Tracks, on the other hand, are for quick-gliding drapes, slippin' and slidin' along, easy openin' and closin'. There are many varieties of tracks—invisible, visible, cording and overlap, double valance—so scope out your local home decorator depot for the look you want and follow the kit instructions. Tracks are often cut to order, so it's important to measure the curtain space properly.

Before deciding on the kind of track or pole you use, ask yourself these three key questions:

1. Where will the poles be attached: inside the window sill; outside the window; around a curved corner; on the ceiling?

2. Will they support the weight of the curtains?

3. Are they visible? If so, make sure the look of the pole or track matches your room or it is covered.

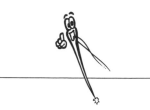

Sew Far, Sew Good

Decorators usually show fabrics in books filled with miniscule swatches. How could anyone make an educated choice with so little to go on? Instead, go the extra yard—buy a yard of fabric and live with it for awhile. Hang it up. Look at it in different lights. Pretend it's surrounded by people at a party. Does it live up to your lifestyle?

Noteworthy Notions

If you want to keep your curtains on track, buy quality tracks. Most are made from lightweight plastic, so be sure they can support the weight of the curtains. Also check that the gliders or runners move with the greatest of ease so that your curtains don't get all hung up.

Hang 'Em High: Pole Placement

Pole and track placement is determined by the construction of the window and the look that you want the curtains to achieve. When you assess your curtain situation, take a good hard look at the windows and where they are. The most common pole placement is on the wall above the window. Is there space for the pole? Can the pole be attached or does the wall's construction make it difficult? If you get the thumb's up for this placement, you need to decide on the length of the pole. It has to extend far enough past the window for the curtains to fall neatly to the side. For sheers and lightweight curtains, you need a side clearance of at least 6 to 10 inches. Heavier and fuller fabrics need upwards of 10 inches.

You can also attach the poles or tracks to the ceiling above the window. This is especially useful if the top of the window is very close to the ceiling. Make sure to buy poles that attach on the top rather than the sides for this placement.

If you have a recessed window, you can attach the pole to the window casing, the top of the window, or with a wooden batten.

Another option is a pole or a track with overlap arms and what is called "returns" on the side. This track gives the curtains room to blow in the breeze, extending out from the window with ease.

Stitch in Your Side

Always look before you sew! Check and see where the hook holes are, and make sure they're facing out. Sewing the tape on to the wrong side is a real gathering gaffe.

Sew Far, Sew Good

Make sure you position the tape correctly; if you have two curtains that meet, make sure the pleats start an equal amount into each curtain so they're evenly spaced.

Ahead of the Game: Curtain Headings

If you've got a head on your shoulders (and what sewer doesn't?), you'll want to get a handle on heading tapes, a quick and easy way to tailor your curtains with pleats and gathers.

Heading tapes are ready-made strips of stiff fabric that you attach along the top border of curtains. They either have drawstrings to form even gathering or pockets for hooks that create different pleats (such as triple pleats or box pleats) without any complicated stitching on your part.

They're a total pleasure to use, and can create a complex and tailored look by simply stitching into place; the pleats or gathers form automatically with either a quick pull of the drawstring or the addition of hooks to the headers. Since the fabric doesn't lie in a flat sheet, you will have to calculate the amount of extra fullness needed to create the folds. Following are the most common gathering tapes and the fabric fullness required.

Groovy Gathers: Standard Gathering Tape

Standard gathering tape is a relatively thin (usually 1 to 2 inches) tape that creates even, soft gathers. You will need $1^1/_2$ to 2 times the track length of fabric fullness.

Noteworthy Notions

If you're attaching heading tape to slightly flimsy fabric, add some stiffness with a strip of interfacing. Your heading will stand at attention, doing away with droop.

Three Times As Nice: Triple-Pleat Tape

When you want to pull out all the stops and create formal, tailored curtains, nothing beats a triple-pleat tape. It's a deep, stiff tape with slots at the bottom for triple-pronged hooks that slip into the pockets, gathering the curtains into perfectly-placed pleats with spacing in-between. The fabric fullness required is two times the track length.

Picture-Perfect Pleats: Pencil-Pleat Tape

This tape creates thin, even pleats that are gathered together with cording. The fabric fullness required is $2^1/_4$ to $2^1/_2$ times the track length.

Drop-Dead Gorgeous: Measuring the Drop

You've figured out the hard stuff—hanging, headings, and even fabric—now comes time for the hard math. Before cutting the fabric, get out your tape measure instead of your calculator. You need to measure up by first figuring the *drop*. This is the length of the finished curtain from where it will hang (whether on a pole or track) to the bottom. The length of the curtains, or the drop depends on the window style. Follow these guidelines:

➤ *Sill length.* Drapes should end $^5/_8$ inch to 1 inch above a sill for clearance.

➤ *Below-the-sill.* Usually ends 2 to 4 inches below the window itself, depending on what's underneath the sill and the look you want.

Sew You Were Saying ...

The **drop** is the measurement of the finished curtains from where they will hang to their length.

Sill-length curtains.

5/8-1"
clearance

Below-the-sill curtains.

2"-4"
overhang

➤ *Recessed curtains.* Recessed curtains are used with a recessed window—that is, a window that's set into the wall rather than flush with the wall. Since the window has its own set-in area, the curtains need to fit inside as well. Give a $^5/_8$-inch to 1-inch clearance.

Recessed curtains.

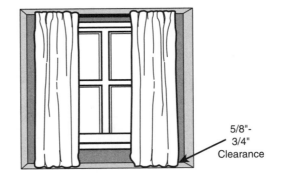

5/8"-
3/4"
Clearance

➤ *Floor length.* For the curtains to hang flat, leave a 1-inch floor clearance.

Floor-length curtains.

1"
Clearance

Noteworthy Notions

Going for the glam look, or a bit of drama? Instead of ending your floor-length curtains right below the floor, let them pool in a plush "puddle." Add anywhere from 2 to 10 inches to your drop length for a classic puddle. I personally love that word so much I want almost all my curtains to puddle, but I guess that's not practical.

Full-Blown Fabric Measuring

Curtains strike fear into the hardiest sewing hearts because of the amount of fabric involved. What if a miscalculation in width costs you not only an arm and a leg, but many feet of fabric?

Expensive mistakes can be avoided with some handy calculating rules. They may look complicated, but once you dig in and start doing the math, you'll be whipping up café curtains in your spare time. Just remember this hard and fast rule: Measure for fabric only after you've decided on the fabric, attached the poles or tracks, and figured out the style of curtain, including the heading. Then, and only then, are you ready to whip out your tape measure.

Figuring Fabric Length

1. Measure the drop from where the curtain hangs to the finished length.

2. Decide on the casing/heading. Determine the top hem. For most curtains, a 3-inch top hem will suffice.

3. Determine the bottom hem. This amount is usually 3 to 6 inches.

4. Add up the total *length* of fabric needed.

Figuring Fabric Width

1. Determine the finished width. Measure the rod only where the curtain will hang (not any additional decorative elements). Be sure to measure the returns if you have them.

2. Multiply the width by the fullness amount.

3. Add the side hems. A standard hem, which you may alter, is a double-turned 1-inch hem, or 4 inches total for one panel. This is the total *width*.

Figuring Fabric Yardage

1. Divide the total *width* of the finished fabric by the width of your fabric (be it 54", 60", etc.). This amount is the number of fabric widths that you need.

2. Multiply this number by the fabric *length* from above.

3. Divide this number by 36". This is the total number of yards needed to complete your curtains.

Sew Far, Sew Good

Now that sewing has inched its way into your life, your plastic tape measure always seems to be on hand. But for curtain measuring, only your steel or wooden tape measure will do for long-distance accuracy.

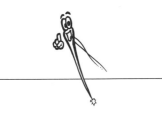

Sew Far, Sew Good

It may seem like a money-waster, but always add more when estimating curtain fabric. No one likes to be left with the shades up, exposing one's lack of fabric savvy, by buying too little. That's the real waste of money.

Sheer Magic

There's nothing better than a beautiful sheer curtain blowing in the wind, letting light in while adding an aura of decorative flair. Sheer curtains look best hanging on a rod with a simple casing rather than a fancy or complicated construction. And the real beauty is the bucks you'll save; these will cost a fraction of cookie-cutter curtains and come in just the color and size you want. Here's how to calculate the fabric measurements:

➤ *Bottom hem:* A double-turned 1-inch hem (2 inches total).

➤ *Side hems:* A double-turned $1/2$ hem on each side for each panel (1 inch total per panel).

➤ *Top hem and casing:* Measure the rod width by wrapping a ribbon around the rod; mark and measure. Add three inches ($1/2$ inch for the hem turn and $2^1/2$ inches for some give) to the rod width for the total top hem.

➤ *Panels:* If you need to sew panels of fabric together, this is where your beautifully bound French seam comes in handy. Add $5/8$ inch for each side of a panel you plan on using.

➤ *Fabric fullness:* Multiply the rod length by 2 to $2^1/2$ times to achieve a full rather than flimsy look for sheer curtains.

Length: Add the drop length plus the rod width plus 3" plus 2".

drop length: ___ + casing width: ___ + top hem (3") ____ + bottom hem (2") = ___

Width: Rod length multiplied two to two and a half times, plus hems of one inch for each side, plus $5/8$ inch for each panel side that will be sewn together.

rod length: __ × 2 (or $2^1/2$) + hems (2" + $5/8$" for each panel side that will be sewn together): _____

Now that you have your fabric measured, it's curtains time! Follow these simple steps for sewing sheer curtains.

1. Sew together each panel that you need to connect. Use French seams with a $5/8$-inch seam allowance.

2. Double-turn a $1/2$-inch hem on each side.

3. Double-turn 1 inch for the bottom hem.

4. Make the casing. Turn under $1/2$ inch, press, and stitch into place. Turn over the rod width plus $2^1/2$ inches and stitch into place.

5. Press. Slip your rod into place, hang those bad boys, and watch them blowing in the wind with great satisfaction.

The Café Way

Unlined is the way to go when you want good looks fast. Imagine you're in an Italian bistro, and the cotton curtains are wafting in and out of the window along with the smell of coffee and biscotti.

They're hung on strips (or loops) of fabric, and their simplicity seduces you. Okay, maybe it's the wine and the gorgeous brunette. Either way, café curtains set the scene, and you can carry them into your kitchen with or without the brunette and biscotti.

Café curtains have very little gather, so they're great when you don't want to spend a lot of money on a lot of fabric.

➤ *Bottom hem:* A double-turned 2-inch hem (4 inches total).

➤ *Side hems:* A double-turned $^1/_2$-inch hem (2 inches total).

➤ *Top hem:* A double-turned 2-inch hem (4 inches total).

➤ *Panels:* An additional $^5/_8$-inch seam for each panel that needs to be joined together. Use a French seam if the fabric is sheer.

➤ *Fabric fullness:* The rod width plus 4 to 10 inches, depending on the fabric and the amount of fullness you would like.

  Width: Rod length plus four inches plus $1^1/_4$ inches plus $^5/_8$ inch for each panel

  Length: Drop length plus eight inches

Here I provide instructions for creating café curtains with fabric loops. These curtains don't require fussy finishings; they're hung on simple loops of fabric. The general rule is that one loop is sewn flush to each end, and then they're spaced evenly about 4 to 6 inches apart.

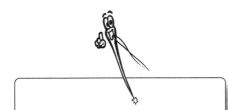

Sew Far, Sew Good

Even if your inner artist hasn't seen the light of day recently, get out a paper and a pencil, and sketch your café curtains. Decide on the loop placement on paper, playing with the measurements ahead of time, rather than wasting time marking and sewing and remarking on the fabric.

1. Follow steps 1 through 4 for making sheer curtains.

2. Cut a strip of fabric 5 inches wide and long enough to make the number of loops you need. Their length is a matter of taste, depending on how low you wanna go. To the finished length of the strips, add 2 inches for stitching on to the curtain. Multiply the loop length times the number of loops and you've got the total length of the strip.

3. Fold the strip in half with the right sides together and edgestitch $^1/_4$ inch along one side.

4. Cut the loop lengths. Stitch across one end at $^5/_8$ inch, trimming to $^1/_4$ inch and grading the corners. Turn inside out and press.

5. Position the strips in place. Put one strip on each end and evenly position the rest of the strips in between, spacing them about 4 to 5 inches apart.

6. Place each loop on the wrong side of the curtain with the unfinished edge about one inch down from the top edge and baste into place. Bring the finished edge over the raw edge and topstitch into place, making a neat square. Keep going until you've completed all the loops.

7. Hang 'em and wallow in your craftiness.

Romancing Roman Shades

While curtains can really draw you in, shades are an easy alternative, adding simple style with less effort and fabric. They're particularly fun and functional in a kitchen or bathroom, or wherever you want clean lines and a quick draw (up and down, that is).

When it's up, light has easy access; when it's down, the view is blocked in a neat way. And all you have to do is pull the cord.

There are a bunch of different shade types, from the simple, flat kind that zip up and down a roller, to balloon shades that have inverted pleats and a puffy look. But the most versatile are Roman shades.

These shades hang flat when closed, and pull up in horizontal folds, drawing up into neat sections when opened. It's best to line them for wash 'n' window-wear ease and a more finished look.

Sew Far, Sew Good

Since shades hang absolutely flat, you need to measure the fabric absolutely accurately. Here's where your grainline lessons come in handy; always locate the grainline and make sure the cutting lines are at perfect right angles.

Noteworthy Notions

If one width of fabric won't do it and you have to use connecting panels, make sure you use an entire panel in the center with the cut panels on the side. But here's the tricky part where you should go that extra distance: Match the lining panel seams to the curtain seams. Why? Light often slips through a seam, and you don't want too many showy lines.

Whereas living room or bedroom curtains are often stately or staid, kitchen shades can really push the style envelope. They're great for fun and funky remnants that add spice and color to a kitchen. The Roman shade in my kitchen is made out of a 1950s linen that's a map of California, hand-painted in glorious yellow, white, and red Technicolor. Who cares if it says that Mt. Whitney is the highest point in the U.S.? It's the attitude, not the accuracy, that counts.

Batten Down the Hatches

Roman shades are attached to the top of the window by a batten, a small plank of wood that stabilizes the curtain, allowing for clearance for smooth shade sailing. The standard batten size is one inch wide by two inches deep by the length of the window. Buy a batten at any lumber or well-stocked hardware store (they will cut it to order), and attach it to the wall or window casing with metal L brackets.

Need to know how long your batten will be? Decide where your shade will be positioned with these two quick tips:

➤ If it'll hang in a recessed window, make it 1 inch shorter than the recess with the batten flush to the top of the recess. This ensures side clearance.

Recessed Roman shade batten.

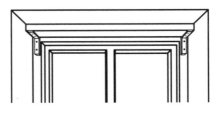

Recessed batten

➤ Got a window that's flush with the wall? The batten should go on the wall above the window, extending 2 inches on each side. This ensures side coverage.

Roman shade batten.

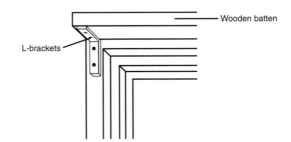

Wooden batten

L-brackets

224

Shady Business: Measuring

Shed some light on your shade measurements with these tips:

➤ Calculate the width by measuring the batten and adding a side hem allowance of 2 inches (1 inch for each side).

➤ Calculate the length by measuring from the top of the batten to the sill. For a recessed shade, subtract one inch for clearance. For an outside-the-window shade, add 4 inches, plus 2 inches for the top and bottom hem (1 inch for each). You now have the length and the width.

➤ Here's where your shade math can get shaky, so pay attention. The lining is longer than the shade fabric. This is because the folds of the shade are formed with rods that are inserted in pockets in the lining that pleat when pulled with a cord.

➤ To calculate the rod pockets, get out your sketch pad and make a panel plan. Draw the finished curtain length. Make a horizontal line four inches up from the bottom. Divide the rest of the curtain into sections of about 12 inches, adjusting for the amount of fabric you have.

➤ For each line you make, you need to create a pocket that the rod will slip into. Add an extra $2^{1}/_{2}$ inches for each rod (this accounts for a rod or dowel of about $^{1}/_{2}$ inch wide, which you can pick up at the hardware store).

➤ Add top and bottom hems of one inch each (a double-turned $^{1}/_{2}$-inch hem).

➤ Add it all up, and get stitching!

If you're feeling out of kilter and askew, drop the Roman shade sewing and wait until you're on track. These shades need absolutely straight lines for the rod casing so that they don't dip and droop; one rotten rod ruins the whole bunch. A shake of the wrists, a head-clearing stretch, with maybe a quick samba around the living room, and you should be ready for steady rolling.

Easy Hardware Rules: How to Hang Your Shade

Set aside your sewing machine and get out your toolkit for this part of the job. Anyone is handy enough to hang a shade without calling in a pro or getting out the power tools. Put these items on your shopping list: Velcro strip, three screw-in hooks and eyes, drapery cording.

1. The easiest way to attach the top of the curtain to the batten is with Velcro tape. Simply cut the tape the same as the length of the batten and stick on both the batten and top of the curtain. If need be, sew the Velcro to the curtain fabric for a secure hold.

225

2. The shades will draw up with a cord that's attached to plastic rings that are sewn onto each pocket. Position the rings two inches from each side and in the center (add additional rows if you have an extra-wide shade). Sew 'em on with heavy-duty thread.

Noteworthy Notions

To conceal a wooden batten, why not add a fabric flourish? Using a staple gun, get a grip on your fabric with the satisfying "kachung" of the gun. Or, for an even easier way, slap on a fresh coat of paint.

3. Screw a hook and eye into the batten directly above each row. Place one additional hook and eye 1 inch from one side of the batten.

4. Get out your curtain cording (this is special cording that's available at drapery stores). Tie one strand to the bottom plastic ring and thread it through each ring, then through the hook and eye, and over to the side hook and eye. Tie another cord to each bottom ring, threading it through the plastic rings and hook and eyes.

5. Cut the cords the same length, making sure they're long enough to wrap around a cleat or a hook when the shade is pulled up and long enough to hang freely when the shade is down.

Roman shade hardware.

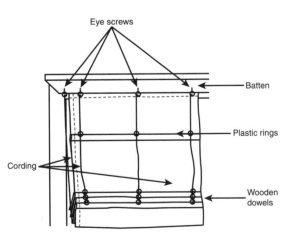

So, you've battened down the Roman shade, conquered easy breezy curtains, and gotten rid of café-curtain gaffes. You've seen the light of creating your own curtains, and your home is now bathed in fabric beauty, all without turning your trust fund over to your decorator.

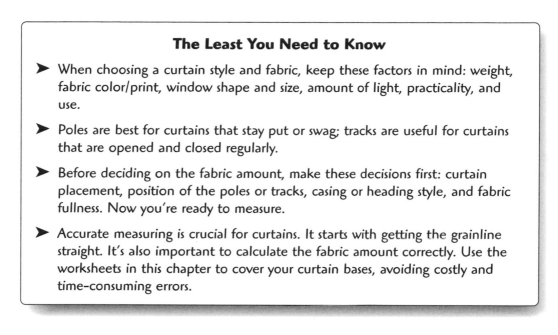

The Least You Need to Know

➤ When choosing a curtain style and fabric, keep these factors in mind: weight, fabric color/print, window shape and size, amount of light, practicality, and use.

➤ Poles are best for curtains that stay put or swag; tracks are useful for curtains that are opened and closed regularly.

➤ Before deciding on the fabric amount, make these decisions first: curtain placement, position of the poles or tracks, casing or heading style, and fabric fullness. Now you're ready to measure.

➤ Accurate measuring is crucial for curtains. It starts with getting the grainline straight. It's also important to calculate the fabric amount correctly. Use the worksheets in this chapter to cover your curtain bases, avoiding costly and time-consuming errors.

Chapter 18

The Well-Dressed Home: Pillows and More

> ### In This Chapter
>
> ➤ Pillow talk: the European sham
>
> ➤ Divine duvet covers
>
> ➤ The well-dressed table: tablecloths and linens
>
> ➤ It's raining shower curtains

Your home is your castle. But that medieval, spare, unembellished look is outré: The bare wooden benches, the monk's bed cot, and the Spartan table all need a little sprucing up.

This is where fabric enters the picture. A striking duvet cover, a couple of overstuffed pillows with a glam European sham, or a crisp linen tablecloth with matching napkins can turn the barest of homes into a plush and princely place, full of comfort. It's amazing the way a splash of fabric can transform any room, inviting you to sink into a cushioned seat, lie back against a pillow, and take a load off.

And all this can be accomplished without a load of trouble. Home decorating details are costly additions when you have to go out and lay down the cash for them. Just taking a stroll around a department store and doing a quick inventory of some new home additions will confirm your worst monetary fears—fancy-schmancy pillows can easily cost $50 and up, with tasseled and tied beauties running into the hundreds. Ditto for linens and bedclothes. Not so when they're home sewn!

Do-it-yourself decorating with fabric is the simplest of all sewing tasks; you already have all the skills you need. With a few cut-and-dry measuring, cutting, and stitching shortcuts, you'll be throwing together throw pillows in no time, putting your personal stamp on your most personal place—your home.

Pillow Talk

My brother once asked me, "What is it about chicks and pillows?" Well, we love 'em. And so do many of the male persuasion, mostly because they add color, richness, and a plush look with so little effort.

With the addition of a few nice pillows, a couch can go from drab to dramatic; side chairs can change from staid to stately; and a bedroom can become a full-fledged boudoir. Pillows use small amounts of fabric, and are the ideal use for remnants, flea-market finds, and leftover pieces from your major sewing projects.

If you can't afford a raw-silk bed cover, you can certainly cover your simple bed with silk throw pillows, creating the illusion of luxury—without the cost.

Noteworthy Notions

Pillow forms come in all sizes and materials, from the least costly foam variety to down-filled softies. The price variable is dramatic, so do some comparison shopping before investing in costly forms. Check out your local department stores, the foam and futon listings in the Yellow Pages, and designer outlets. A little know-how never hurts ....

When you're looking around for pillow forms, you'll come across loose polyester fiberfill stuffing that's sold in bulk. Avoid it. It may seem like a cheap alternative, but no matter how you stuff a pillow with it, it never seems to hold the right shape, and turns out to be a lumpy mashed-potato pillow rather than a taut, neatly encased looker. Unfortunately, this is one time that you get what you pay for. Here's the low-down on pillow stuffings, from goose down right on down the price line:

➤ *Down:* The most luxurious pillow stuffing, down, is made of cleaned, de-quilled goose or duck feathers. It's available loose from specialty stores or in premade plain pillows of varying sizes.

➤ *Polyurethane foam:* You can find foam in sheets of $^1/_2$ inch to 5 inches in precut sizes or cut from bulk pieces. The quality and density of foam varies—try to buy the most dense that you can find (this is one of the few times that dense is a good thing!). Bear in mind that foam has hard, sharp corners and edges so the shape has to suit the use. For example, foam is great for seat cushions, not as great for bedding pillows.

➤ *Polyester forms:* The best all-purpose pillow bet. You can find polyester forms in all shapes and sizes.

➤ *Polyester fiberfill:* Loose polyester stuffing that's wadded into a pillow form. As I said, steer clear of this if you want a pillow that retains its shape after repeated pillow fights.

European Sham Glamour

A simple pillow is a welcome addition to any home, but a European sham—a pillow with a fabric border—really makes a statement and calls attention to itself. With a little extra effort, you'll have a real decorator's touch.

1. Cut the fabric with the following measurements:

   Pillow front: The length is the pillow length plus 5 inches; the width is pillow width plus 5 inches.

   Pillow back: The length is the pillow length plus 10 inches; the width is the pillow width plus 5 inches.

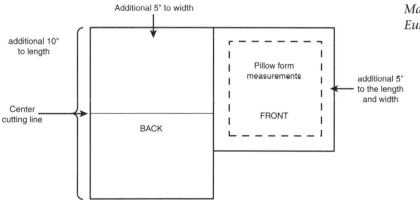

Marking and creating a European sham.

2. Fold the pillow back piece in half lengthwise and cut across the foldline. These two pieces will create the back opening and overlap.

3. Double-turn a $^1/_2$-inch hem on the edges of the overlap. Press and edgestitch.

Noteworthy Notions

You can take the instructions for creating a European sham down a notch and make a simple pillow cover. Just subtract the 2-inch border and the $^1/_2$-inch seam allowance all around and stitch a plain pillow cover. Stitch all the seams, right side to right side, leaving 3 inches on one side open. Turn, insert the pillow form, and slipstitch the opening.

Sew Far, Sew Good

Is your fabric a little floppy? Will the edges of your sham droop? Fix this problem by adding some interfacing to the edging so that it stands at attention.

4. Align the front piece and the two back pieces, right side to right side. Pin in place.

5. Stitch a $^1/_2$-inch seam around the entire pillow. Trim the seam allowance and corners. Turn right side out.

6. Mark a 2-inch border around the pillow with chalk or a marker. Topstitch. Stuff it—the pillow, that is.

Making a simple overlap on the back of the pillow is the easiest way to create an opening. If you want a finished look, nothing beats buttons. I love to add vintage buttons to my pillows for that one-of-a-kind look.

Because the pillow instructions give you enough room for buttonholes on your overlap, simply mark and create the buttonholes before sewing the front and back pillow pieces together—the buttons come last. Usually, two will suffice, but you might need three for an extra-big pillow. Be sure to position them evenly along the back opening.

Another closure that can be completed with ease is Velcro tape, which is inserted in the back openings. Simply position the tape on the edge of each back opening, stitching around the tape to secure it in place.

When measuring your pillow, don't pull too tight, or you'll be sorry later when you have to huff and puff to stuff your pillow into the case.

Pillows can complement your fabric decor or add a contrasting color and look, depending on the effect you want. For example, the oversized European pillows that anchor my bed are the reverse side of my curtains, with seafoam green dominating the curtains and the reverse, white, ruling the pillows. You want just enough variety for depth, and just enough unity to tie it all together.

Making the Case for Pillowcases

Let's face it: Most pillowcases are pretty drab affairs, cotton-poly blends without much goin' on. And the really nice ones—all-cotton, sateen, or linen—are pretty pricey. So, you'll want to seek out great medi-umweight cottons that feel nice against your skin; ditto for silks or linen.

Pillowcases are a breeze because they can be made out of one piece of fabric that's simply folded and stitched. Here's how to do it:

1. Cut the fabric with the following measurements: The width is the width of the pillow plus $1^1/_4$ inches; the length is twice the length of the pillow plus 9 inches.

2. Hem the edge of the pillow opening by double-turning $^1/_2$ inch and edgestitching.

3. Turn each edge 3 inches. Topstitch into place.

4. Fold the fabric in half lengthwise. Sew French seams on each side (not the pillow opening, obviously). Turn the pillowcase right side out, place a downy white pillow in it, and sigh with satisfaction.

Stitch in Your Side

Keep your head when choosing pillowcase fabric! A creamy silk may be sexy, but does it need to be dry-cleaned? Think how often you'll be marching back and forth to your local cleaners. Or that elegant linen—do you really want to iron your pillowcases? That's a requirement for a heavy linen. Closely-woven cottons are always a good bet for a good night's sleep.

Noteworthy Notions

This is where your flea-market savvy really pays off …. Old linens that are still in good shape can be cut down to create beautiful pillowcases—nothing beats the weight and feel of vintage linens, especially if they're worn in without being worn, threadbare, or yellowed.

The Well-Made Bed

If you've ever flipped through home decorating magazines (and who hasn't?), what really stands out are the well-made beds, beds that people drool over and dream about. But it usually isn't the actual beds (meaning the frame) that arouses the bed envy. It's the bed dressing—the fluffy duvets, the overstuffed pillows, and the perfectly turned sheets.

If you're like me, you might own a menial bed: Mine's a platform made out of not-so-nice pine. But who would ever know? The 1940s dupioni silk duvet and the flood of pillows would cover even a cot in luxe finery. It makes you want to jump right in, which is exactly what a bed should say to you.

How to Do an A-OK Duvet

The fastest and easiest way to dress up a bed is with a duvet cover. Even more than a bedspread, a duvet is a luxurious blanket, which you can blanket in a luxe fabric to add allure and attitude. Furthermore, a duvet covers a multitude of sins, including an unmade bed; just toss a duvet over a bed with a quick snap of the wrist, and you're set. No tucking, no Army corners—what could be simpler?

A duvet cover is essentially a big rectangular bag that I like to fasten together with buttons, snaps, or Velcro. And even though you're working with a lot of fabric, the sewing is relatively simple.

1. Cut the fabric according to the following measurements: The width is the width of the duvet plus $1^1/_4$ inches; the length is the length of the duvet plus $3^1/_8$ inches. You will need to cut two matching panels.

2. Make the top hem and border first. Turn the top edge over $^1/_2$ inch, and press. Create a double-turned 1-inch border. Topstitch into place. Sew the same on the other top edge.

3. Align the two pieces. Sew a French seam on the bottom and sides of the duvet using a $^5/_8$-inch seam allowance.

4. Edgestitch 12 inches from each side of the top of the duvet cover. The center opening is where you'll insert the duvet. You can go wild with whatever closure you desire. If you use buttons, place them at regular intervals in the opening, sewing the buttonholes first and then stitching on the buttons. Snap tale or Velcro also works well, especially with kids' covers that need more frequent trips to the laundry room. Better pick a closure that rips or snaps in a sec.

Noteworthy Notions

Although I'm partial to a clean look and favor buttons or Velcro as a duvet fastener, a lot of people prefer ties. If you like this fancy fastener, just cut strips of fabric that are about 6 inches by 3 inches. Fold the strips in half lengthwise, and stitch across the top and down one side with a $1/2$-inch seam allowance, leaving one end unstitched. Trim, and turn inside out. Turn the cover inside out, turn the edges, and topstitch. Stitch about 1 inch into the duvet cover in a rectangular fashion, positioning one tie on each end and spacing them about 4 inches apart. That's the way to tie one on with style!

The Well-Dressed Table

Wouldn't it be nice if dining room tables were disposable? It's my fantasy that, after a dinner party (especially one where your three nephews and their best friends have a food fight on your teak masterpiece), a new table shows up on your front doorstep. But life doesn't work that way. This is why we have tablecloths.

Besides protecting your favorite table, tablecloths add style and a stately presence to your parties, tying together your decor with a small detail. Choose the fabric carefully—if you live with a couple of messy kids, you may want to use stain-resistant, permanent press fabric for easy care. Stay away from loud prints that need to be matched. Remember—home sewing is supposed to simplify your life.

Before you decide on the fabric amount, you need to decide how low you want to go. Or, put another way, how close to the floor you'd like the tablecloth to reach. You calculate this by determining the amount of the "drop." The drop is the length from the edge of the table to the floor. Take into account a couple of factors when determining drop: the overall proportions of the table and room; how much leg room you'd like to give your guests; the look of the table; if you have anything to hide (an unsightly card table, for example); and the cost of the fabric. Decide on your drop before dropping a bundle on pricey fabric!

The Angle on Rectangular Tablecloths

Faced with a rectangular shape to cover? Have no fear!

1. Cut the fabric according to the following measurements: The length is the length of the tabletop plus twice the drop plus 2 inches; the width is the width of the tabletop plus twice the drop plus 2 inches.

2. Double-turn a 1-inch hem, press, and edgestitch. Now your table is Pouilly-Fuisse-proof!

Noteworthy Notions

To finish off your tablecloth with a flourish, add some crochet cotton cording around the edge in a complementary color. Lay it over your hem stitching line, on the right side of the fabric, and zigzag stitch it in place. To double your flourish fun, add the cording to your matching napkins as well.

All-Around Easy Round Tablecloths

Round tablecloths are perfect for hiding imperfections. A round tablecloth will turn anything into an elegant side or dining table, whether it's a cardboard table or a slab of glass on top of an old step stool.

1. Cut the fabric according to the following measurements: the diameter of the table plus twice the drop length plus $1/2$ to 1 inch all around. Cut the fabric in a square.

2. Fold the fabric in half and then in half again. Pin in place. Draw an arc from corner to corner by measuring at regular intervals and marking. Cut through all four layers.

3. Sew a narrow-rolled hem. Snap your circular tablecloth into place. Add flowers, crystal, wine, and a few guests. You've got a party!

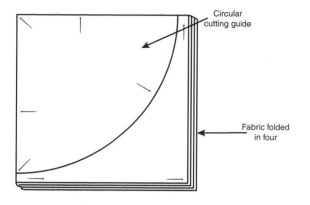

Circular
cutting guide

Fabric folded
in four

Round tablecloth template.

Lapping-Up Napkins

Sure, you can buy a stack of 100 paper napkins at your grocery store for a handful of pennies, but wouldn't you rather dab the corners of your mouth with some clean cotton napkins, the kind that are simple to sew and easy to wash—and that also cost pennies? Here's how:

1. I'm a fan of a real laptop napkin, the kind that covers your lap in the event of a real spill. They look and feel luxurious, and save your suit better than those little pocket-square-size napkins. The standard sizes are 14- and 17-inches square. I personally like a bigger napkin that really does a lap justice, and often opt for a 20- to 24-inch square.

2. This is where your narrow-rolled hem comes into play (see Chapter 11, "The Bottom Line: Hems"). If you don't have a narrow-rolled hem attachment, double-turn $1/4$ inch to finish off the napkins.

Make sure to use the appropriate fabric for napkins—a crisp cotton, linen, or a cotton blend. Don't use anything too heavy, or the napkins will be too uncomfortable; anything silky or too light won't hold the shape.

Sew Far, Sew Good

Instead of those vinyl placemats you've been using for years, why not make some new ones out of some stiff fabric (or some fabric that's stiffened up with a double layer with an interfacing in the middle). A common size is 16 × 14 inches—finish the edges by binding it in the napkin fabric and your table is as color-coordinated as your closet.

It's Raining Shower Curtains

If you're putting off making your own shower curtain, you'll be cured of cold feet by a quick trip to Bed, Bath, and Beyond. Go directly to the shower curtain section, finger a plush terry curtain, and flip through a lovely linen. Now check the price tag. See what I mean? Why spend a small fortune on what is essentially a square of fabric?

Sew Far, Sew Good

Shower curtain fabric doesn't need to be waterproof, but it *does* need to have the right H_2O stuff to withstand the water treatment. This is not the time or place for 100–percent silk or pane velvet. Save your silks for scarves, and stick to bathroom friendly fabrics.

Shower curtains do more to create atmosphere than any other bathroom accouterment. This means you can change the mood of your most-used room lickety-split by whipping up a new curtain. If you're having a mood indigo, confine your blue period to your bathroom, swaddling your shower in moony blue. I have a bathroom bathed in luminescent silvery gray, which makes every morning a treat. Treat yourself and your family by taking the following steps:

1. Cut the fabric according to the following measurements. The width is the width of the shower rod plus 4 inches. The length is the measurement from the shower curtain rings to at least 6 inches below the sill of the tub plus 10 inches.

2. Double-turn a 1-inch side hem on each side, press, and stitch.

3. Double-turn a 3-inch hem along the top and stitch; double-turn a 2-inch hem along the bottom and stitch.

4. A standard shower curtain uses 12 shower curtain rings. Thus, you need to make 12 buttonholes, positioning the first two $1/2"$ in from the sides. Now measure in between the two side buttonholes and divide by 10. This is where each buttonhole will be placed.

5. Mark each buttonhole. Place them $1/2"$ from the top of the curtain, making them $1/2"$ long.

6. Hang your curtain, along with a waterproof liner, and revel in your ingenuity.

The home-sewn details described in this chapter are just the start of what you can do for your home; use the tips and hints from the other chapters to cradle your home in all sorts of fabric creations.

Noteworthy Notions

Create a couture commode—match your shower curtains to your towels. For example, you can use a fantastic fuschia terry, piping everything in white cotton for contrast. Move over, Mario Buatta.

The Least You Need to Know

➤ Pillows are a great way to create luxury without a huge time and money investment. Whether it's a glamorous European sham or a basic pillow cover, a splash of color on a bed or sofa can turn a ho-hum home into an attractively accented abode.

➤ The narrow-rolled hem really helps on the home front. Use it for napkin and tablecloth finishes that you can fly through.

➤ Napkins are a neat way to use leftover pieces of fabric, especially beautiful cottons and linens that you've used for garments or other home accents. Napkins and tablecloths don't need to match. Let your imagination take you.

➤ Need a new look in your bathroom? Create a shower curtain. Use fabric that wears well with water. Measure properly, sew the side and top seams, and secure to the rings with buttonholes.

Crafty Gift Giving

Nothing says you care more than a home-sewn gift. Sure, anyone can go out and drop a bundle on a fine crystal decanter from a department store, a fancy French wine, or a glittery gold bauble. Now, I'm not knocking any of these beautiful store-bought presents; you can't beat them for last-minute occasions or quick pick-me-ups. But when you want to show that special family member or friend that you think they're not exchangeable (unlike the crystal decanter), give them something you've made with your own two hands.

I know from experience that home-sewn goes over big on the gift-giving front. It's so satisfying to whip up a holiday hoo-ha for your favorite Secret Santa, and then see her squeal with delight when she unwraps your homemade gift. And you don't need to wait for a special occasion; a lovely silk scarf with fancy fringe, a delicate pocket square, a home accent, or even a crisp pair of boxers are all easy to make, and appreciated any time of year.

The great thing about home-sewn gifts is that they're personal. In other words, they're made with someone special in mind, taking into account their own particular taste and quirky interests. You're free to customize your present, matching both the utility and style to your recipient's likes and dislikes. I love gathering fabric and notions that

I know will suit particular people, and then putting them aside for special occasion gifts. And the nice thing is that you don't need to do anything too fancy or too time-consuming; you can follow the simple steps you've learned so far to create a few elegant and easy gifts that are sure to make a good impression.

Noteworthy Notions

When I found a remnant of psychedelic pane velvet in my sewing box, I knew exactly what to do with it. I sat down at my machine and made a pair of pajamas for a groovy girlfriend whose taste is decidedly '60s redux. She loves padding around her apartment in her out-of-this-world print, pretending she's been transported to Austin Powers's boudoir. Personalized gifts mean so much more than an off-the-rack purchase, so let your creativity and generosity run rampant!

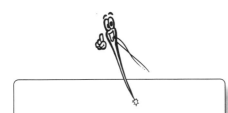

Sew Far, Sew Good

Does your favorite chef have a penchant for plaid? Make a gorgeous green and red Glen-plaid apron, put it into a steel mixing bowl along with some Scottish shortbread, and wrap it all in red transparent paper, using leftover fabric to make a matching bow. It's a wrap!

Cooking Up Something Special: The Chef's Apron

Know someone who loves to cook? Instead of heading to your local department store for a special skillet or expensive kitchen gadget, how about making an apron? You can whip one up in about an hour, and you don't need any extra notions.

The Raw Materials

The only thing you need to make an apron is one yard of fabric (at least 35" wide). When choosing your fabric, bear in mind that it's going to have to endure a lot of wear and tear. Between tomato-sauce splatters and greasy hand swipes, the fabric needs to be durable enough to withstand kitchen duty and regular washings. I prefer heavyweight cotton, poplin, canvas, or duck. You may want to use fabric that's treated so that it's stain-resistant, making it extra kitchen-proof.

The Works

1. Fold the fabric in half along the grainline.

2. Using a fabric marker and your tape measure, mark the apron measurements, as in the following illustration.

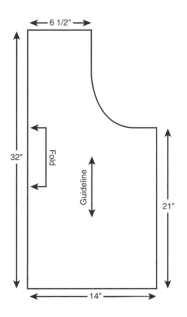

Easy apron measurements.

3. Measure and cut the ties. The two strips that fasten the waist are $1^1/_2$" × 26", and the neck strip is $1^1/_2$" × 24".

4. Sew the ties. Fold $^1/_4$" on each side of the strips, press into place, and then fold in half and press in place. Stitch close to the edge. There's no need to hem the ends of the waist strips—just tie them in a knot at the end and trim. If they start to unravel, use a drop of seam sealant such as Fray Check.

5. Hem the top of the apron by double-turning $^1/_2$" and stitching.

6. Hem the straight sides by double-turning $^1/_2$" and stitching.

7. Double-turn a $^1/_2$" hem on the sloping side of the apron (equivalent to the armhole if it were a shirt). Before stitching, pin the neck loop into place (making sure it's not twisted!), and the waist ties. Stitch, securing the ties.

Stitch in Your Side

Don't be left with a too-tiny apron ... make sure you preshrink the apron fabric, especially if you're using 100–percent cotton. It pays to shrink cotton two or three times so you're not stuck with an itsy-bitsy apron.

243

Noteworthy Notions

A home-grown apron is a great His and Hers gift that can be shared by both sexes. Just remember to match the fabric for the use—if your recipient du jour is a big barbecue fan, make sure you use seriously heavy fabric; if your cook is into delicate desserts, bear that in mind when choosing the fabric weight and appearance.

A Dandy Gift: The Pocket Square

I know several self-styled dandies—men who like to dress to the nines, complete with three-piece suits, an occasional pair of braces, and the obligatory pocket square. Believe it or not, a fancy French pocket square can cost as much as $80 at a fine clothing shop—all that for a simple silk square! You can make one in less than a half hour, using only 19 square inches of fabric.

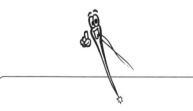

Sew Far, Sew Good

Because pocket squares use such a small amount of fabric, you can finally put those leftover swatches of luxurious silks to good use. So set aside your leftovers in a special place—you'll be thrilled to discover them right before Father's Day.

The Raw Materials

This is where your personal flair and affinity for fabric come into play. Pocket squares are all about the fabric—the feel, the color, and the print. Use the finest fabric you can, deciding whether your man (or dandy woman) is a silk or cotton kind of person.

The Works

1. Measure and cut a piece of fabric that's 19" × 19". Be very careful when cutting slinky silks—slippage can be a problem, causing you to create pocket ovals instead of squares!

2. The key to a well-done pocket square is a neat, narrow hem. Switch to the narrow-rolled hem foot and stitch a narrow-rolled hem on each side of the square.

Fit to Be Tied: Scarves

Scarves are the all-time, all-purpose, tried and true crowd-pleasing gifts. They're a perfect use for stray pieces of fabric, they're quick and easy to make, and they can be as simple or as elaborate as you want. The possibilities with scarves are endless—get your creative juices going by checking out the scarves at your favorite store. You can take the basic, oblong scarf and dress it up with any number of notions: Put a tassel on each corner, sew rickrack along the top and bottom, or make a patchwork quilt scarf out of swatches.

The Raw Materials

You can concoct a scarf out of almost anything—beautiful cottons, luxe satins, gauzy silks, nubby wools, summerweight wools, plush synthetics—the sky's the limit. First, you need to figure out your scarf mood; if you want a warm and fuzzy scarf, go for heavy wools. If you'd like a lean and sophisticated style, try an elegant white satin or silk jacquard.

When you've decided on the mood, you can match the look and weight of the fabric to the use: Long, flowing scarves are mostly decorative, an accent to an outfit; short, squat scarves are great for warmth and utility. Following are some common scarf measurements. These are the finished measurements, so be sure to add 1" all around for the seam allowance.

➤ Stylish outdoor scarf: 10" × 42"

➤ Longer outdoor scarf: 18" × 52"

➤ Flowy accent scarf: 12" × 75"

➤ Wrap scarf: 50" × 75"

The Works

There are two simple ways to make a scarf. The first is to cut a piece of fabric, fold it in half lengthwise, stitching around the open ends to create the scarf. The second—and, in my opinion, preferable—way is to cut two pieces of fabric, sandwiching them

Stitch in Your Side

When the gift's as simple as a pocket square, presentation plays a big role. Purchase some flat, square boxes and colored tissue, press the pocket square properly (taking extra care not to get any water stains on silk), and place the square in the box. Take that, Charvet!

Stitch in Your Side

If you go for a two-toned look—a scarf made of two different fabrics—try to pick fabrics that are about the same weight. The sewing gets tricky when you match a plush velvet with a sheer silk, with one fabric feeding through the machine at a much different pace than the other. If you don't pin everything carefully in place, checking your progress as you go, you'll end up with unequal pieces of fabric and a cockeyed scarf. Better to avoid that trap altogether and stick to similar fabrics.

together and stitching around the edges to create the scarf. We'll stick to this method because I like the way these scarves hang and look. They also provide you with the opportunity to have two different pieces of fabric, making the scarf two-toned, reversible, and just plain snazzier. Just follow these steps:

1. Measure and cut two pieces of fabric according to the type of scarf you're creating. Make sure both pieces are cut along the same grainline, which should be parallel to the long side of the scarf.

2. Pin the pieces, right side together. Stitch around the edges with a $1/2$" seam allowance, leaving a space open to turn the scarf right side out. The space you leave depends on the weight and amount of fabric. If you have a very large wrap scarf made of heavy wool, leave about 5" open. If you're making a small silk scarf, you only need to leave about $1^1/_2$". Trim the seam allowance.

3. Turn right side out, and then press.

4. Slipstitch the opening by hand, hiding the stitches inside the seam of the scarf.

Noteworthy Notions

You can add some extra oomph to this scarf with four tassels, one on each corner, stitched into place when you're done; or, you might add a row of tasseling on each end. Just sandwich the tasseling between the layers when you're pinning the sides together, stitching the seams and tasseling into place in one fell swoop. When you turn the scarf right side out, the tasseling will appear.

It's a Wrap: A Festive Wrap

If you want a more dramatic look (and who doesn't?), you can create a wrap that drapes elegantly over the bare shoulders of the holiday reveler. I love making this wrap, both as a gift and for myself because it's so cost-effective and attractive. You get a huge fashion bang for the bucks you've invested in the fabric, and the sewing time is short.

Wraps can completely change any look, creating a Cinderella-like transformation to even the simplest black sheath. I particularly favor lacy and luxe fabrics for this (red satin, off-white lace, and so on), but you can use a standard wool if you want a more traditional look.

The Raw Materials

You'll need a piece of fabric that measures 43" by 94", which you can piece together or cut in one fell swoop if the fabric you have is large enough (always the easiest and cleanest option).

Noteworthy Notions

My best wrap, the one that gets the most "oohs" and "ahs," is made out of one of my favorite fabrics—Ultrasuede©. This '70s fabric is perfect for a wrap because it needs no hemming (you just cut the edges), and there is no raveling or mess. Ultrasuede is also the ultimate in carefree maintenance—simply hand wash and drip dry. No dry cleaning allowed. I knew I had a winner when someone rushed up to me with my lavender Ultrasuede wrap and asked if Halston designed it!

The Works

This is the easy part: Double-turn a $1/2$-inch hem on all sides. You've made an elegant and easy evening wrap, one that's fit for the queen for the night.

In the Bag: Evening Clutch or Coin Purse

A simple fabric evening clutch is a wardrobe staple; a black velvet number works with almost any outfit, a richly embroidered brocade makes a statement, and a metallic quicksilver is an eye catcher. Why spend a lot of money on something so simple and easy to make? The same goes for an even tinier purse for coins and cosmetics.

The Raw Materials

For an evening clutch, you'll need two pieces of fabric that measure 6" × 8"; for a coin bag, you

Sew Far, Sew Good

Ever take a good look at most cosmetic bags? Most of them need their own cosmetic coverup because of unsightly plastic, ungainly canvas, and bad construction. There's no need to be embarrassed by your minibag when it comes out of your handbag. The new vinyls and waterproof materials are perfect for toting your lipsticks, and they're simple to sew.

need two pieces that are 5" × 8". Also, you need a zipper that measures 7". (I suggest using an invisible zipper in a matching or complementary color.)

The Works

1. Measure and cut two pieces of fabric.

2. The best zipper to use with this bag is an invisible zipper. This means that you will stitch the zipper into place first, and then stitch the rest of the bag. See Chapter 10, "Win One for the Zipper," for easy instructions.

3. After inserting the zipper, align the pieces right side to right side and stitch around the remaining three sides, allowing for a $1/2$" seam allowance. Trim the seam allowance, turn the bag right side out, and you're ready to roll.

Noteworthy Notions

This is a great little bag for a piece of fantastic beaded fabric. Beaded fabric requires a little bit of special sewing care; here are some pointers: Remove the beads from the seams so you don't stitch over them; use a zipper foot; don't steam beads—they curl and wilt.

The Stockings That Dreams Are Made Of: Christmas Stockings

I never owned a store-bought Christmas stocking as a child. My seamstress grandmother made new ones every year, transforming this relatively mundane holiday tradition into its own special event. My favorite was a stocking in the shape of a pink princess puppet, complete with a shiny tiara and a bejeweled bodice.

After you've created the basic stocking shape, go for the decorative gusto, from gluing on some glitter to making an animal shape to embroidering a few decorative fillips. Check out your local trimmings store and grab whatever sparks your imagination.

The Raw Materials

You can use any fabric you want to make a stocking—from crafty felt to rich cashmere—depending on whose stocking you're stuffing. The same goes for the notions: Be as creative as you like when adding decorations.

The Works

1. Enlarge the illustrated stocking pieces to the desired size (see the following figure). Mark and cut two pieces of the stocking and cuff, and one piece of the strip, which becomes the hanging loop.

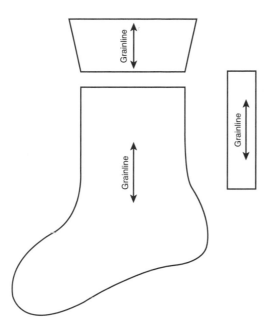

Simple stocking form.

2. Pin the right sides of the stocking together and stitch with a $\frac{1}{4}$" seam allowance, leaving the top open. Turn the stocking right side out.

3. Fold the hanging loop in half lengthwise (with the right sides together) and stitch along one side, leaving the ends open.

4. Pin the cuff pieces with the right sides facing each other and stitch on each side with $\frac{1}{4}$" seam allowance. To attach the cuff to the stocking, tuck it inside the stocking so that its edge aligns with the top of the stocking. Make sure the side seams face each other, not the stocking. Stitch along the edge. Pull out the cuff and roll it down.

5. Turn the loop right side out and attach it to the inside of the stocking with a quick hand or machine stitch.

Give Me a Hand: Quick Hand Puppets

Hand puppets are a crowd pleaser; you can enlist the help of little hands during the cutting and construction of these fun crafts (just as long as you stay on sewing machine duty). Making them is half the fun; the rest comes when the puppeteers slip them on, and you can sit back and enjoy the show.

The Raw Materials

The best fabric for hand puppets is felt. Of course, you can use any fabric you want as long as it's stiff enough to hold the shape of the puppet—no sheer or silky fabrics allowed because you just end up with, well, a hand. Felt is also great because you don't have to worry about finishing the seams—just sew and trim; because felt doesn't ravel, you don't even have to turn it inside out if you're in a rush. The notions are up to you and your creative side.

The Works

1. To determine the size of the puppet, perform this quick test: Put your puppeteer's hand on a piece of paper and draw around it, leaving some finger wiggle room. Add $1/2$" seam allowance all around to your rough puppet shape.

2. Here's where your imagination comes into play. I personally like a pig puppet, so I've illustrated how to make this little piggie with just a little glue, a magic marker, and a pipe cleaner.

Pig puppet.

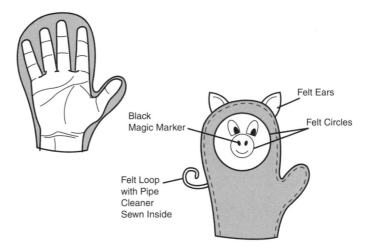

Black Magic Marker

Felt Ears

Felt Circles

Felt Loop with Pipe Cleaner Sewn Inside

The Mane Thing: Scrunchies

Hair scrunchies are all the rage, the hair tamer of choice whether you're 6 or 60. The reason is that they're fun, easy, and a real hair preserver. (The rubber bands I used to wrap around my teenage mop left a lot to be desired.)

Sometimes it's hard to find scrunchies in the fabric you want, so making them yourself is the answer. They're really quick, and a great gift for the hair-impaired.

The Raw Materials

A strip of fabric (1$\frac{1}{2}$" × 19") and a band of elastic cording ($\frac{1}{8}$") is all you need (along with a little help from a small swatch of fabric).

The Works

1. Fold the fabric strip in half, right sides together, and stitch along the long edge with $\frac{1}{4}$" seam allowance. Leave the ends open, and turn the fabric right side out.

2. Cut a 10" length of elastic cording. Thread the elastic through the fabric tube. Scrunch up the fabric so that it leaves you room to work on the elastic. You need to overlap the edges of the elastic slightly and sew them together. The best way to do this is with a small swatch of stable fabric. Place it under the overlapped elastic, wrap it around, and stitch back and forth over the overlapped edge.

3. Pull the fabric around, insert one open edge into the other, fold under one edge, and slipstitch by hand to secure the end.

We've just completed a quick course in home-sewn gift giving—but there's no need to stop here. There are plenty of other easy options for showing (and sewing) your generosity. Check out the pattern catalogues for more ideas—from plush terry robes to silky dressing gowns to scruffy slippers to crisp boxers—and let your sweet side show to your lucky friends and family.

Sew Far, Sew Good

I prefer a pig puppet, but you and your young puppet master might have other ideas. If you want a witch, a Pokémon hero, Mickey Mouse, an evil sorcerer, or Bettie Boop, try to think of these characters in simple, easy-to-assemble shapes. Reduce them to geometric figures that can be cut from other pieces of felt, notions that can be glued on, and so on. Preserve your artistic integrity by cutting down on the drawing and painting.

The Least You Need to Know

➤ Hand-sewn presents win you a very large and appreciated "A" for effort. Plan ahead for special events and fit stitching into your life so that you can present your new godchild with a homemade romper. It'll go over big.

➤ Scarves are a fantastic gift—simple to sew and great to give. You can use all sorts of leftover fabric, from the most luxe to the simplest cotton and dress it up in any number of ways.

➤ Even if you're the designated sewing machine driver, making hand puppets and other kid-oriented crafts is an opportunity to have some fun with your young friends. They love to dig into the fabric, play around with glitter, and create their own puppet characters. Go wild.

➤ I've given you a few simple guidelines for gifts, but don't stop there. You can create so much that's tailored to your recipient—just think what strikes their fancy and work with it.

Glossary

apex The point of the bust. It's also the very tip of a dart (whether a bustline dart or not).

baby hem A seam finish or hem in which the fabric is double-turned a tiny amount ($^1/_8$ inch to $^1/_4$ inch maximum) and stitched.

backstitch Just like backing up a car, this is when you stitch in reverse. Your sewing machine has a button, knob, or switch that activates the reverse. Backstitching a couple of stitches will secure the beginning and end of your stitch lines so they don't come undone.

bartack A few stitches back and forth that secure your stitch lines. Some machines have a bartack setting.

basting stitch A temporary stitch that secures your fabric before the real stitching. You almost always use the longest stitch possible for basting since it's meant to be removed.

basting tape Double-sided sticky tape that holds fabric in place temporarily without the hassle of stitching. Great for zipper placement.

bias This is the line that runs diagonally across fabric. The true bias is always at a 45° angle to the crosswise and lengthwise grains, and is the fabric's stretchiest point.

bias tape Prepackaged, commercially sold tape that is used to bind seams or hems. The tape comes in different sizes and colors, so buy accordingly.

bias-bound seam Also known as a Hong Kong seam, this is a seam finish in which you bind the raw edges of the seam in a bias-cut strip of fabric.

blind hem A hem in which the stitches don't show on the right side of the fabric. You can accomplish this by hand or by machine with a special presser foot attachment.

blindhem stitch   Machine stitching, using a blindhem presser foot, that creates a blind hem with the use of straight and zigzag stitches.

bobbin   A plastic or metal spool that holds thread; it's inserted in the bobbin case, usually under the machine where it loops with the needle thread to create the stitches.

bolt   A large roll of cloth or fabric of a specific width.

buttonhole bead   One side of buttonhole stitches.

buttonhole chisel   A small tool with a sharp metal blade (usually $1/2$-inch wide) used to cut a buttonhole open in one fell swoop. You need to use the chisel with either a self-repairing mat or a wooden block.

clapper   A pressing tool that's a flat wooden block used to create serious creases. After using an iron, pressing with the clapper flattens that area while drawing the heat out of it, "setting" it in place.

crosswise grain   This is the fabric line that runs from selvage to selvage, perpendicular to the lengthwise grain. It's also known as the weft and always has more give or stretch than the lengthwise grain.

dart   A tapered tuck sewn into a garment to create contouring. Usually V-shaped, the tuck narrows to the apex or the tip, and is most often placed at a bustline or waistline.

double needle   A double-pronged needle that's joined in one shank for use with your machine. It creates a double row of evenly spaced stitches on the top while the bottom zigzags between the rows. Perfect for hemming, decorative topstitching, and working with stretchy fabrics.

drop   This is the length of a finished curtain from where it will hang (whether on a pole or track) to the bottom.

ease   This means a few things in sewing terminology. First, it applies to any time you need to fit a longer section of fabric to a shorter one. This almost always happens with a set-in sleeve, the cap of which needs to be eased to fit into the armhole, or a long hem where the top or folded fabric needs to be eased to fit the bottom fabric. Second, it's the difference between your body's measurement and the garment measurement, or the allowance the garment gives you to move.

edgestitch   Stitching that's placed a maximum of $1/8$ inch from a turned edge, whether a hem or a fabric detail like a pocket.

elastic thread   Finely wound elastic that's used in place of regular thread.

European sham   A pillow cover with a flat border of about 2 inches around the edges.

feed dogs   The teeth on the throat plate of your sewing machine that rise and fall back and forth, gripping the fabric and moving it as you stitch.

flat-fell seam   A seam finish in which you stitch the right sides of the fabric together, trim one seam allowance and turn the other under, topstitching it into place, creating a double row of neat stitching and an encased seam. Good for reducing bulk in your seam finish.

free arm   The "arm" of your sewing machine is usually created by removing a detachable casing, exposing a narrow section that supports the needle and bobbin mechanisms. This enables you to sew tight circular areas like sleeves and cuffs without straining.

French seam   A completely encased seam that adds a finished, couture look to your home-sewn seams. The seam is sewn on the right side of the fabric, turned, pressed, trimmed, and encased, after which the wrong side is sewn. Imperative for see-through fabrics so the raw edges don't show.

fusible interfacing   Interfacing that is backed with a heat-activated resin that bonds with the fabric when ironed and steamed properly.

grainline   The direction of the weave of fabric.

heading tape   Ready-made strips of stiff fabric that you attach along the top border of curtains. They either have drawstrings to form even gathering, or pockets for hooks that create different pleats (such as triple pleats, pencil pleats, or box pleats) without any complicated stitching on your part.

Hong Kong finish   Another name for a *bias-bound seam.*

interfacing   A layer of fabric that adds shape, stability, durability, and control to garments. It's usually used on the edges of clothes—armholes, necklines, or the edges of jackets and blouses—and on special details, such as collars, cuffs, and pockets, so they maintain their crisp look. The two basic kinds of interfacing are fusible (iron-on) and sew-on.

invisible thread   A sturdy, clear plastic thread. I keep a bobbin wound with invisible thread on hand so that I can sew quickly with any thread without worrying about matching the color of the thread to the fabric.

ironing press   A fantastic pressing tool for pressing large areas at once. This machine looks almost like a Xerox machine cover with a handle; pull down, placing the fabric on the bed, and the press provides about 100 pounds of pressure with almost no effort on your part. Great for fusing interfacing.

lengthwise grain   Running parallel to the selvage, this is the all-important grainline. When commercial patterns indicate the grainline, they're referring to the lengthwise grain. It's the strongest and has the least amount of stretch. Also known as the *warp.*

long-staple polyester thread   The best polyester thread that differs from all-purpose polyester in that it uses longer thread filaments (from 5 to 6$\frac{1}{2}$ inches) so that it's stronger and shinier.

magnetic seam guide   A small magnetic "shelf" that sticks to your machine throat plate, providing a stitching guideline to keep your seams straight.

metal sewing gauge   A 6-inch metal ruler with a sliding plastic marker; an essential tool.

mock French seam   A seam finish in which you turn the raw edges of the seam and sandwich them together, stitching the edges.

narrow-rolled hem   Another name for a *rolled hem.*

needleboard   A bed of nylon bristles that preserves the nap of heavily piled fabrics while pressing. Place the fabric face down on the bed and the fur, velvet, and the like fall in between the "needles," maintaining their fluffy appearance.

notions   A loose term that applies to all the parts of a sewing project besides the fabric, from thread to pins to needles to interfacing.

pinking shears   Shears with serrated blades that cut a toothy, zigzag edge. Often used to prevent raw edges from unraveling or for a decorative finish.

placket   A V-shaped opening or slit in a garment, usually at the sleeve or neckline. The most common placket is in a menswear-style sleeve that allows it to slip over the wrist and attach with a cuff.

point turner   A small utensil with a pointy edge that allows you to turn fine points—as in collars, cuffs, and pockets—fully so that you get that very last, tiny bit of fabric turned and pointed to perfection. The most common ones are made of bamboo or wood.

press cloth   A thin piece of fabric, often see-through, that's placed between your iron and your fabric to protect the fabric from damage or shine. It's a necessity for certain fabrics and for fusing interfacing.

presser foot   A sewing machine attachment that exerts pressure on the fabric, holding it in place while stitching. Presser feet are detachable, and there are many specialty presser feet, the most common of which are the standard foot that accompanies your machine and the zipper foot.

pressing mitt   A padded, double-sided mitt that slips over your hand while pressing, protecting your hand from heat.

rolled hem   This is a tiny, evenly rolled hem that's created with a special narrow-rolled hem presser foot. The fabric is fed into the funnel of the presser foot, turned, and then stitched.

Roman shade   A window shade that pulls up in horizontal folds, hanging flat when closed, and drawing up into neat sections when opened.

rotary cutter   Essentially an X-Acto knife that's shaped like a pizza wheel. As you roll it along, it accurately cuts fabric without lifting the cutter from the cutting surface. It must be used with a self-repairing mat—and yes, these little innovations actually repair themselves by "healing" the cut marks after you're done!

scissors   As opposed to shears, scissors are shorter and have the same size finger loops. Use them for cutting patterns, stray threads, etc., but not for cutting fabric.

seam allowance   This is the amount of fabric added to your pattern to allow for stitching and trimming. Or, a little less technically, it's the space between where you've cut the fabric and where you stitch it. Almost all commercial patterns use a $5/8$-inch seam allowance, but you can vary it according to your sewing needs.

seam ripper   Basically a tool with a two- to four-inch handle and two prongs—a crescent-shaped blade and a shorter blunt edge—that's used to safely rip out the threads from a seam. If you're using it, you've made a mistake, which happens a lot.

seam sealant   A clear resin that's used to prevent edges from fraying. It's especially useful on buttonholes.

serger   This is a machine that stitches the seams, cuts the excess fabric, and finishes the seams with an overcast stitch all at once. As a supplement to your traditional sewing machine, it's great for creating a finished, professional look.

set-in sleeve   The most common tailored sleeve in which the sleeve is slightly bigger than the armhole, meaning it must be eased or "set-in" to fit and hang properly. The other types of sleeves are raglan and kimono, both of which require no easing techniques.

shank   When referring to a button, this means the ring-like projection on the back that's sewn on to the garment. You can create a shank, or a raised area behind the button, out of a column of thread. A shank can also mean the top of the needle where it attaches to your sewing machine.

shears   Your most important sewing tools. These are special scissors that are longer than six inches and have a larger upper finger loop for cutting ease.

sleeve roll   A sausage-shaped hard cushion that's perfect for pressing sleeves and other circular or curved areas of a garment.

sloper   The master pattern that a commercial design company uses.

stabilizer   A temporary sheet of material that's applied to fabric when stitching to provide support and stiffness. There are three varieties: tear-away; water-soluble, like Sulky or Super Solvy; and heat-soluble, like Heat-Away. They're all stitched in place, and then removed by various methods, leaving only the plastic stiffness in the stitches, not around the fabric. They're perfect for buttonholes, which need extra reinforcement, especially when using silk or other lightweight fabrics.

staystitch   A row of stitching for curved areas like collars, necklines, and seams that have a tendency to stretch when stitched. Before stitching your seam, you first "stay" the fabric with a staystitch just inside the permanent stitching line (usually about $1/2$ inch).

stitch in the ditch   A stitching technique that allows you to stitch in the seam well formed by joining garment pieces (collars, cuffs, waistband, and so on) so that the stitching doesn't show on the front of the garment.

tailor's chalk   Chalk used for marking hems, transferring pattern markings, and indicating stitching lines. Make sure you buy real chalk, rather than chalk/wax combinations, which can melt into the fabric.

tailor's ham   This is a thick, heavy, ham-shaped cushion that's used for pressing open seams, especially in curved areas like darts, sleeve caps, collars, and waistbands.

tension   The resistance or "pull" between the top and bobbin threads that creates even knots or stitches that lie in-between the fabric pieces. Proper tension is essential for flawless stitching.

throat plate   The metal plate on your sewing machine that surrounds your needle hole. It's usually marked with lines at graduated $1/8$-inch settings to gauge your seam allowances.

topstitch   Straight stitching sewn about $1/4$ inch from the seam or finished edge. Can be a decorative finish or utilitarian.

twin needle   Another name for a *double needle*.

Universal point needle   The most common needle size for use with most fabrics.

warp   Another name for the *lengthwise grain*.

weft   Another name for the *crosswise grain*.

zigzag stitch   Just like it sounds—a zigzag stitch that's sewn as a seam finish to prevent unraveling or for stretchy fabrics because it has more "give" than a straight stitch.

When the Sewing Gets Tough— Finding Help and Resources

Professional to the Rescue

For a complicated sewing fix, seek out someone who knows his or her stuff.

Head of the Class

When more know-how is needed, there's nothing better than taking a class from a pro. So much of sewing is tactile; you need to watch a pro in action and then put your own fingers to the test.

➤ Many of the larger cities have design schools that offer continuing education to people who aren't in the biz. In New York, Parson's and the Fashion Institute of Technology offer professional-level courses to anyone. I supplement my skills every semester at Parson's, where I'm amazed at how much someone who's immersed in the industry can teach any home sewer.

➤ There are also one-on-one tutorials and sewing schools. Check out your local Yellow Pages, the internet or ask your favorite tailor for teaching tips.

The Sewing Bee

Quilting bees have never gone out of style, but sewing bees are a new twist on an old-fashioned way of getting together, gossiping, and getting some serious sewing done.

➤ Young urban professionals have recently started gathering to throw together a skirt or two, sharing sewing tips as well as stories.

➤ People in their 20s and 30s are sewing more than ever before, and see it as a hip alternative to store-bought items. You may want to start your own group, inviting friends to bring their fabrics and patterns, sharing supplies and machines.

Sewing Associations

American Sewing Guild, Inc.
9140 Ward Parkway
Suite 200 Dept. TH
Kansas City, MO 64114
Phone: 816-444-3500
Toll free: 1-877-I CAN SEW (422-6739)
Web site: www.asg.org

Home Sewing Association
1350 Broadway, Suite 1601
New York, NY 10018
Phone: 212-714-6333
Fax: 212-714-1655
Web site: www.sewing.org

Resourceful Resourcing

If you're not blessed with the variety of notions, fabrics, and machinery that New Yorkers have, you need to be resourceful about where you get your supplies. You can get catalogues, swatches, and—at the very least—generous phone ordering help from many suppliers. Here's the rundown of some of the best resources.

Rotary Cutters/Mats

The Sewing Emporium
PO Box 5049
Chula Vista, CA 91910
Phone: 619-420-3490
Toll free: 1-888-742-0471

This is a great place to go for any number of sewing essentials, so you'll see this name pop up a lot!

Sew/Fit Company
5310 West 66th Street
Unit A
Bedford Park, IL 60638
Phone: 708-458-5600
Web site: www.sewfit.com

This store has a terrific selection of cutting tables, self-healing mats, and tables that work with the free arm of your sewing machines.

Fabric

B&J Fabrics
263 West 40th Street
New York, NY 10018
Phone: 212-354-8150

This place is filled with designer, specialty, and high-quality fabrics. They allow for student swatching (where you can go and get samples of any of the fabrics they have in stock) one day per week, so call and check.

Fabric Depot, Inc.
700 SE 122nd Ave.
Portland, OR 97233
Phone: 503-252-6267
Toll free: 1-800-392-3376
Web site: www.fabricdepot.com
Email: fabricdepot@worldnet.att.net

This is an enormous online fabric store. While they don't have a catalogue, they do have great customer service.

Fabric Direct
PO Box 194
Mount Marion, NY 12456
Web site: www.fabricdirect.com

This Internet site has close-ups of fabric swatches to make your fabric choice easier.

G Street Fabrics
Toll free: 1-800-333-9191
Web site: www.gstreetfabrics.com

Terrific and very expansive Web site offering fabric swatches, notions, and courses. There are two store locations in Virginia and one in Maryland.

Paron Fabrics
56 West 57th
New York, NY 10019
Phone: 212-247-6451

They also have three other New York City locations and a big selection of half-priced designer fabrics at all times.

RJR Fashion Fabrics
13748 Gramercy Place
Gardena, CA 90249
Toll free: 1-800-422-5426
Fax: 310-217-9898
Web site: www.rjrfabrics.com
Email: info@rjrfabrics.com

Thai Silks
252 State St.
Los Altos, CA 94022
Toll free: 1-800-722-7455
Web site: www.thaisilks.com
Email: thaisilk@pacbell.net

Great selection of specialty silk fabrics.

Vogue Fabric by Mail
Toll free: 1-800-433-4313

Thread and Notions

Banasch's
2810 Highland Avenue
Cincinnati, OH 45212
Toll free: 1-800-543-0355

Bernina
3500 Faircourt
Aurora, IL 60504
Toll free: 1-888-Bernina
Web site: www.berninausa.com

Bernina sells machines (sewing, embroidery, and sergers) and a whole supply of notions and sewing gadgets. Call for their catalogue.

Coats & Clark, Inc.
8 Shelter Drive
Greer, South Carolina 29650
Toll free: 1-800-241-5997
Phone: 864-877-8985
Fax: 864-848-5603
Web site: www.coatsandclark.com

Galaxy
224 West 38
New York, NY 10018
Phone: 212-944-7331
Fax: 212-921-4815

This store specializes in buttons. They will make customized covered buttons and buttonholes.

Greenberg & Hammer
24 West 57th
New York, NY 10019
Toll free: 1-800-955-5135

G Street Fabrics
12240 Wilkins Avenue
Rockville, MD 20852
Toll free: 1-800-333-9191
Web site: www.gstreetfabrics.com

Fabrics, notions, books—all sorts of sewing resources.

Mettler Thread
400 East Central Ave.
Mount Holly, NC 28120
Toll free: 1-800-847-3235
Fax: 1-800-847-323
Web site: www.amefird.com

Nancy's Notions
PO Box 683
Beaver Dam, WI 53916-0683
Toll free: 1-800-833-0690
Web site: www.nancysnotions.com
Email: nzieman@aol.com

This is Nancy Zieman's notions catalogue, and it offers more than 4,000 products, including books, videos, and sewing supplies. Just call the 800 number and the catalogue will arrive within days.

Professional Sewing Supplies
PO Box 1472
Seattle, WA 98114-4272
Phone: 206-324-8823

Gingher, Inc.
PO Box 8865
Greensboro, NC 27419
Phone: 336-292-6237
Fax: 336-292-6250

The best maker of all kinds of professional quality scissors and shears.

Mundial
PO Box 99
Norwood, MA 02062
Phone: 781-762-8310
Fax: 781-762-0364

Prym/Dritz Corporation
PO Box 5028
Spartanburg, SC 29304-5028
Toll free: 1-800-845-4948
Fax: 1-800-574-3847
Web site: www.dritz.com

Gutermann of America
PO Box 7387
Charlotte, NC 28241-7387
Phone: 704-525-7068
Fax: 704-525-7071
Web site: www.gutermann.com

Sewing Notions
PO Box 980707
Ypsilanti, MI 48108
Toll free: 1-800-334-4241
Web site: www.sewingnotionsinc.com

The Sewing Place
18476 Prospect Place
Saratoga, CA 95070-3651
Toll free: 1-800-587-3937
Fax: 1-408-252-8445
Web site: www.thesewingplace.com
Email: webmistress@thesewing place.com

Sulky of America, Inc.
3113 Broadpoint Drive
Harbor Heights, FL 33983
Toll free: 1-800-874-4115
Fax: 941-743-4634
Web site: www.sulky.com

Sulky products as well as the Sulky Sew Exciting courses are offered around the country.

Sewing Machine and Ironing Supply Companies

Elna, USA
1760 Gilsinn Lane
Fenton, MO 63026

Euro-Pro
178 West Service Rd.
Champlain, NY 12901
Toll free: 1-800-798-7398

An excellent supplier of steaming and pressing equipment.

Husqvarna/Viking
PO Box 308
Mt. Olive, NJ 07828
Toll free: 1-800-358-0001
Web site: www.husqvarnaviking.com

Pfaff American Sales Corp.
1077 Third Avenue
New York, NY 10021
Toll free: 1-800-99-PFAFF (997-3233)
Web site: www.pfaff-us-cda.com

Rowenta, Inc.
196 Boston Ave.
Medford, MA 02155
Phone: 781-396-0600
Toll free: 1-800-769-3682
Web site: www.rowentausa.com

Singer Sewing Company
PO Box 7001
4500 Singer Rd.
Murfreesboro, TN 37129
Toll free: 1-800-474-6437
Fax: 615-893-3061
Web site: www.singerco.com

Pattern Companies

Burda Patterns, Inc.
1831-B West Oak Parkway
Marietta, GA 30062
Toll free: 1-800-241-6887
Fax: 770-423-9103

KWIK SEW
Web site: www.kwiksew.com

Patterns, books, courses, and more.

McCall's Pattern Company
11 Penn Plaza
New York, NY 10001
Phone: 212-465-6800
Fax: 212-465-6814

Simplicity Pattern Company
Consumer Relations
901 Wayne St.
Niles, MI 49121
Toll free: 1-888-588-2700
Web site: www.simplicity.com
Email: info@simplicity.com

Vogue/Butterick
161 Avenue of the Americas
New York, NY 10013
Phone: 212-620-2500
Fax: 212-620-2746
Web site: www.butterick.com

Further Reading

The great thing about sewing is that there is no one right way; there are many ways to beat a sewing challenge. I've scoured books for new techniques and have found that you can always learn and update your skill library.

With all the time-saving techniques out there, everyone still seems pressed for time. That's why so many of the newer books focus on fitting sewing into a busy schedule. There are hundreds of books that can give you help and advice, but I've read and reread (and passed on to you) the truly great quick-sewing hints found in these books and magazines:

Beyond the Pattern: Great Sewing Techniques for Clothing by Threads, compilation, Taunton Press, Inc., 1995.

Essential Sewing Guide, Nancy Zieman, Oxmoor House, Inc., and Leisure Arts, Inc., 1998.

Fabric Savvy, Sandra Betzina, Taunton Press, 1999.

Fantastic Fit for Every Body, Gale Grigg Hazen, Rodale Press, Inc., 1998.

High-Fashion Sewing Secrets from the World's Best Designers, Claire B. Shaeffer, Rodale Press, Inc., 1998.

Mother Pletsch's Painless Sewing: With Pretty Pati's Perfect Pattern Primer and Ample Annie's Awful but Adequate Artwork, Pati Palmer and Susan Pletsch, Palmer/Pletsch Associates, 1997.

No Time to Sew: Fast & Fabulous Patterns & Techniques for Sewing a Figure-Flattering Wardrobe, Sandra Betzina, Rodale Press, Inc., 1997.

Pillows, Curtains, and More, Myra Davidson, Quarto, Inc., 1993.

Sew Fast, Faster, Fastest: Timesaving Techniques and Shortcuts for Busy Sewers, Sue Hausmann, Rodale Press, Inc., 1998.

Sewing Tips & Trade Secrets, compilation, Taunton Press, Inc., 1996.

Simplicity's Simply the Best Sewing Book, The Simplicity Pattern Company, Inc., HarperCollins/Perennial Library, 1998.

10, 20, 30 Minutes to Sew, Nancy Zieman, Oxmoor House, 1992.

Singer's Sewing for the Home, Singer Sewing Co. with Cowles Creative Publishing, Inc., 1995. This is one of the many books in the *Singer Sewing Reference Library.* Other books focus on window treatments, quilting, tailoring, lingerie, etc.

The Vogue/Butterick Step-by-Step Guide to Sewing Techniques, Butterick Company, Inc., 1998.

All of these titles, as well as about 800 others, can be ordered on the Internet and be at your door in a matter of days. You should also look at some of the sewing Internet sites for ideas and book updates, such as www.tauntonplus.com.

In addition to *Threads* magazine, Taunton publishes some of the best, most up-to-date books, which you can keep up with online. For orders, you can reach Taunton at 1-800-888-8286. Write them at: Taunton Direct, Inc., 63 South Main St., PO Box 5507, Newton, CT 06470-5507. There are also a million (okay, maybe not a million, but pretty darn many) Internet sites for sewing information, classes, and resources. Just seek with your search engine and ye shall find.

Sewing Publications

Sandra Betzina
Web site: www.sandrabetzina.com

***McCall's Patterns* Magazine**
11 Pen Plaza
New York, NY 10001
Phone: 212-465-6800
Fax: 212-465-6814

Palmer/Pletsch
PO Box 12046
Portland, OR 97212-0046
Phone: 503-294-0696
Toll free: 1-800-728-3784
Web site: www.palmerpletsch.com
Email: patipalmer@aol.com

Sew News
Box 56907
Golden, CO 80322-6907
Toll free: 1-800-289-6397
Web site: www.sewnews.com
Email: sewnews@sewnews.com

Simplicity Pattern Co.
Consumer Relations
901 Wayne St.
Niles, MI 49121
Toll free: 1-888-588-2700
          1-800-334-3150
Web site: www.simplicity.com
Email: info@simplicity.com

***Threads* Magazine**
Taunton Direct, Inc.
63 South Main St.
PO Box 5507
Newton, CT 06470-5507
Phone: 203-426-5507
Web site: www.threadsmagazine.com

Vogue Patterns
161 Avenue of the Americas
New York, NY 10013
Email: mailbox@voguepatterns.com

I'd like to acknowledge my overwhelming debt to Nancy Zieman and Mother Pletsch (okay, to Pati Palmer and Susan Pletsch) for their invaluable tips that have helped me on every single project I've ever sewn. Their books are filled with practical, no-nonsense info that has saved my sewing but many a time. Try out their Web sites and notion catalogues, and you'll learn that you're just one sewer amidst many, many confident and accomplished sewers.

Index